HT
governance
management of
your p's
man. contr !.
uhaurivity

The Marketization of Employment Services

The Marketization of Employment Services

The Dilemmas of Europe's Work-First Welfare States

Ian Greer, Karen N. Breidahl, Matthias Knuth, and Flemming Larsen

OXFORD
UNIVERSITY PRESS

OXFORD

UNIVERSITY PRESS

Great Clarendon Street, Oxford, OX2 6DP,
United Kingdom

Oxford University Press is a department of the University of Oxford.
It furthers the University's objective of excellence in research, scholarship,
and education by publishing worldwide. Oxford is a registered trade mark of
Oxford University Press in the UK and in certain other countries

First Edition published in 2017
Impression: 1

Published in the United States of America by Oxford University Press
198 Madison Avenue, New York, NY 10016, United States of America

British Library Cataloguing in Publication Data
Data available

Library of Congress Control Number: 2016960176

ISBN 978–0–19–878544–6

Printed and bound by
CPI Group (UK) Ltd, Croydon, CR0 4YY

Acknowledgments

We would like to thank the Hans Böckler Foundation for funding this research. In particular we want to thank Claudia Bogedan, then our contact within the foundation, now Senator for Children and Education in Bremen, and President of the Standing Conference of the Ministers of Education and Cultural Affairs of the Länder in the Federal Republic of Germany. We also thank the University of Greenwich for funding a pilot phase for this research in 2011–12 that allowed us to pilot our interview questions in Germany and Britain, and John Ward and Mark Stuart for working with us during the pilot phase.

One advantage of working with the Böckler Foundation is that the funding includes many opportunities for intellectual exchange with researchers and practitioners. One part of this is the Advisory Committee (*Beirat*), in which our findings and interpretations were discussed and debated. We are grateful to Ingo Bode, Dorte Caswell, Damian Grimshaw, Sebastian Jobelius, Henning Jørgensen, Thomas Kruppe, Janine Leschke, and Jay Wiggan for their interventions. A second forum in which the project was discussed was the final workshop. This involved two days of debate, and we are especially grateful to the presenters: Hans-Peter Eich, Damian Grimshaw, Christina Grøntved, Richard Johnson, Eva Katarina Sarter, Els Sol, Wolfgang Uellenberg-van Dawen, and Sharon Wright. In addition there were three national workshops, and we would like to thank participants in these.

To collect the data we depended heavily on the openness of our interviewees and their willingness to share their time, experience, and views with us. We particularly thank the people responsible for purchasing at the Federal Employment Agency, senior executives at most of the large "prime" providers, staff and lay officials in the trade union PCS in Britain, and interviewees in Denmark who patiently answered our naïve questions in English.

We want to thank our colleagues who provided administrative support during the project, including Shanaz Sumra and Maria Alejandra Rodriguez at Greenwich and Anders Eeg at Aalborg University. We also thank Sebastian Pehle for analyzing tendering documents and Bettina Mosler for transcribing interviews at IAQ.

Finally we would like to thank those who helped us to bring the manuscript to fruition. This includes members of the project team who helped to co-author specific chapters. Lisa Schulte contributed to Appendix B and Johannes Kirsch and Graham Symon to Chapter 5. Shanaz Sumra was instrumental in the final submission of the manuscript. We also thank Clare Kennedy at Oxford University Press, who advised us, offered encouragement, and tolerated delays, as well as Dawn Preston and Vaishu Venkatesan, who supported us in the final stages of production. Finally, we thank six anonymous reviewers who offered valuable critical advice.

Contents

List of Figures

List of Tables

List of Abbreviations

ALG I/II	Arbeitslosengeld I/II (Unemployment Benefit I/II)
ALMP	Active Labor Market Policy
AMS	Arbejdsmarkedsstyrelsen (Labor market authority)
BA	Bundesagentur für Arbeit (Federal Labor Agency)
BAG	Bundesarbeitsgemeinschaft (Federal Working Party)
CVT	Continuing Vocational Training
DS	Dansk Socialrådgiverforening (Danish Association of Social Workers)
DWP	Department for Work and Pensions
ERSA	Employment Related Services Association
ERSS	Employment Related Support Services
ESA	Employment and Support Allowance
EU	European Union
GEW	Gewerkschaft Erziehung und Wissenschaft (Union for Education and Science)
HK	Handels- og Kontorfunktionærernes Forbund i Danmark (National Union of Commercial and Clerical Employees)
IEP	Institute for Employment Professionals
JSA	Jobseeker's Allowance
NAO	National Audit Office
NPM	New Public Management
NVQ	National Vocational Qualification
OECD	Organisation for Economic Co-operation and Development
PbR	Payment by Results
PCS	Public and Commercial Services Union
PES	Public Employment Service
REZ	Regionales Einkaufszentrum (Regional Purchasing Center)
SGB II/III	Sozialgesetzbuch II/III (Social Law Book II/III)
TUPE	Transfers of Undertakings and Protection of Employment
Ver.di	vereinte Dienstleistungen (United Services Union)

1

Introduction

Across Europe, market mechanisms are spreading into areas where they did not exist before. In public administration, market governance is displacing other ways of coordinating public services, such as place-based networks of non-profits or direct hierarchical control by the state. In social policy, the welfare state is retreating from its historic task of protecting citizens from the vicissitudes of the market and taking on the opposite task, namely of compelling citizens to participate in the labor market. In the workplace, trade unions, collective bargaining agreements, and employment-protection legislation are losing their ability to protect workers from the pressures of the labor market, because of declining coverage and functional weakening where they still operate. Large swathes of the European and national policy communities have proclaimed their faith in the powers of "the market."

This neoliberal reorientation applies as much to national economies classified as liberal or coordinated and as much to welfare states classified as liberal, conservative, or social democratic. It has continued past the financial crisis, raising the question of whether policymakers learn from the mistakes of past neoliberal policies. It has had a hold on center-left social-democratic parties at least since the 1990s.

It is tempting to argue that European countries are converging on a shared neoliberal model. There is indeed strong evidence of a liberal bias in European-level legislation (Hartlapp et al. 2014), its interpretation by the European Court of Justice (Höpner 2011), and its application in the workplace (e.g. Lillie 2010). A common trend to liberalize can be observed at the national level in a wide range of policy areas and countries (e.g. Höpner et al. 2009; Baccaro and Howell 2011).

One fertile area for the empirical study of marketization has been publicly funded employment services for the jobless (e.g. Considine 2001; Sol and Westerveld 2005; Van Berkel and Van der Aa 2005; Bredgaard and Larsen 2008; Davies 2008; Hipp and Warner 2008; Rees et al. 2014; Zimmermann et al. 2014; Wiggan 2015; Klenk and Pavolini 2015; Heidenreich and Rice new 'public' man. vs the work-1st welfare state.

2016). This literature located marketization of employment services on the intersection between new public management (NPM) and the work-first welfare state. NPM replaced the existing hierarchies and procedures with contractual relationships, competition, and performance management. The work-first welfare state tightened the link between the entitlements of citizens to out-of-work benefits linked to job-search activities. While the use of market mechanisms promised to improve performance of these services and reduce costs, this literature noted problems such as high transaction costs and quality problems such as creaming and parking and increasing standardization.

The marketization of employment services did not happen everywhere simultaneously. Australia and the Netherlands reformed their employment services along market lines in the 1990s (Bredgaard and Larsen 2008), Great Britain, Germany, and Denmark began market reforms in the early 2000s. Britain was in some ways a laggard, with its current market fully in place only since 2010. Countries also vary in the way they marketize, including the degree to which they empower private providers and the ways that they hold providers accountable (e.g. Jantz et al. 2015). This variation in timing, speed, and power dynamics of marketization can also be found in other areas of welfare-state provision (Gingrich 2011) and economic policy (Prasad 2006).

Such variation also exists within countries. In industrial relations there is a longstanding recognition in institutional differences by sector (Dunlop 1993; Bechter et al. 2012) and dualization models positing differences between high-productivity "core" and low-productivity "peripheral" sectors (Berger and Piore 1980; Emmenegger et al. 2012). Empirical studies on vertical disintegration and its effects on industrial relations suggest that the boundaries between well-organized and unorganized kinds of work are not as clear as the sectoral image suggests or as fixed as the dualization image suggests (Doellgast and Greer 2007; Brinkmann 2011). In employment services it is common to have multiple segments, each one with different funders and funding arrangements and diversity in the kinds of providers, services, and working conditions for staff (Greer et al. 2011).

Our study seeks to explain between- and within-country variation in these services. We rely on data we collected for a comparative research project in Denmark, Germany, and Great Britain funded by the Hans Böckler Foundation. In addition to gathering publicly available statistics and reports, we carried out dozens of interviews with managers, policymakers, front-line workers, and other actors in each country. We asked three questions:

1. What does marketization mean in practice in these three countries? What, in other words, is happening "inside of welfare markets" to "the interactions between politicians, bureaucrats, and managers of marketized welfare providers"? (Klenk and Pavolini 2015: 263–4) Building on

Welfare

past research on the marketization of employment services, we locate marketization in this context as part of the parallel development of public administration and social policy across the developed world (e.g. Bredgaard and Larsen 2008). Drawing on Williamson (1999) and Le Grand (2006) we focus on a particular feature of governance that plays a prominent role under marketization: the modes transaction between public purchaser and external provider.

2. What are the broader effects of marketization on services and governance arrangements? How are front-line workers managed in contracted-out providers, many but not all of them for-profit firms and commercially minded non-profits; and how do workers respond to management practices such as performance targets? As the street-level bureaucracy literature points out, it is the front line where policy is enacted from the perspective of service users (Lipsky 1980). Looking at the organization level leads us to look at dilemmas discussed by funders and providers alike, such as price versus quality.

3. How does variation in marketization and its effects map against the theoretical national "regime types" commonly found in comparative literature? National history, institutions, and culture matter; nevertheless, debates on the persistence, roll-back, or transformation of past practices tells us little about the new market arrangements that are reshaping workplaces and public services. In this study we map the market segments in this sector, which vary within countries, and show how market arrangements found in them shape workplace outcomes.

The Conceptual Background: the Political Economy of Welfare and Work

Our research team has two different starting points, with backgrounds in the applied fields of industrial relations and social policy. Some team members have a history of working with trade unions to improve wages and working conditions for workers and working in the fields of industrial relations and sociology of work; others with civil servants and policymakers to improve the effectiveness of active labor market policies and have worked on the boundary of social policy and public administration. From different perspectives we have approached a shared set of issues of welfare and work, as they played out in employment services and marketization. A shared concern, however, is comparative political economy, which conceptualizes the interaction of markets, states, and societies in ways that have shaped debates on both labor and policy.

While there is a history of research examining welfare states and the workplace in an integrated way, the communities studying these two issues have, at least since the 1970s, been quite separate in the English-speaking world (Greer 2016). This is not to say that social-policy literature always neglects the workforce, as the title of a recent update on street-level bureaucracy research, *Work and the Welfare State*, demonstrates (Brodkin and Marston 2013). Given the participation of labor economists in the evaluation of welfare-to-work schemes and the many studies of unemployed people in sociology of work journals such as *Work Employment and Society*, it would be equally misleading to argue that labor scholars consistently ignore welfare states and unemployment. However, where members of one research community venture onto the turf of another, it is rare to see anything like intellectual cross-fertilization.

Industrial relations is an applied field with a rich theoretical tradition grounded in the canon of institutional political economy (Commons 1909; Webb and Webb 1897; Kerr et al. 1960). In recent years it has been deeply influenced by varieties of capitalism theory (Hall and Soskice 2001). The expectation that the latter theory produces for comparative employment relations is that liberal countries such as the UK and US are market-driven and are likely to remain so, while coordinated market economies such as Germany and Denmark will resist liberalization pressures. As a result, employers in the latter group lack the incentive to challenge worker protections and trade unions seen in the former group. Comparative industrial relations work has come to hinge on characterizations of countries centered on broad differences in the workings of markets and expectations of divergent trajectories in their development.

More recent scholarship has had to cope with apparent marketizing changes by discussing common trends in institutional change across different regime types, including the erosion of collective bargaining and decline in trade union membership (Baccaro and Howell 2011) and the increasing incidence of low-wage work (Gautié and Schmitt 2010), and the effects of marketization trends such as privatization, open migration, free trade in goods and services, and financialization (e.g. Doellgast 2012; Lillie 2010; Greer and Hauptmeier 2016; Brinkmann and Nachtwey 2013). At the core of these debates is an attempt to understand a shift in the relationship between markets and the institutions that once protected workers' terms and conditions of employment, in which the former undermine the latter. Typically they analyze the retreat or disorganization of non-market social protection, but increasingly they also examine the market dynamics behind this retreat.

The intellectual roots of social policy mingle with those of industrial relations. In Britain, Sidney and Beatrice Webb (1909) made seminal contributions to social policy and industrial relations and Marshall's (1950) account of citizenship neatly integrated the development of welfare states with that of industrial relations systems. The most influential international-comparative typology in social policy, Esping-Andersen's *The Three Worlds of Welfare Capitalism* (1990), points to the strength of working-class organization as an important explanation for longstanding differences between welfare states. This theory has provided the underpinning for a vast literature explaining persistent national differences between countries representing liberal, conservative, and social-democratic welfare regime types, such as Great Britain, Germany, and Denmark, respectively. This characterization of the welfare state hinged on its decommodifying properties for workers: the degree to which it protected them from the disciplines of the market.

The past two decades of policy studies have documented a trend that is nearly the opposite of decommodification: the rise of the work-first welfare state. Social policy has been reoriented to institutionalize labor-market flexibility and to move jobless people into paid work (Peck 2001), and this has taken place in countries representing the full range of theoretical regime types (Lødemel and Trickey 2001; Lødemel and Moreira 2014). These schemes are almost always administered using the performance-management and contracting practices associated with NPM (Clarke and Newman 1997; Brodkin and Marston 2013), with overall principles of governance and the securing of accountability that are increasingly market-based (Jantz et al. 2015). Policy writers have labeled this trend "contractualism," pointing to the rise of "back-to-work agreements" between advisors and jobseekers and contracts between funder and provider as means to apply pressure to produce the job-placement outcome (Carney and Ramia 2002; Sol and Westerveld 2005). Other writers use the term "marketization" for these shifts in social policy, which entail an operational shift towards competition and results-orientation and a substantive shift towards participation of welfare clients in the labor market (e.g. Zimmerman et al. 2014).

Applied interdisciplinary social-science fields are thus host to a vast number of studies looking at the effects of marketization in a wide range of workplaces and policy arenas. Labor and policy scholars are struggling separately and in different ways with three questions:

(1) What is the change in markets that matters?
(2) What are the consequences of marketization?
(3) How do these dynamics vary between and within countries?

What Is the Change in Markets that Matters?

One difficulty in sketching the literature on marketization is that most studies of phenomena that increase market competition do not use the term marketization. In American industrial relations literature on globalization, for example, the increasing scale of competition from national to international has led to pressures on managers and trade unionists to increase flexibility and negotiate worker concessions (e.g. Kochan et al. 1986). In the international literature on contracting, there is an increased focus on the problems that contracting causes for regulating the workplace, because they create scope to shift work out of the scope of collective agreements (Doellgast and Greer 2007, Lillie 2010) or because they create difficulties for government regulators to police standards in the workplace (Weil 2014). Some recent British studies on government contracting emphasize the importance of cost pressures in explaining employment outcomes (Vincent and Grugulis 2009; Lonsdale et al. 2010). These are just a few of many studies that identify features of markets that matter—in the first case its openness, the second case the degree of non-market regulation, and the third case price pressures—but not in the context of a broader framework for understanding the making and structuring of markets and of market change.

A second problem is that users of the term "marketization" have differing definitions. Often terms such as "privatization," "liberalization," "commodi-fication," "neoliberalization," and "marketization" are used interchangeably or defined tautologically; but even where the meaning of the term is clear, it varies. In studies on non-profit management "marketization" refers to organizational shifts in values and methods towards commercial revenue generation, performance-based government contracting, and the adoption of an entrepreneurial approach to management (Eikenberry and Kluver 2004). In British studies on health care, "marketization" typically refers to the creation of organizational boundaries, mainly within the public sector, that are supposed to stimulate competition, increase private-sector involvement, and turn ser-vices into a commodity rather than an entitlement of citizens (Krachler and Greer 2015). Quasi-markets theory often emphasizes customer choice as a means of improving the quality of services (Le Grand 2006). In employment services, studies using the term tend to highlight overall patterns of public-sector "governance" that mimic the management tools of the private sector, placing a premium on price, competition, and results (Jantz et al. 2015). As with "contractualization," these studies use a definition that includes both the management of the services and the expectation that clients partici-pate in the labor market (Zimmermann et al. 2014). These literatures all suggest that markets are increasingly staged in the production of public services, but their emphasis varies depending on the academic subfield: the cash nexus, organizational model of providers, the transaction, customer choice, and over-all governance principles, respectively.

A synthesis is needed, because there is a common thread that runs through literature on the various phenomena called marketization. Our synthesis centers on the modes of transaction. This builds on the theory of quasi-markets that forms the backdrop of much of the social policy literature, which suggests that policymakers create a divide between purchaser and provider as a means to discipline non-compliant or unresponsive staff and create incentives for efficiency (Le Grand 2006). It also builds on the literature on different modes of governance, which points to the implementation of NPM principles in practice, for example payment by results (Rees et al. 2014) and consumer choice (Hipp and Warner 2008). It builds, finally, on a nascent strand of industrial relations literature that points to principles of competition built into the funding of public services that, by putting downward pressure on costs, undermine existing collective bargaining structures leading to greater within-country diversity in labor-management relations (Greer et al. 2013).

We conceptualize the diversity in markets in terms of transaction *modes*: (1) grants, in which governments allocate money for a particular purpose, usually specialized or experimental services delivered by non-profits and local government; (2) purchasing, in which a public authority pays for an input or outcome, usually a less specialized service; and (3) vouchers, where the government issues a document that entitles a client to a government-funded service. The most common of the three modes in our sample is purchasing, which, along with vouchers, is usually more marketized than grants. Public purchasing can also be subjected to detailed EU-level regulation in the form of the 2004 and 2014 Procurement Directives, as well as some national rules governing labor and environmental standards for contractors (Jaehrling 2015). We will discuss transactions in some detail in Chapter 3.

Our analysis of marketization focuses on four dimensions: openness to new market participants, the price mechanism, the standardization of service involved, and the frequency of the transaction. Public authorities can increase or reduce the degree of marketization by altering these variables, in three ways. First, they can switch away from grant making to procurement or vouchers. Second, they can alter the way a transaction works, for example by changing the length of contracts, changing the weighting of price versus quality in tendering, or eliminating barriers to entry such as accreditation. Third, they can change the make-or-buy decision by privatizing public-sector functions or assets (creating a new potentially market-mediated boundary in the production of the service) or insourcing work (abolishing that boundary).

Our first contribution is thus to provide a workable definition of marketization that can be applied to studies of market change in a range of different academic fields and empirical contexts. This includes a classification (transaction modes) and four dimensions along which a marketized transaction differs from a non-marketized one. It provides a vocabulary for market change that will be useful beyond employment services and that we hope different disciplines can use to make their findings mutually intelligible.

What Are the Consequences of Marketization?

These changes to transactions have obvious implications for providers of employment services, and not all of them are the consequences intended by the public authority. Economic analyses of transactions tend to follow Williamson's (1985) assumption that the nature of the task sets the parameters for exchange. While this has some plausibility—a simple service is more conducive to competitive price-based exchange than a more complex one—causality also runs the other way. Just as Polanyi (1944) saw the rise of labor, land, and money as "fictitious commodities" transforming the character of the thing being commodified, the marketization of employment services alters the services being provided.

Furthermore, exchange between public purchasers and providers is shaped by political and legal considerations in addition to economic ones. Public purchasers must demonstrate that competing bidders are treated in transparent and non-discriminating ways, as per the principles of procurement law, and where a service is bought in order to satisfy citizens' entitlements or expectations vis-à-vis the state, both the perceived quality of the service and the perceived responsibility for potential flaws of the service are political issues. The service bought may not only be the profiling of job-seeking customers or the provision of debt counseling, but may also help the public authority shift the blame associated with limited resources for escalating client needs. The procurement procedure chosen is not only shaped by the task of profiling or counseling but also by safeguarding legality of the procedure and producing legitimacy first for the decision to outsource this function and second for entrusting particular providers with it. Thus, legality, legitimacy, and blame shifting influence the design of transactions between a public authority and a service provider at least as much as efficiency.

One common problem with quality highlighted by policy writers has to do with the assessment and sorting of clients. Because staff have to make decisions about the exact service needed and the kind of job that would be suitable, there is to some degree sorting for "employability" and "opportunity" (Paugam 2002). The problem is that the former comes to dominate. "Creaming and parking" is a longstanding concern in public-administration studies on the consequences of numerical targets: staff sort their clients into easy-to-serve and difficult-to-serve categories and focus their attention on the latter in order to meet their targets (Lipsky 1980). This can happen within public bodies driven by outcome targets, but payment-by-results arrangements built into contracts with external providers create even stronger incentives to neglect clients who are not likely to receive a job outcome, since the cost of serving them cannot be recovered from the funder and in general would eat into surpluses (Rees et al. 2014). Germany's job-placement vouchers create very similar incentives, although here it is called "cherry picking," since clients are sent back to the job center and not "parked" as part of the provider's case load (Doerr and Kruppe 2014).

These are not the only problems with marketized employment services highlighted in the literature. There is a problem with innovation, for example, in which contracts reduce the resources and discretion to do new kinds of work by squeezing prices and clearly specifying the work. As Rothstein (1998) points out, innovation is important in employment services, since active labor-market schemes entail detailed intervention in a complex and changing context. There is also a problem for local networks of non-profit providers, which function by virtue of jointly developing work and referring clients. Evaluation evidence on vouchers in the United States and Germany shows that they tend to undermine the cooperative relationships between providers that allow the information flows that would allow informed choices by voucher holders (Hipp and Warner 2008).

A different approach is to focus on the labor process and the institutional regulation of workplaces. A squeeze on prices and resources can in many cases be passed by management on to workers in the form of lower pay or through bonus systems that make pay contingent on performance. This can be mitigated by encompassing wage-setting institutions such as statutory minimum wages or collective bargaining (Doellgast 2012), or by writing compliance with such standards into tender specifications (Jaehrling 2015).

A second problem with job quality is insecurity. The relationship with contracting is equally obvious here, since winning contracts, attracting voucher-holding customers, or triggering outcome payments involve uncertainty. Management can pass this uncertainty onto employees through temporary contracts or freelance contracts, which are very widespread in German employment services (Enggruber and Mergner 2007; Dobischat et al. 2010). Open-ended employment contracts, however, are no guarantee of job security, especially in Britain and Denmark where statutory employment protection is weak. Job and employment insecurity can be mitigated by transfer of undertakings rules that protect terms and conditions of staff moving from one contractor to another or the creation of pathways for progression at the sector level.

A third consequence in the workplace has to do with the intensification of management control. In general, NPM and welfare markets shift control away from workers; and there are some concrete features of contracting that help to explain this (Clarke and Newman 1997; Gingrich 2011). One is deskilling, or the devaluing of professional qualifications. While work with vulnerable clients is arguably a task for trained social workers and teachers, a work-first focus tends to violate their occupational ethos. Consequently it is common for employment-services providers to employ staff with a wide range of occupational backgrounds and formal qualifications, including former clients without formal qualifications and staff with backgrounds in sales. The occupational autonomy of professionals may be undermined in other ways as well, for example through intensive monitoring by electronic systems using quantitative performance indicators, the weakness of formal worker representation, and the (above-mentioned) insecurity of these jobs (Baines 2004; Esbenshade et al. 2016).

One effect of marketization that we do *not* examine is that on performance: how it affects clients' income levels, probability of being in paid employment, and amount of benefits received. This may seem strange given that many of the methods that feed into marketization—more clearly specified contracts, payment by results, and competition generally—are intended to improve performance and outcomes. But this has already been subject to a very large empirical literature. Sympathetic reviewers of the evaluation literature show that the effects of active labor market schemes are mixed, small, and contingent on many program-design variables such as the clientele, whether it is a make-work scheme, and the narrowness of the work-first focus (Schmid 2008; Stephan and Pahnke 2008; Card et al. 2015). Performance effects of marketization may exist, and may very well be traceable to the organizational dynamics it unleashes that we are exploring qualitatively; however, the evaluation literature looks at privatization rather than marketization and finds only weak effects. It suggests that this may be because such effects are overdetermined by other factors such as caseloads and other features of program design (Krug and Stephan 2016).

Our second contribution is to sketch the dilemmas and tradeoffs of work-first welfare states generated by marketization. Drawing on discussions with policymakers, managers, and front-line workers about problems generated by the marketization process, our synthesis of the problems outlined above focuses on the following dilemmas and tradeoffs: price versus quality, payment by results versus equal access to services, customer choice versus compulsion, and bureaucracy reduction versus fairness and transparency. Each will be discussed in Chapter 6.

How Do These Dynamics Vary between and within Countries?

As a comparative book it would seem natural to set up our analysis as being about national similarities and differences. For us, however, there is the problem of within-country variation in the main outcomes of interest. In Denmark the employment-services market varies due to the power of local government; in Britain due to the dualized nature of the contracting market; and in Germany due to the different legal frameworks governing various kinds of employment services. Our argument is that the features of the transaction help to understand within-country differences between these organizations, especially in Britain and Germany.

Varieties of capitalism and welfare regime typologies provide clear expectations about the varying nature of markets in different countries. Welfare regimes theory, which remains highly influential in comparative policy studies, is centered on the decommodifying character of the rights granted by the welfare state, which are closely related to the real functioning of the state and its interaction with family structure (Esping-Andersen 1990: 21). Varieties of capitalism theory, which remains highly influential in comparative industrial relations, nests this idea in a broader view of the regulation of capitalism, arguing that it is rooted in particular forms of employer coordination, which reflect business interests in sustaining diverse industrial relations and welfare-state arrangements (Estevez-Abe et al. 2001). These are not implausible as starting points, and there is nothing inherent in this approach that prevents the analysis of within-country variation; indeed, in Przeworski and Teune's (1970) seminal contribution to comparative research methods, explaining differences in within-system variation is part of the definition of the method. While this approach in its original formulation is static, more recent reformulations have reconciled its core concepts with transformative change in institutions and their outcomes (e.g. Thelen 2014).

But any attempt to use these typologies to understand the topic at hand would face two challenges. The first is the timing of the diffusion of marketization across countries' employment-services landscapes. The first movers in the 1990s were liberal Australia and the conservative Netherlands. Social-democratic Denmark and conservative Germany followed suit in the early 2000s. Marketization in liberal Britain remained experimental until the late 2000s and even when it was fully in place after 2010 it placed strict limits on the amount of competition. If liberal regimes were more market-driven, we would expect Britain and Australia to marketize first and other countries to do so later.

The second challenge would be to understand the kind of marketization. It entailed quick and large-scale privatization of public services in the Netherlands and Australia; in Denmark and the UK it led to piecemeal privatization of particular services for particular groups over a few years; and in Germany it meant a change in the management of already external services rather than privatization. The British and Danish markets are dominated by for-profits; the German and Australian markets have a higher degree of non-profit participation. Employment services in countries classified as liberal have not had deeper privatization, more intense competition, or a greater profit orientation than conservative or social-democratic ones.

An alternative narrative would point to neoliberal convergence, another conveniently straightforward narrative that would allow us to see how macro-level social change leads to changes at a more micro level. This would have some plausibility, since marketization is readily observable in all three of our countries, along with the rise of NPM and work-first welfare states. But these too are insufficient to explain what we see. Why did the British landscape shift from fragmentation to centralized control by for-profit firms (Wiggan 2015)? Why do German providers have such a severe problem with wage dumping and insecure jobs (Dobischat et al. 2010)? Why have Danish providers had to change their services and approach so radically over the years (Breidahl and Larsen 2015)? Something is happening aside from a creeping convergence driven by deregulation.

Such macro-level theories are not well suited for understanding the uneven way that societies are being reshaped by neoliberalism. This unevenness has been captured by such labels as "variegation" (Peck and Theodore 2007) or "converging divergences" (Katz and Darbishire 2000); but behind these labels are no analytical frameworks illuminating conditions under which we observe the outcomes of interest. Drawing on the policy and industrial relations literature, we aim to provide a key ingredient for such an analysis.

Because policy writers tend to focus on the structure of the state as a key determinant of marketization dynamics, there is considerable room for within-country variation. Zimmermann et al. (2014), for example, find in a study of Italy, Germany, and Britain that the degree and kind of marketization is shaped by the discretion and willingness of local actors to implement it. They find variation within Germany depending on the kind of work and whether work is governed by vouchers or competitive tendering, and they find the top-down control of the British state as important in imposing a particular pattern of marketization. Knuth (2014a) similarly identifies a difference between services in the two tiers of the public employment service in the wake of the Hartz reform: an insurance-based logic for claimants of income-related unemployment benefits and a social-assistance logic for those of tax-funded benefits. Wiggan (2015) finds variation in marketization practice in the UK, with strong for-profit corporate control in Great Britain and more public control in Northern Ireland. There is thus a strong reason to see within-country variation in the kinds of markets, dependent on politics of place and kind of service.

Industrial relations writers typically focus on sector-specific differences in competitive pressures and non-market worker protections. Brown et al. (2008) and Hauptmeier (2010) have argued for product-market competition as an important contextual feature explaining workplace outcomes, and there is a longstanding convention in comparative industrial relations to point to the internationalization of markets as an important contextual factor and then to differentiate between sectors that are exposed (e.g. export-oriented manufacturing sectors) from those that are sheltered (e.g. public services). Similarly, writers on dualization distinguish between high-productivity large firms in the core of the economy from low-productivity small firms; while the former may have unions, collective bargaining, and lifetime employment, the latter usually do not (Berger and Piore 1980; Emmenegger et al. 2012). One problem is that distinctions between industrial sectors have broken down, due to the vertical disintegration of corporate structures (Doellgast and Greer 2007) and the encroachment of competitive pressures in once sheltered sectors such as health services (Greer et al. 2013; Krachler and Greer 2015). But the insight remains: holding country constant, the intensity of economic competition is causally related to the institutional regulation of work and the kinds of jobs.

Our third contribution is to highlight different degrees of marketization as a cause of within-country variation in the quality of services and jobs. Such variation is most evident in German employment services, where there are different transaction modes at work simultaneously. As we will see in Chapter 5, the different market segments that result have very different kinds of organizations, jobs, and services. This effect is also evident wherever there is a change in the way that a transaction works. The municipalization of services in Denmark, the rise of vouchers and the public purchasing function in Germany, and the concentration of power in the hands of prime contractors in Britain are all examples of this. In Chapter 4 we will show how changes in transactions transformed the landscape of providers delivering employment services.

Methods

Our research design is qualitative and comparative, with three national case studies constructed from the available literature and statistics, and from interviews with policymakers, managers, and front-line staff. The country cases vary according to the conventional national regime types discussed above, and we selected establishments to visit to represent the within-country diversity in the transaction modes and kinds of providers. Because of differences in the organizations in the three countries, there were differences in the kind and amount of information that was available and the willingness of interviewees to speak with us and participate in the workshops in which findings were discussed. In the end, however, we gathered information that allows a meaningful comparison, not only between the countries, but also between the different kinds of markets and providers within the countries.

In order to discuss case selection it is important first to say what externalized employment services are.

By *externalized* we mean that they are not carried out directly by the staff of the responsible public authority or authorities, the Public Employment Service (PES), normally charged with organizing job-search assistance and paying benefits. We exclude services provided in house by the PES, but include work carried out by other public-sector bodies funded by the PES. While employment relations literature is concerned with procurement, purchasing, or contracting out (e.g. Jaehrling 2015, Grimshaw et al. 2012), not all services we examined were governed in this way. Germany, for example, used vouchers, in which the funder delegates the choice of provider to the client. There are also longstanding traditions of cost reimbursement and grant making in all three countries, which were funding arrangements with external providers that did not involve market competition. While much of the discussion of externalized services refers to privatization, this was often not an immediate issue at the providers and public agencies we were visiting. More commonly the market pressures faced were due to changes in funding arrangements between purchaser and provider that reshaped a relationship that already existed.

By *employment services* we mean that the PES is one of the responsible public authorities and that the purpose of the services is to move unemployed people into, or closer to, paid work. (Whether the services have this effect is a different matter.) Tasks include assessing clients, providing advice and guidance, training them, placing them in jobs, and organizing make-work schemes. Employment services include many of the organizations that implement Active Labor Market Policy (ALMP) as conceptualized and measured by bodies such as the Organisation for Economic Co-operation and Development (OECD), but does not include other spending items such as benefits payments to clients or subsidies to employers. We exclude services that apparently have this function but are not funded or regulated by the PES (such as programs to combat unemployment and social exclusion funded by the European Social Fund and administered by regional governments) and those that are funded by the PES but do not have this function (such as German sheltered workshops for the disabled or outsourced ancillary services for PES operations such as cleaning or catering). The purpose is to study work in the three countries that, if not organized identically, is at least comparable by virtue of shared institutional responsibility, a shared goal, and a shared set of tasks. Still, some cross-country difference remains with regard to the importance of vocational training in the portfolio of national ALMPs; eliminating vocational training from our definition of employment services would result in the exclusion of training voucher schemes in Germany, which would have been a loss in empirical richness of our study.

Our original data consist of 114 qualitative interviews with the funders and providers of these externalized employment services. Interviewees included managers (at the strategic and operational level, and personnel and contract managers if possible) and front-line staff working with the unemployed (including advisors and trainers). Establishments were selected for variation that mirrors the variation in funding in the different national contexts. A second source of data was interviews with people involved in the making of markets, including civil servants involved in the design, procurement, and the management of contracts. Third, we talked to other experts, including representatives of umbrella bodies for providers and worker representatives (trade union staff and works councilors).

Table 1.1 provides an overview of our interviewees. For Germany and Denmark, it includes interviews over the course of the project (2013–14); for Great Britain and Germany it also includes interviews during the project's pilot phase (2011–12); for Denmark it includes a round of follow-up interviews with front-line staff and managers in 2015.

Most interviews were carried out by the national teams in their home countries and in their native languages; however, each team visited the other two countries and carried out interviews together in English. British team members participated in several German-language interviews in Germany. In all cases, the other national teams spoke to national-level policymakers, and in most cases they also spoke to respondents involved in

Table 1.1. Research interviews and interviewees

		Germany	Great Britain	Denmark
Public authorities	Ministry/politicians	3	1	2
	PES management	8	8	3
	Which levels of management?	*Local and national*	*National only*	*National and local*
Providers	Management	15	12	5
	Front-line staff	13	15	3
	Works councils/shop stewards	2	5	0
	Which providers?	*For-profit/ Non-profit*	*Prime providers/ subcontractors (non-profit and municipal)*	*For-profit/ Non-profit*
Other	Trade union headquarters	1	3	2
	Umbrella bodies	5	1	1
	Other	1	2	1
	What is "other"?	*Federal labor inspectorate*	*Welfare claimants' groups*	*Association of municipalities*
Total interviews		50	47	17
Total interviewees (including interviews with 2–4 respondents, subtracting repeat interviews with the same respondent)		67	55	19

managing provision, either direct management of providers or umbrella bodies representing providers. The British team also had conducted interviews with German policymakers, providers, front-line workers, and claimants groups in earlier projects. All of the interviews have summaries in the languages in which they were carried out, and some have word-for-word transcripts as well.

Including both funders and providers was crucial for understanding marketization—how the transaction is organized by the government funder, and how providers respond to these pressures. It was also useful as a triangulation technique, as the two gave us very different views on the same phenomenon, allowing us to improve the reliability of our case-study writeups. Speaking to front-line staff similarly helped us to clarify our thinking about management practices in the workplace.

Our sample is selected to represent the internal diversity of the three countries in terms of market segments and the kinds of providers. In Denmark we spoke to municipalities engaging both "partnership" and "competitive tendering" methods in organizing services, as well as providers operating under both arrangements. In Germany we spoke to national and municipal purchasers, as well as providers operating under the two voucher schemes, competitive tendering, and grants. In Britain we spoke to policymakers responsible for national tendering, large providers responsible for the bulk of contract management and in most cases provision, and their non-profit, public-sector, and for-profit subcontractors.

In each country we assembled what publicly available information existed on contracting and the sector. We drew on a strong tradition of academic work describing and evaluating various aspects of active labor-market policies, including the organizational and market dynamics of interest to us. We also collected statistics on the size of the market (in terms of spending, participant numbers, and employees working at providers) and its structure (kinds of services, public-private-non-profit mix in provision, structure of supply chains, and different modes of transaction). We also collected tendering documents. We discuss these data in Chapter 3 and the Appendices.

Municipalization and payment by results made it difficult to obtain spending data in Denmark and Britain; in Germany the statistics were available but difficult to interpret. Because the purchasing of Danish employment services is handled by ninety-eight municipalities with only limited central oversight, our assessment of the market draws on a national survey of municipal jobcenter management we carried out. Because of the difficulty of getting information in Great Britain, we rely on publicly available information on the Work Programme—which is voluminous and covers roughly half of spending on external employment services—as well as data provided by the government in response to a Freedom of Information Act request. Because of these differences in available data, we have summarized our findings on the markets in three appendices, one for each country.

The third part of our study was to present and discuss preliminary findings in workshops with practitioners and academics. This included national workshops in all three countries and a final workshop in April 2015 in Düsseldorf with participants from all three countries. In each case we invited academics and practitioners—funding bodies, providers, umbrella bodies, and trade unions—from the respective countries to comment on our findings. These discussions were useful for encouragement and for sharpening our thinking, and in some cases we received valuable updates and data points on developments in our countries, which we cite in the book.

The national differences in dissemination were telling about the three countries. In Great Britain the national workshop was in June 2014 at Greenwich and included ten participants, including trade unionists and academics, with apologies from claimants' groups, representatives of providers, and PES representatives. This reflects the high degree of conflict and low level of trust, not only between government and activists who might resist marketization and corporate control of services, but also within the activist camp. In Germany and Denmark, by contrast, there was strong and broad participation. Twenty-three people attended the April 2014 workshop in Germany, including representatives of umbrella organizations, providers, the PES, trade unionists, and academics. The Danish team presented findings from the survey in two practitioner-oriented workshops, including one in March 2014 with sixty representatives from the unions, providers, national, regional, and local labor market authorities, insurance funds, and others with interest in employment services, and one in June 2014 organized by the umbrella body of private providers including forty of its members as well as representatives of the PES.

The Book and its Findings

The following chapters begin with some context, including the task of employment services and the overall trajectories of the three countries. Chapter 3 and the Appendices address the question of what exactly marketization is, by spelling out the different transaction modes and the varying degrees of marketization among the transactions in the sample. Chapters 4, 5, and 6 deal with the consequences of marketization for the sector, the workplace, and for the principles of governance. Chapters 4 and 5 also grapple with the issue of how different transactions for employment services lead to within-country variation in the landscape of organizations and the employment relations and labor process. Chapter 6 explores the consequences of these effects on providers for the governance of services and lays out four dilemmas found under marketization. We conclude with implications for policy, politics, and research.

Chapter 2 summarizes the national stories and depicts employment services as a task. It is common in comparative research for national stories to be shaped by conventional national typologies: Denmark the social-democratic regime, Britain the liberal one, and Germany the conservative Bismarckian one. Although the issues highlighted by the conventional theory do play a role, we do not succumb to the temptation to rely on the national stories repeated in the literature. This is due to the nature of the task, which has little relation with the traditional concerns of the decommodification of labor or skill protection; it is nearly the opposite, since it combines very basic training, counseling, and job placement with an eye to move a very wide range of claimants into the bottom of the labor market.

Next we depict the three marketization trajectories. In Denmark we narrate three waves of market change—a first experimental one that begins in 2002, a second centrally regulated and highly competitive one (2005–10), and a third municipalized, deregulated, and less competitive phase (2010–present). In Britain the story since the New Deals beginning in 1997 is one of centralization, privatization, and a particular form of market competition limited by non-market coordination, taken to an extreme by Conservative-led governments since 2010. In Germany the story begins with the Hartz reforms (passed and implemented in 2002–5), which created a highly fragmented and varied market and precipitated the creation of a powerful procurement apparatus within the PES.

In Chapter 3 we unpack the meaning of marketization at the level of the transaction. We begin with a discussion of the relationship between public authority, service provider, and client. This includes a discussion of why employment services exist external to the state (and it is not always due to past privatization) and the mixture of choice and compulsion, or rights and responsibilities, that define the role of clients. We then discuss some of the elements of the transaction, including its openness to new competitors, its frequency, the degree of standardization of the service involved, and the power of the price mechanism. We conclude by discussing different transaction modes that we observe in our sample that vary along these dimensions. We argue in this chapter that different kinds of transactions have different implications for providers, since they create different degrees of uncertainty and resource constraint and shape providers' capacity to mitigate them.

After Chapter 3 comes three appendices which present data that did not fit into the comparative structure of the book's chapters, but which will give the reader a more in-depth view of the cases. It includes deeper discussion of the survey of Danish municipalities, the Work Programme tendering process and resulting provider structure, and the workings of German voucher and tendering arrangements.

In Chapter 4 we examine the implications of marketization at the level of the sector. We find variation in the sector's composition and internal power relations and the degree of power and influence that providers have in policymaking. We argue that marketization redistributes power, and that this effect varies due to differences in transactions. The British market structure tends to empower private providers by giving them centralized control both over the market and discretion in devising their own services. In Germany transactions have the opposite effect, since they themselves are tightly managed by the public authority and they operate as a means of tightly controlling management within providers (although the situation is somewhat different under vouchers and grants). Furthermore, the diversity of contracting arrangements tends to fragment the sector. In Denmark providers have little power at the level of the market but often have considerable discretion in how they organize provision in-house (although this varies depending on the municipality and contract).

In Chapter 5 we examine the implications of marketization for front-line workers at the level of the organization, in providers. We include two trends highlighted by the employment-relations literature: the disorganization of industrial relations institutions (worker voice, pay, employment contracts, and professional regulation) and the assertion of managerial control of the labor process (including work organization and the interaction between clients and staff). The British market has tended to produce disorganized employment relations due to the turnover of contracts and the inadequacy of transfer of undertakings rules in mitigating the effects, and to reinforce management control in for-profit firms by giving them immense discretion. British providers have worked collectively to mitigate the problems of disorganization by creating an "Institute of Employment Professionals." Germany has a highly diverse landscape of front-line work, although generally the tight control of the funder over provision tends to undermine management control (by specifying the work in detail and requiring the use of trained social workers) while promoting disorganization (by squeezing prices and ensuring uncertainty). At the initiative of trade union-affiliated providers, lawmakers have responded with a sectoral minimum wage, albeit one with significant challenges for the labor inspectorate. Denmark has quasi-disorganized employment relations, with widespread use of freelancers and temporary employment contracts but high collective bargaining coverage; and typically very tight managerial control over the labor process.

Chapter 6 presents the implications of our analysis for governance. We find no evidence that any form of marketization is highly effective in achieving the policy goal, of low-cost but effective services to move unemployed people into jobs. Instead the chapter introduces four dilemmas. The first is price versus quality. Squeezing prices is a crucial part of extracting "value for money" from contracted-out services. But its consequence is to reduce the capacity of providers to innovate, which is crucially important given the complex and changing nature of the task. Second is payment by results versus equal access to services. Payment by results is attractive because it allows governments to claim that all spending is for services that are effective, but the consequence is usually "creaming and parking." Third is customer choice versus compulsion. Customer choice is a central justification for introducing markets in public administration, but this cut against the spirit of active or "activating" labor market policy, which is to compel clients to use particular services to move into paid work. Fourth is bureaucracy reduction versus open and transparent markets. The reduction in bureaucracy is a key justification of marketization, but markets that are open and transparent require considerable administrative effort, i.e. transaction costs. One way out of these dilemmas can be observed in Germany and Denmark: the insourcing of the services by the public sector. While understanding this is a matter for further research, we argue that it is neither panacea nor a return to the "bad old days."

The concluding chapter summarizes our findings and comparative analysis and presents the questions for future research that follow from them. It concludes with implications for the future of employment services, and the marketization project more generally, in Europe.

2

Employment Services

Three Marketization Stories

Given the spread of work-first welfare states and new public management across diverse countries, it is unsurprising that the marketization of welfare services is found in these three very different countries. And they are not the only countries where this has happened. The two most frequently analyzed cases in the literature, Australia and the Netherlands, marketized through a near-complete transfer of employment services from public to external providers. Denmark, Britain, and Germany, by contrast, retained most in-house provision of services. Here, marketization refers mainly to changes in existing externalized services, which may include increases in private-sector provision, but more importantly include changes to the workings of transactions between purchaser and provider.

These services vary widely, both within and between countries. Differences exist in terms of the exact task and clientele, the ownership and size of the provider, the quality of jobs and services, and the extent and kind of market mechanisms involved. These differences reflect the different history, institutions, and culture of the three countries. But before we can explain why these services vary, we need to say what the services are and what this variation is. In this chapter we take a first step by introducing employment services and the three country cases.

In Denmark marketization took place in three waves: a preliminary experimental one (2002–5), a second in which arms-length price-based competition was imposed from the national level managed by the national labor market authority, the Labor Market Authority (*Arbejdsmarkedsstyrelsen*—AMS)[1] (2005–10), and a third in which municipalities were handed responsibility for

---

[1] Arbejdsmarkedsstyrelsen has from 2014 been given a new name: STAR: Styrelsen for Arbejdsmarked og fastholdelse—Danish Agency for Labor Market and Recruitment.

organizing the services, with consequently some of them reducing the degree of marketization (2010–present). In Denmark marketization initially involved a huge part of the providers being affiliated with trade unions, but they became displaced by a for-profit sector that had to adapt to quick and radical changes both in the amount of funding and the kind of services provided. In recent years management of the market has been passed to the municipalities, including developing other ways of contracting and insourcing of parts of the services.

In Germany the main changes took place around the same time. The very public face of work-first welfare reforms were the Hartz reforms, which from 2002 and 2005 reshaped the benefits system, labor market regulation, and administration of employment services; it coincided with the much more quiet introduction of voucher schemes and the subjection of contracts to procurement law. This was followed by incremental changes imposed by lawmakers and the BA (*Bundesagentur für Arbeit*), in particular its procurement arm (the *Regionale Einkafszentren* (REZen)). While the landscape of providers had a similar composition after these reforms (aside from the new job-placement firms), the market became organized by a new actor, the REZ, and purchasing became accordingly more centralized.

The British story begins in 1997 with the creation of large labor market programs under the New Deals and privatization experiments starting in 2000. The more rapid changes, however, took place after 2007 with a push towards centralization of control and privatization of services, and the current market was brought about by the radicalization of this policy by the Conservative-led government under the Work Programme, launched in 2011. Over the latter period the landscape of provision was transformed from a diverse and fragmented one to one dominated by a few large firms known as "prime contractors" (or "primes"). A single market was created under the joint control of the responsible ministry, the Department for Work and Pensions (DWP) and the primes.

This chapter introduces employment services and the differing actors and institutions that constitute them in these three countries. We examine the ebb and flow of marketization and the dominance of for-profit providers in social-democratic Denmark, the proliferation of vouchers and competitive tendering in violation of the subsidiarity principles of conservative-continental Germany, and the rise of centralized control and strictly limited competition in neoliberal Britain. We show that these processes play out in uneven ways within these countries: Denmark has strong municipal control, Germany has extreme diversity and fragmentation, and Britain has tightening central control. Finally we show that the process is not irreversible: in Denmark and Germany there is evidence of externalized services being brought back into the public sector.

What Are Employment Services?

In Chapter 1 we defined employment services abstractly, in terms of the policy goal of moving jobless people into or closer to the labor market, the tasks of assessment, advice, training, job placement, and the organization of make-work schemes, and the role of the public employment service as a "public authority" responsible for funding and managing these services. But what does this mean in terms of the daily work of front-line staff?

In most countries a PES is responsible for paying benefits and providing job-search assistance for unemployed people eligible for insurance-funded benefits. In Britain this would be the local office of Jobcentre Plus and in Germany the local employment agency (*Arbeitsagentur*, and before the Hartz reforms, the local *Arbeitsamt*). In Denmark the municipal job center (and earlier a national PES) is not responsible for paying benefits (located at insurance funds or municipal benefit offices), but does play a crucial role in the assessment of entitlements in relations to fulfillment of obligations. Because the vast majority of these clients find work with no government-funded assistance, the intensity of services for new claimants is relatively low. Programs serving these clients usually suffer from "dead-weight effects," in which clients deemed highly employable find jobs without any service; evaluators often deduct these from overall program effects.

As the spell of unemployment lengthens, intervention intensifies. Clients receive advice from advisors in the job center. As part of these discussions job-seekers agreements are devised spelling out the actions that the client must take to look for a job and the support provided by the job center. This agreement is backed up by a threat of sanctions, i.e. having benefits payments stopped. The required actions might include applying for a certain number of jobs or attending training courses. In Denmark it was these kinds of services, for the insured and therefore relatively short-term unemployed, that were contracted out in the early phases of marketization.

Most marketized employment services in our countries, however, are for clients deemed to be more distant from the labor market, and who fall outside of the unemployment insurance system. These include long-term unemployed people whose entitlement to insurance-funded benefits has expired and who are deemed "needy" by means tests. Britain's largest contracted-out scheme, the Work Programme, also includes claimants of "inactive" benefits who have been reclassified as jobseekers. It is for clients who have been claiming the mainstream unemployment benefit, Jobseeker's Allowance (JSA), for at least twelve months, plus claimants of Employment and Support Allowance (ESA, the main sickness benefit) who are deemed work-ready with the aid of a "work-capability assessment" (which itself is contracted out). In Germany, numbers of participants in employment services are roughly equal between claimants of contribution-based Arbeitslosengeld and means-tested Arbeitslosengeld II (ALG II, known colloquially as Hartz IV), even though the latter claimant group is much larger.

For clients deemed distant from the labor market, intervention becomes more complex. There is also a strong element of compulsion, in line with the weakening of entitlements and tightening of conditions attached to benefits that define the work-first welfare state. Front-line workers in employment services for these clients carry out the following tasks, in all three countries.

Assessment and Sorting

In employment services assessing and sorting is inevitable because providers have to determine what kind of service is needed and what kind of job would be appropriate. For most schemes this is the first task after a client is referred from the job center. Assessment can be very in-depth and involve multiple one-on-one meetings; or it can be through a quick meeting or self assessment using an online tool. Sorting can be purely to identify suitability for job placements or also according to a broader assessment of needs and available services. German training providers, for example, will check whether clients showing up with a training voucher possess the general educational background needed for participating successfully in the kind of vocational training stipulated on the voucher.

Advice and Guidance

Behind work-first welfare states is the assumption that unemployment is caused, not only by problems in the macro economy to be addressed by fiscal or monetary policies, but also by individual problems that can be addressed through interventions in clients' lives. This can be very specialized, as with debt or drug and alcohol counselling; it can also be very broad, with advisors involved offering career coaching and identifying needs and monitoring progress on an ongoing basis. This is the core task carried out by university-educated social workers, but is also carried out by front-line workers with lower qualification levels, such as in Britain with the National Vocational Qualification (NVQ) level 3 for Information, Advice and Guidance (Crawford and Perry 2010: 8; see also Grugulis 2003).

Training

Low skill levels are another commonly cited barrier to work; and training for the unemployed takes two forms. There is professional training, such as the acquisition of formal qualifications, and general skills training, such as CV preparation, language training for foreigners, and basic computer skills. While much of the policy literature might see potential in employment services for "human capital investment," the countries in our sample have reduced skills training for the unemployed often to very brief courses. In Britain's "skills conditionality" scheme, for example, courses last a few weeks or days, and within Work Programme providers they may be briefer still. Denmark traditionally has had relatively extensive training opportunities for the unemployed (and probably comparatively still has), but over the last decade training has increasingly emphasized "activation" as the main instrument to labor market reintegration. Germany, traditionally a country placing great emphasis on vocational training, saw a massive decline of this in the wake of Hartz reforms, and courses aiming for certified skills declined even more. After a slight recovery, they were crippled after 2008 by budget cuts.

Job Placement

Because they are embedded in the work-first welfare state, job placement is the end goal of employment services. In all three countries, much effort goes into "employer engagement": convincing firms to hire unemployed clients, organizing meetings between clients and potential employers, and making follow-up phone calls to sustain the job placement (Ingold and Stuart 2015; McGurk 2014). Sometimes the same staff who are counsellors also do this work; other providers create separate employer-engagement and counselling functions. The job placement sustained over a specified amount of time (six months with German placement vouchers, two years under Britain's Work Programme) is the basis of payment by results in employment services in all three countries.

Organizing Make-Work Schemes

The so-called "second labor market" aims to overcome the isolation of clients and expose them to the disciplines and rhythms of work. Make-work schemes are diverse. They include sheltered employment in workshops for the disabled (as with Remploy in Britain, most of which was closed down during the period under study); schemes for public-benefit work for people who are difficult to employ (as with the German one-euro jobs, also recently scaled back); or work-for-benefit schemes in which a private employer receives claimants who are not being compensated (as with Britain's politically important but numerically small Mandatory Work Activity scheme). In Germany, subsidized waged employment (with a labor contract and with social insurance contributions paid) was implemented at a huge scale during the 1990s but was marginal during the period of our study; the more frequently used one-euro jobs compensate clients with an allowance that is a benefits top-up rather than a wage.

Combining and Governing Tasks

These tasks are combined in various ways in particular "schemes" that public authorities fund. Many combine most or all of the tasks listed above as an "end-to-end" service for a particular clientele. German one-euro jobs, for example, are make-work schemes that provide compensation to the client along with additional support services, including training and guidance, organized by the provider. Danish municipalities contract out end-to-end services for particular client groups, in the context of supported employment and work-first job-placement schemes. The British Work Programme similarly moves all counselling, training, and job-placement services that a client will receive over a two-year period to an external provider. German and Danish public authorities often contract these services out for a narrowly defined group of clients, usually young people, single mothers, disabled people, older jobseekers, or immigrants in a particular region, city, or neighborhood; in Denmark a scheme can be purchased for a very small number of clients. The Work Programme, by contrast, does so for a large and extremely diverse clientele numbering in the tens of thousands for each contract.

Other schemes focus on a single task. Most German schemes funded through procurement or vouchers, for example, are organized in this piecemeal way. A local job center will purchase a training program for a particular occupation or a general skill (e.g. CV writing or German language) for its clients in its territory and refer them to that service. Or a job center advisor will issue a voucher for a particular training course or for assistance from a private placement firm. It is also common for Danish municipalities to purchase these kinds of schemes. The DWP does this on a larger scale: it outsourced the reassessment of sick-benefits claimants nationwide (the so-called Work Capability Assessments) to determine who should be reclassified as a jobseeker and potentially mandated onto the Work Programme. Defining tasks narrowly gives the public authority the power to determine the mixture of services clients receive. Narrow definitions of client groups supposed to be rather homogenous limit providers' scope for the "creaming" of relatively job-ready clients.

Finally, these services are funded and regulated by the public employment services in varying ways. Some services are tightly controlled by the funder, like those purchased by the German BA and in the second wave of marketization in Denmark, discussed in the next section. Others give the provider discretion to design services as with the British Work Programme, the first wave of marketization in Denmark, and partnerships between municipalities and non-profit providers funded by grants in all three countries. As we will see in Chapter 3, there is variation in the degree to which providers are subject to competitive pressures.

The rest of this chapter introduces the three country contexts.

Denmark

Denmark shows how marketization takes place in a Nordic welfare state dedicated in theory to equality and social protection. But it also shows that marketization is not an irreversible, universal trend. Marketization was initiated by a center-right government with the agreement of Social Democrats in 2002 in response to criticisms of the public employment services as excessively bureaucratic, expensive, and ineffective. Services could be shifted to "other actors" (*Andre aktører*), a label that signaled that it was not purely a "privatization" using private, for-profit providers, but also an opportunity to use non-profit providers, such as union or union-driven insurance funds or training institutions or even new types of union-driven organizations. Unions saw this as an opportunity to regain influence and resources, prompting them and the Social Democrats to support a marketization agenda that they otherwise would have contested.

The quasi-market for employment services was created in Denmark between 2002 and 2005, primarily through the reform of services for the insured unemployed. While vocational training was always delivered by non-public providers, what were contracted out here were the employment services delivered by the PES, including contacts, interviews, guidance, job-search activities, availability checks, coaching, finding job training, and small basic training courses. The fourteen regional public employment service offices, corresponding to the present counties, were given free rein to decide what types of service and target groups of insured unemployed to contract out. The regional PES offices were required to purchase these services, but had discretion in the organization of contracts (e.g. length, provider obligations, monitoring, etc.) and pay models. Their only obligation was that at least 10 percent of the unemployed should be in services fully or partly provided by non-public providers.

This *first wave* of the marketization of employment services was almost unregulated by the national authorities, as regional public purchasers were provided with the cash and freedom to contract out all services and target groups to create a market. The market for contracted services grew significantly after its initial creation, invigorated by the mandatory obligation to contract services out for the unemployed. In 2005, around 46 percent of all insured unemployed persons were transferred to non-public providers, reflecting the stretched in-house capacity of the job centers (Bredgaard and Larsen 2008). Although a market was created, the national audit office and other evaluations (AMS 2004) criticized the lack of transparency or price-based competition. This first wave of creating an unregulated and non-transparent market was, hence, followed by public reregulation to make the market more transparent and competitive. At the same time, however, the public authorities wanted to gain greater control over the type of tasks and target groups being contracted out to non-public providers.

A *second wave* of marketization occurred following the discovery that it was difficult to establish and legitimate accountability relations (in relation to how the regional authorities engaged with non-public providers) while at the same time documenting cost savings, stimulating price competition, and promoting innovation (AMS 2004). In response to criticism from the National Audit Office, a reform was launched in 2005 that introduced strong central regulation on the market, imposed national tendering with price-based competition, and mandated that 80% of payments be performance-based. The AMS was in charge of the tendering, making framework contracts with providers from which local job centers could pick services. At the same time, non-public providers should no longer do administrative tasks formerly done by the PES, but instead "make a difference" in the contact with and service for the unemployed. Market incentives were thus enforced, while at the same time more "traditional" public regulation was put back in place to reregulate the deregulated market (Bredgaard and Larsen 2008). A more transparent and competitive market was created by public reregulation.

This reform nearly halved the number of insured unemployed persons being transferred to non-public providers (Bredgaard and Larsen 2007). As the new pay model intensified price competition and the focus on short-term job outcomes, the union-based providers and CVT (Continuing Vocational Training) institutions gradually disappeared from the market, being replaced by private, for-profit providers (Bredgaard and Larsen 2006). The union-based providers and CVT institutions each initially had around a 25 percent market share, shrinking to only 6 percent for the CVT institutions and 4 percent for union-based providers in 2009. Today, very few of these providers are left in this part of the market. Private, for-profit providers had an 89 percent market share in 2009 and today, the contracted market for employment services remains mainly based on private providers. This was probably due to the focus on short-term employment effects and the need to reduce investments in the services, which was unacceptable for many non-profit and union-affiliated providers due to their professional ethos and their need to remain in good standing with their members.

National tendering and performance-related payment models were mandatory up until 2011. Although the model was argued to improve effectiveness and efficiency, the results were disappointing. The combination of price-based competition, high risks for providers (waiting up to six months for full payment), and the drive to create short-term employment outcomes led to poor services from many of the private providers. Providers were also given much discretion in the design of their services as long as they could deliver job outcomes. Instead of the expected innovative market providing individualized services to the clients, however, this market produced standardized services centered on interview preparation and job-search activities.

Hence, providers competed on the basis of the price of their services rather than the innovative solutions they provided. This was especially a result of the performance-related payment model, as many of the providers found out that they could rely on substantial dead-weight effects to claim outcome payments. Although there were variations among the providers, media-reported "scandals" revealed examples of inferior services and what was seen as silly and humiliating forms of "activation" for the unemployed (Larsen and Wright 2014). Trade union activists collected and disseminated examples of poor service quality, leading to conflict with the for-profit providers that were often mentioned in interviews. This gave for-profit service providers a bad reputation and, as found in our interviews, undermined the confidence in market solutions among political and administrative decision makers.

The *third wave* of marketization took place from around 2010 and was related to another reform, which dissolved the PES and transferred employment services to the municipalities. Until then, the municipalities had little experience with the marketization of employment services. As municipalities had previously only contracted out limited parts of their services, the government feared this would harm the marketization process. And rightly enough, it seemed, since the market for transferring insured unemployed persons to market providers declined as a consequence of an experiment allowing some of the municipalities to assume responsibility for employment services from 2007 to 2009. In 2009, economic incentives for the municipalities to bring the unemployed into activation (for as much of their unemployment period as possible), at the same time as special economic incentives for using "other actors" were introduced, reigniting the growth of the quasi-market. Spending doubled for the insured unemployed, and more non-insured social-assistance recipients were transferred to external providers. Furthermore, national tendering was maintained and supplemented with a mandatory requirement to refer certain target groups to the market-based providers. With these initiatives, the government attempted to encourage municipalities to marketize services and the market briefly experienced a new "golden" period.

With the fiscal crisis and as part of a national restoration plan for the economy, however, the center-right government in 2010 removed most of the economic incentives for the municipalities to use external providers for employment services, although keeping the national tendering and the requirement to use market providers for certain target groups. The market was under severe pressure due to problems with low-quality services delivered by the market-based providers and declining political and administrative faith in such a market. Hence, when a Social Democrat-led government came to power in 2011, it dissolved national tendering and the requirement to use market-based providers for certain target groups, made tendering a matter for the municipalities to decide, increased municipalities' discretion in the purchasing of employment services, and exempted employment services from EU procurement rules.

Consequently, the Danish market for employment services has become much less regulated by central public authorities since 2011. While the regulation of providers was always relatively weak, deregulation has extended to the purchaser. The decision to contract out services and how to do so is, with a few exceptions, in the hands of the local authorities whereby the national authorities let the municipalities decide on using non-public providers. The extensive decentralization of the market for employment services makes it more difficult than in Germany and Britain to capture recent developments in the market, as there are no overall statistics for the municipal use of non-public employment service providers.

Our interview data and the national survey of municipal purchasers indicate considerable diversity in local practice, but an overall decline in both the volume of work and use of market mechanisms. (For more detail on our survey findings see Appendix A.) Of the sixty-six municipalities that responded to our survey, nine reported no longer using "other actors," and only six reported using them for more than 35 percent of clients. Of the fifty-one municipalities responding to our questions about purchasing practices, twenty-four reported no longer using the national tendering framework and sixteen reported abandoning competitive tendering altogether. This may reflect a learning process: 78 percent of respondents reported at least one instance of a contractor failing to live up to the requirements of the contract.

The decline of the market is due to less money spent on employment services and the municipalities being more reluctant than central government to use market solutions. Hence, as Table 2.1 shows, the vast majority of respondents report a decline in the use of other actors as well as a decline in the use of tendering. At the same time, respondents indicate that a shift in the type of services that are contracted out has taken place from using the non-public providers for generalized services to using them for more specialized services. This also involves a shift in target groups for the services to be contracted out, moving from the more easy to place (e.g. insured unemployed) to harder to place (e.g. disadvantaged, uninsured social-assistance recipients). Finally, respondents confirm our interview findings that a type of locally

Table 2.1. Danish municipalities' views on the development of the market (numbers of responses)

	Strongly agree	Partly agree	Neither agree or disagree	Partly disagree	Strongly disagree	Don't know
The use of other actors have decreased considerably	28	22	3	0	0	3
The abolishment of national tendering has reduced the use of other actors	17	21	4	8	2	4
The use of tendering has decreased	18	18	8	3	2	7
Other actors are more used for specialized tasks for weaker unemployed compared to generalized services for stronger clients	12	20	6	9	5	4
The involvement of other actors have been more partnership-based and less tendering- and contract-based	9	17	14	9	1	6

driven, more partnership-based contracting is increasing, leading to less price-based competitive tendering.

According to interviews with central civil servants, the evaluations which have been made in Denmark to assess whether "other actors" are more effective in terms of outcomes and costs than the public employment authorities have found that contracting out is neither more effective nor cheaper than keeping services in-house (AMS 2009; Deloitte 2009; National Audit Office 2013; Skou et al. 2008). The above-mentioned scandals facilitated this shift in the market model, as the limit on the exemption for political and administrative responsibility for the services appears to have been reached. Towards the end of its term, the Conservative government rolled back the market and the new Social Democrat-led government reduced it further in 2011 by abolishing the obligation for municipalities to contract out services for unemployed graduates, thereby abolishing the market at the national level. While this will reshape Denmark's trajectory, the Social Democrats supported the introduction of an employment-services market back in 2002 and the center-right government began rolling back the market in 2010. Consequently, the attraction felt by national politicians to markets and non-public providers disappeared, on both the left and right.

To anticipate the next chapters, three points can be made about Denmark. First, Denmark has had many different kinds of contracting practice since 2010 and at present has a varied market with both competitive tendering and partnership-based contracts. Second, marketization is reversible, with some municipalities using the framework of competitive tendering as promoted by AMS with others preferring a "partnership" approach, as well as "insourcing" of services. Third, the waves of marketization were due in large part to changes in the power of regional, local, and central levels in the governance of these services; while there is some learning taking place about how best to manage employment services, the lessons drawn differ from municipality to municipality.

Great Britain

British employment services are unusual due to their high degree of centralization and private-sector power. Prior to 1997, however, services for the unemployed not carried out in-house by Jobcentre Plus and its predecessors were managed by regional bodies or municipalities. Training and Enterprise Councils, for example, organized among other things voucher schemes to train unemployed young people. Using their own funds and national funding streams for urban regeneration, municipalities commissioned local schemes run by non-profits as well as maintaining in-house employment services (Finn 2015). For a decade afterward, a series of pilot programs tested concepts such as payment by results and private-sector provision of end-to-end services, alongside other activation schemes funded by devolved governments in Wales, Scotland, and Northern Ireland; regional agencies in England; and municipalities. In the wake of recommendations by investment banker David Freud (2007), under both Labour and Conservative governments, the market assumed its current structure.

The "New Deals" began in the immediate aftermath of the 1997 election of a Labour government. These schemes were carried out mostly in-house by the job centers, but partly by the same providers working on other schemes: local government, educational institutions, charities, and for-profit companies. These were market incumbents with a history of organizing training, advice, guidance, subsidized job placements, and other services for the unemployed. While the New Deals created a sudden shift in requirements for jobseekers—initially young ones—and increased the scale and political salience of active labor-market schemes, they did not immediately alter the landscape of service provision.

In 2000–7 experiments took place in privatized welfare-to-work provision. The "Employment Zones" were the seminal experiments in commissioning. Unlike Denmark, where marketization began with the short-term unemployed, Britain's early experiment with private providers involved services for long-term unemployed people in thirteen of Britain's most deprived areas. Far more than the large-scale national programs that replaced them, the Employment Zones relied on local partnership relationships between providers, local governments, job centers, and other regional bodies (Wiggan 2009: 1033).

While private providers did perform better than their public-sector comparators, this seems to have been because they were granted greater flexibility and more generous funding, and because of numerous job center advisors working for them on secondment (Davies 2008). There was a strong political will to move ahead with further privatization. Indeed, in 2000 the government created Working Links, a for-profit firm, as a joint venture with Manpower and Ernst & Young Consulting. It transferred numerous civil servants into this new private-sector market player, which became a major player in the Work Programme. Sensing an opportunity for increased contracting business from the government, the non-profit Association of Chief Executives of Voluntary Organizations joined with the mainly for-profit Employment Related Services Association (ERSA) to lobby for more privatization.

From 2007 to 2011 the market evolved toward greater centralization and privatization as part of a broader centralization trend in government. After 2007 the government moved the contracting function into central DWP offices, bypassing the local job centers, and reduced the number of organizations with which it directly contracted. This was motivated by parallel drives to reduce the number of contractors and professionalize the procurement function (Gershon 2004). Local control was further eroded with the abolition of regional funders in England (the Regional Development Agencies and Learning and Skills Councils) and the imposition of a 30 percent cut on funding to municipalities after 2010 (Local Government Association 2013). In 2011 the centralization of authority in the DWP was pushed further by abolishing the organizational separation between the ministry and its operational arm, Jobcentre Plus, demoting the latter as a "brand" within the ministry.

The market also changed due to specific ideas about how to organize welfare-to-work schemes articulated by Freud (2007). While Gershon had called for improving the in-house procurement function (2004: 13–14), Freud called for outsourcing it to prime contractors (2007: 17). The Labour government began to implement Freud's operational principles with the "Flexible New Deal," which used larger contracts and payment by results. These principles were enshrined in the welfare reform acts of 2007 and 2009, which created ESA, a new benefit for disabled people, reassessed claimants of sick benefits for job readiness, and moved large numbers of lone parents to JSA, preparing the way for these groups to enter the same mandatory schemes as other jobseekers.

Advised by the same David Freud, the Conservative-led coalition government that came to power in 2010 pushed these principles further. It quickly cancelled several of Labour's activation programs, including the Flexible New Deal and Pathways to Work (the latter for the disabled) and replaced them

Table 2.2. DWP-funded programs in 2013

Scheme	Indicative annual value (£)	Number of lots	Per year starts
Work Programme	500m	40	633,142
Skills conditionality (with SFA)	–	–	320,113
Health assessment framework	150m	5	n/a
Work choice	92m	28	19,716
Families with multiple problems (ESF)	67m	12	–
Community Action Programme	42m	18	7,000
Youth Contract	36m	12	ca. 80,000
Flexible support fund	32m	–	–
Innovation fund	10m	5–20	14,640
Mandatory work activity	8m	11	29,302
New Enterprise Allowance	6.3m	20	18,918

Note: SFA is the Skills Funding Agency; ESF is the European Social Fund

Source: Compiled from <http://www.gov.uk/contracts-finder> and <https://www.gov.uk/government/organisations/department-for-work-pensions>, own calculations

with the so-called Work Programme, also rolled out in 2011. Table 2.2 lists the DWP's schemes during the time of our research.

One early move by the government was to establish a small group of providers with which it would have direct contracting relationships. In September 2010 providers submitted tenders for the Employment Related Support Services (ERSS) Framework, with eleven lots covering all of Great Britain. Successful bidders would be eligible to bid for upcoming contracts directly with the DWP, including the Work Programme. One of the qualifying criteria was "sufficient [turnover] to sustain a contract of this size—a minimum [turnover] of £20 million is required unless further risk mitigation offered." This disqualified all but the largest players. Criteria also included supply-chain management, implementation, stakeholder engagement, and various statutory compliance issues (DWP 2010a).

In February 2011 providers on the ERSS framework submitted their bids for Work Programme contracts, which was divided into forty lots in which two or three "prime" contractors would manage the scheme in each of eighteen different "Contract Package Areas." Half of the points were attached to qualitative aspects of the bids (including supply-chain management, minimum service levels, and a description of the delivery model) and half to price (discounts offered by providers based on indicative price tables published in the tendering documents) (DWP 2010b). Eighteen providers won at least one contract as prime provider, with just over 50 percent of market share held by four multinational firms: Ingeus, A4e, Working Links, and G4S.

This process was designed to attract private capital, with the commercial interests of large providers in mind, and its details will be spelled out below. Surprisingly, spending on employment services declined under the Work Programme. This is in part because of the pricing during the tendering process;

the government provided a schedule of prices and then asked for discounts. The firm reported to have made the deepest discount—Deloitte Ingeus—won by far the largest share of the work, 22 percent, and interviewees estimate that discounts built into bids brought down prices by 40 percent. It is also due to the low numbers of outcome payments claimed. Fewer clients than expected were referred onto the program by job centers; of those that were referred there was a lower than expected number of job placements. The indicative annual spend of the Work Programme was around £500 million, about half the annual volume of all other contracted-out programs announced in the early years of the Coalition government. With the annual volume of contracted-out employment service purchasing by the DWP shrinking from £1 billion to around half of that, and the disappearance of other sources of funding, the sector has come under strain.

For the prime contractors, however, this turned out to be a stable market. The resource scarcity that resulted took a form that they could manage, since they had considerable discretion to cut back services. Furthermore, they remained involved in politics and administration, testified in parliament, influenced debate through a lobbying arm (ERSA) and a research arm (Inclusion), and had a relationship with senior civil servants in the DWP formalized as the Work Programme Partnership Forum. While providers are penalized financially for poor performance, by not receiving outcome payments and losing referrals from job centers, they have considerable flexibility to reduce their costs, in part by shifting costs and risks onto contractors and employees. While they can in principle lose their contracts or fail to win new ones, there are few examples of punishing misbehavior and only one example of a prime losing its contract on the Work Programme (a single contract held by the only publicly owned "prime," Newcastle College Group). There were, however, several mergers and acquisitions, including the acquisition of Ingeus and A4e and the merger of the two largest non-profit providers CDG and the Shaw Trust, leading to further concentration of the market and to large payments to the owners.

The municipalities, charities, and small firms that worked as subcontractors were hit hard by the vicissitudes of the Work Programme. These included providers of "end-to-end" services for a particular group ("Tier 1" subcontractors) and for more specific tasks ("Tier 2" subcontractors). It is common for primes, according to our interviewees, to have payment systems with their Tier 1 contractors that mirrored those of prime contractors, i.e. with little or no up-front payment. Interviewees also reported a serious problem with subcontractors not receiving referrals early on in the contract, in some cases leading to bankruptcies. While a complaints-based procedure—the "Merlin Standard"—existed to protect subcontractors, in practice this procedure was rarely invoked. The process of selection of subcontractors by the prime contractors was not subject to procurement law and far less transparent than in a government procurement exercise.

British employment services are unusual in a few ways. First, market competition has been reduced by introducing a five-year contracting cycle and a highly concentrated structure of prime contractors. This was a deliberate strategy to attract private-sector investment, and may have created companies that are too big to fail. Second, the sector has a dualized character, resembling automotive manufacturing more than employment services, with a stable group of prime contractors and a larger group of their subcontractors. Many of the latter are past market incumbents. The DWP has in effect outsourced its relationship with local government and civil society to the primes. Third, the services are standardized and rolled out over a large area, despite the government's intention of promoting innovation. Finally, these arrangements reflect a choice by policymakers for low-cost services delivered on a for-profit basis, with no element of consumer choice or possibility of moving services in-house if privatization did not work. While the other two countries use markets to tighten state control, Britain shifted most purchasing and performance-management functions into the primes.

Germany

Since the introduction of unemployment insurance in Germany in 1927, the functions of registering unemployed jobseekers, of paying contribution-based benefits, of labor market and occupational counselling, of job placement, and of managing ALMPs have been concentrated in the responsibility of the PES, now the BA. The BA is a body of public law with self-administration exerted by representatives of unions, employers' associations, and representatives of Germany's three levels of government. Because of this status there is no day-to-day managerial "steering" of the BA by the government as there is in Denmark via the AMS and in Britain by the DWP. Because government regulation of the BA's operations requires either legislation or ministerial decrees, German labor market policies are meticulously prescribed in law and the overall culture of provision is highly legalistic. It was very common for our interviewees to refer to passages of laws, and several interviewees in management positions in the civil service were trained lawyers.

Owing to the principle of "subsidiarity" in social-service provision between the state and religious as well as secular charities on the one hand and to corporatism in managing vocational training on the other, there is a long tradition of involving "third parties," mostly from the non-profit sector, in the provision of employment services and vocational training for unemployed people. However, until recently they were funded through grants or direct contracting by the local branches of the BA, not through competitive tendering.

The turning point for German employment services was the four laws for "Modern Services in the Labor Market" enacted between 2003 and 2005, known colloquially as the Hartz reforms. While these were triggered by a scandal over the falsification of job-placement numbers within the PES, they had severe implications for externalized services as well. The benefit reform at the heart of the Hartz package created a new means-tested benefit, known as ALG II or "Hartz IV," by merging unemployment assistance (a means-tested but earnings-related follow-on benefit after exhaustion of unemployment benefit claims) with social assistance (a flat-rate and means-tested benefit). The group claiming the new benefit came to be much larger than the group of recipients of the insurance-based unemployment benefit, ALG I, because, as part of the reforms, eligibility for benefits was tightened and the duration of benefits was reduced. In addition, strong labor demand from German employers sharply reduced the number of people on insurance-based unemployment benefits without greatly affecting the number of claimants of ALG II who tend to be more distant from the labor market.

The new benefit follows the logic of social assistance. Although the reform was designed to relieve municipalities of part of their financial burdens for social assistance (Hassel and Schiller 2010), few municipalities were willing to give up their responsibility for serving clients. The political conflict that ensued was resolved by a compromise that eventually led to the division of the PES into two tiers (Knuth 2009; Knuth and Larsen 2010). The first is responsible for claimants of ALG I—normally lasting one year—administered by 156 local offices of BA known as employment agencies. The second tier is responsible for ALG II via 404 local job centers. Three quarters of job centers are "joint facilities" (*Gemeinsame Einrichtungen*) created as separate legal entities by the respective municipality and the regional employment agency, and the remaining one quarter are run by the respective municipality. Because of the constitutional principle of municipal self-government, central government cannot exert managerial control over municipalities and can only steer by detailed legislation. The culture of municipalities is rather different from that of the BA, with a far stronger social-work orientation in the former and labor-market orientation in the latter.

At the time of the Hartz reforms, a variegated scene of providers operated by or associated with religious and secular welfare associations, social partners, business and craft chambers was already involved in providing employment services. There were widespread, though unsubstantiated, accusations of patronage. Since the social partners also sat on local boards of the employment service, it was hinted that procurement decisions resulted from a "give and take" between local management and the social partners. Similar accusations were made regarding organizers of make-work schemes and providers of services in local networks in partnership with municipalities, since many of these providers had connections with politicians and administrators that made funding decisions (Seibel 1991).

Unlike the other two countries, marketization did not entail privatization in the sense of a substantial shift between public and external provision of services; instead "the market" would be used to modernize services in two ways: first, by creating competitive pressure on the BA's in-house services, and second, to shake up the relationship between the public employment service and external service providers (Table 2.3). The law tied specific forms of intervention traditionally known as "instruments" to specific ways of funding them (the "transaction mode"). Under grants, local managers would receive proposals for schemes from providers and approve and fund them. Under vouchers, job centers would issue a document to clients, who would then choose the provider. Under procurement, local managers would specify schemes (*Maßnahmen*), purchase them, or rather have them purchased by a central purchasing unit, and refer clients.

Starting with the Hartz reforms and continuing through consecutive rounds of reforms to these instruments, more and more services were subjected either to procurement via competitive tendering or to payment via vouchers. However, some instruments have remained outside the marketization regime to date, including training centers for disabled youth (cost reimbursement) and various kinds of make-work schemes (grants following applications by providers, who are also the employers).

Figure 2.1 sketches the development of marketization since 2002 by showing the accumulation of instruments funded through vouchers or purchased under procurement law and the years in which specific schemes were introduced or phased out. Although some marketized schemes were phased out,

Table 2.3. Marketized schemes in Germany

Transaction	Scheme	Years running
Vouchers (*Gutscheine*)	Placement vouchers	2002–
	Training vouchers	2003–
	Activation vouchers	2012–
Purchasing (*Vergaberecht*)	Personnel service agencies	2003–8
	Employment integration support	2003–8
	Activation and integration	2009–
	Career start support	2009–
	Apprenticeship preparation	2009–
	Apprenticeship support	2009–
	Vocational training for Hartz IV claimants: optional procurement instead of voucher	2012–

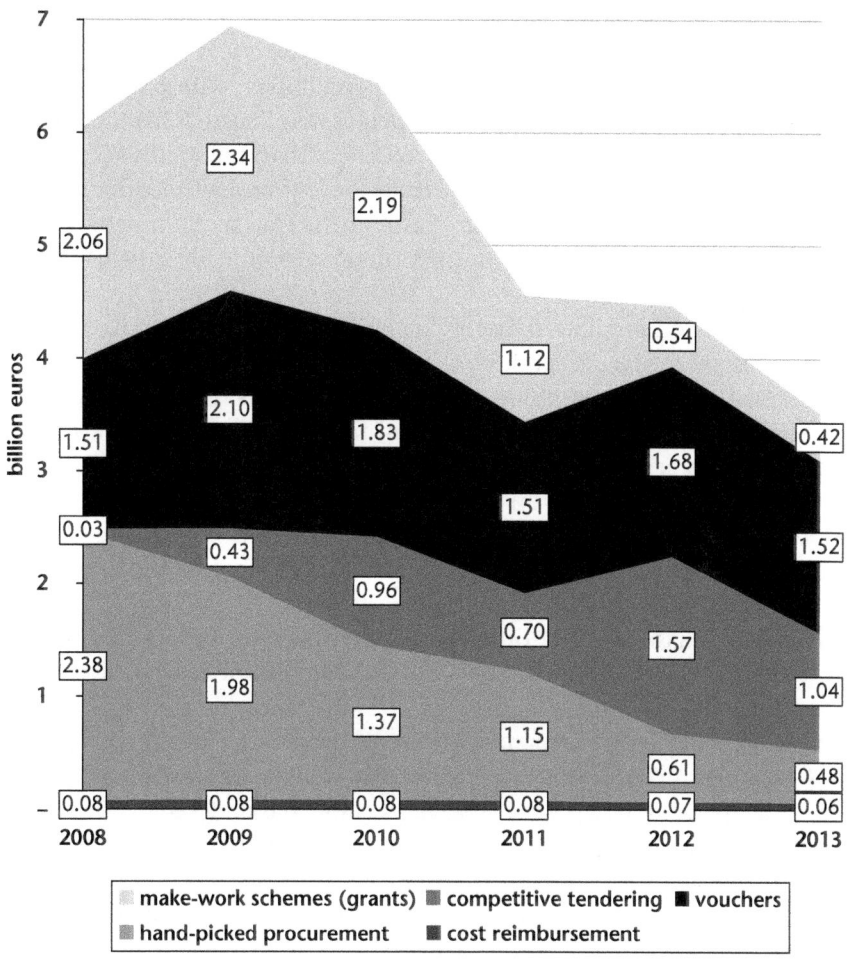

Figure 2.1. Spending by transaction mode in Germany

there was an overall increase in the number of schemes under both transaction modes.

As the number of marketized instruments grew, overall spending shrank. In Figure 2.1 we show the development of spending on schemes governed by different transaction modes as they will be conceptually developed in Chapter 3. Our representation covering 2008–13 is confined to discretionary instruments and excludes measures for disabled people funded via annual grants. It shows cuts to non-marketized make-work schemes from over €2 billion to under €500 million per year. It also shows stability in the amount of spending on vouchers and decline in spending on schemes subject to procurement law.

Job-placement vouchers, the only marketized scheme mentioned in the original Hartz concept (Hartz Commission 2002), represent a marginal market segment. They follow a simple payment-by-result logic, with prices and other parameters fixed in law. Some 330,000 vouchers were issued in 2013, an increase of 32 percent compared to 2012, of which less than one tenth (31,000) led to payments after six weeks, and slightly more than half of these (17,000) survived to trigger payments after six months. Placement vouchers worth €18.5 million were redeemed in 2013 (Bundesagentur für Arbeit—Statistik 2014a and 2014b).

Far more often used are training vouchers, which are worth €1.5 to €2.1 billion annually. The availability of data on these is, however, unsatisfactory since the BA does not publish the number of vouchers issued. In 2014, more than 300,000 persons entered vocational training courses paid by employment agencies or job centers which, according to the legal rules, must have been based predominantly on vouchers. Attrition of training vouchers with about 14 percent of those issued (Kruppe 2009, 12) is much lower than placement vouchers since they are not tied to success but simply to participation in the prescribed course.

Public purchasing is the other path to marketization. Overall spending on externalized employment services has been almost halved from nearly €7 billion in 2009 to €3.5 billion in 2013. Within this shrinking market, competitive tendering expanded from 6 percent to nearly 30 percent, and vouchers from 30 to 43 percent; this went at the expense of grants (from 34 percent down to 12 percent) and "hand-picked" procurement where bidders are chosen in advance by the purchaser (Bundesagentur für Arbeit—Statistik 2014a and 2014b and preceding years; own calculations; see also Figure 2.1). Open competition has thus gone from a marginal position to being the norm.

For the purchasing practices of the job centers the centrally relevant passages of the Hartz laws were those laying out a duty to use procurement law for various instruments. Subsequent legislation expanded the number of strictly marketized instruments (competitive tendering or vouchers). Given the complexity of some of the services and the local politics through which they are specified and funded, the task of compliance was a large one. The BA responded by moving purchasing out of its local offices and into a centralized procurement function. For providers the principal manifestation of this has been the five Regional Purchasing Centers (REZen).

The REZen carry out a professionalized procurement function that must be used by local employment agencies serving ALG I (insured) claimants and may be used by those "joint" job centers serving ALG II (means-tested) claimants managed both by the BA and the municipality. The latter, operating on budgets separate from the BA budget, use the REZ on a fee-for-service basis. (Fully municipalized job centers cannot use the REZ.) There are currently five REZen and a central procurement function in Nuremburg, the seat of BA headquarters, where the fundamental procedure was designed and where regional activities are supervised. In collaboration with the REZen, the procurement arm at headquarters also creates off-the-shelf *Standardprodukte* to be used by local managers as a template for schemes they are purchasing.

The local employment agency or job center is responsible for deciding what kind of schemes are to be purchased. But the REZ plays an important role in the services from the perspective of the provider, for two main reasons. First, it manages the process of evaluating bids, applies a formula according to which cost and price criteria translate into a choice of contractor (see Appendix C for details), and finally draws up and manages the contract with the successful bidder. In response to criticisms from providers—mainly that contracting values low price over high quality—the REZ constantly alters its processes. One current example is the introduction of past performance as a criterion in contracting.

Despite the vast changes in transactions between the BA and the providers triggered by the Hartz reforms, the composition of this landscape remains broadly similar to that prior to the reforms. Its most striking characteristic is its high degree of fragmentation, with specialized private placement providers operating under placement vouchers, private training providers operating under training vouchers and procured training schemes, and a very wide variety of secular and religious non-profits, large and small, delivering various other schemes. Multinational firms have attempted to enter the German market, but without much success; and private placement firms, though new, are restricted to a small market segment.

The German case is marked off from the others in a few ways. First, it is the most diverse and fragmented, in terms of the organization of transactions and in terms of providers. This reflects the localized nature of decision making in the BA, the different legal frameworks covering different services and client groups, and the tendency of BA managers to purchase small narrowly specified schemes rather than end-to-end services covering large numbers of clients. Second, marketization does not entail privatization; external providers have not taken over work previously carried out in-house (with the exception of the small niche for private placement services) but have been subjected to intensified competitive pressures. Third, Germany is the only country in our sample with vouchers, which introduce—or at least simulate—customer choice. Fourth, it is the case with the strongest example of market-making public bureaucracy, the REZ, with a clear formula for choosing providers and a role in designing the work being purchased (discussed in Appendix C).

Conclusion

This chapter shows that the marketization of employment services has developed differently in the three countries. Denmark has had a rapidly changing structure that creates deep uncertainty for providers, resulting in wide variation by municipality. Great Britain developed more gradually a stable national structure favoring a few large firms and creating volatility for hundreds of other providers. Germany has witnessed disruptive change with the Hartz laws and associated reforms, but retains a fragmented structure characterized by intense competition and tight control by the funder. While these changes were associated with intensifying competition, marketization meant different things in different countries and different market segments.

Any explanation for these differences that emphasized the features of welfare regimes would be insufficient. With the adoption of new work-first welfare-state principles, some past principles underpinning welfare service provision were abandoned. Governance of Danish services by the social partners was replaced with competitive tendering and performance management, and provision of services by union-affiliated providers and the public sector replaced with for-profit firms. Public-sector dominance of British employment services was replaced by private-sector dominance, both in terms of provision and regulation. The German principle of subsidiarity, in which services were delegated to civil-society providers on the basis of their politically determined status, was replaced by principles of equal treatment and transparency in the context of market competition. In all three cases the main substantive changes took place after 2000.

This is not to say that the features of welfare regimes typically used by comparativists are unimportant. They help to account for the relatively high per capita spending and the effectiveness of trade union campaigns against the marketization of employment services in Denmark, the eventual willingness by the state to relinquish public control of services to private firms in Great Britain, and the autonomy of the BA and continued large-scale provision by religious charities in Germany. But such an explanation would neglect the competitive dynamics created intentionally by government funders in all three countries and the internal dynamics of providers that result.

The proximate causes of these changes were not only the policies, politics, or principles of welfare states. In all three countries the rise of the work-first welfare state was shaped by New Public Management techniques (contracting and performance management) and austerity (pressures on public spending). Differences were shaped by the state structures involved, often in flux, and not in a common direction. In Denmark the market was shaped by an overall municipalization trend and in Britain by a centralization trend. In Germany marketization took place by central state decree in a context of continued strong local control of the substance of the services. Public authorities do not make markets under conditions of their own choosing, but theories from comparative social science do not tell us what the relevant conditions are.

In Chapter 3 we will draw on other bodies of literature to spell out our alternative line of argument emphasizing marketization. The rest of the book examines the concrete implications that market change has had for policymakers, managers, and front-line workers.

3

Marketization and Transaction Modes

Marketization in this book refers to a change in the way that public authorities fund the services of external providers, i.e. through competitive transactions. The literature defines and operationalizes marketization and related concepts in a variety of ways. Policy researchers tend to emphasize policy principles of states under neoliberalism. A pro-market orientation can be contrasted with past Fordist/Keynesian welfare states (Jessop 1999; Peck 2001) and with governance modes such as bureaucracy or networks (Considine 2001; Jantz et al. 2015). Market competition is sometimes dealt with in practical terms, as part of the managerial tool kit of disciplining staff and clients in the welfare state (Clarke and Newman 1997). Industrial relations writers tend to emphasize a rollback in non-market regulation over private firms by the state or by unions (Baccaro and Howell 2011), the introduction of organizational boundaries within a given production process due to vertical disintegration or privatization (e.g. Marchington et al. 2005; Doellgast and Greer 2007), an increase in the number of competitors selling a specific product (Brown et al. 2008; Hauptmeier 2010), or competition between a firm's locations for investment (Greer and Hauptmeier 2016).

These different ways of discussing the market reflect a way of defining markets and specifying their consequences that is driven by the particular context and available data. We develop below a typology of transactions to grasp the particular features of markets that matter, not only for the workplaces and services we are examining, but also more broadly. In contrast to most policy literature, our focus is on concrete practices of public authorities rather than principles of governance or management. In contrast to most industrial relations literature, we focus on inter-organizational transactions rather than the rules intended to govern the workplace.

We define marketization in terms of the properties of a transaction organized by a public authority.[1] Following quasi-markets theory, our definition

---

[1] We use the term "public authorities" for lack of a better alternative. While some readers may prefer the term "state" or "government funder" as a catch-all term, to other readers these terms

presupposes an organizational divide between purchaser and provider that is mediated by a transaction; this transaction is an exchange of money for services (Le Grand 2006). These transactions vary in how they are organized and how explicitly the give and take between purchaser and provider is spelled out in the legal documents exchanged. Government spending on external services may not be marketized, since transactions may take the form of a grant-making relationship with little or no price-based competition between providers. Even where competitive tendering is used, competition between providers may be limited by a small number of players (Van Slyke 2003), disincentives for investors (Krachler and Greer 2015), and policy reasons for having strong local networks of providers (Knuth 2014b; Schulte et al. 2016). But highly marketized transactions also exist, consisting of open tendering for standardized services with intense competition between providers, short-term contract cycles, and downward price pressures. The transaction is our starting point for moving beyond ad hoc approaches to marketization, because it can be empirically studied, it matters for the nature of public services (both in theory and in practice for our interviewees), and it is important well beyond the context in which we are studying it.

A common assumption is that the organization of business transactions is determined by the nature of the task; this is plausible, since there are differences in what contracting arrangements will be most efficient for differing tasks (Williamson 1985, 1999). As Rothstein (1998: 79) notes, employment services as a task involve intensive state intervention in local labor markets; this means changing operative conditions, with a high degree of complexity and uncertainty concerning the behavior of employers and clients. This should affect make-or-buy decisions and the management of the transaction when an external provider is used. In fact, however, public authorities' actions are not determined by the task or policy environment. Some services are subject to price-based competition and turn them into standardized commodities, while others do not; and this variation can be both within and between countries for similar services.

In Chapter 2 we told the three national stories of employment-services marketization in broad outline. In this chapter we focus specifically on the details of transactions. Our first step is to examine the relationship between the public purchaser, the non-public provider,[2] and the client. We then

---

would refer specifically to central government ministries or departments. Our aim is to develop a theory that applies also to markets organized by subnational levels of government or by national public bodies with some autonomy from central government. The former includes municipalities, which are the main purchasers of employment services in Demark, and the latter includes quasi-public insurance funds, which have this role in Germany.

[2] We use "non-public" and "external" interchangeably. They can be private for-profits, but are often non-profit or even public sector. External public agencies act as a provider and not a public authority responsible for funding and regulation.

examine the main features of the observed transactions, including the legal and policy dimensions that distinguish the three transaction modes—grants, vouchers, and purchasing—and the choices made by funders that affect the intensity of competition—de jure openness, frequency, the price mechanism, and prescriptiveness. Finally, we discuss three basic transaction modes and introduce the examples we observe empirically. The country-specific analyses of transactions that inform this discussion are presented in the three appendices.

Purchasers, Providers, and Clients

Prior to marketization is a "make-or-buy" decision by a public authority. This determines the division of labor between the public authority ultimately responsible for the service and an external provider of the service it is funding. The public authority is responsible for organizing the transaction.

There are countless considerations that inform make-or-buy decisions in public administration. Many are political. The self-interest of external providers, for example, is generally conducive to private provision. Danish trade unions supported marketization in 2002, and one of the main British charity umbrella bodies did something similar in 2008, because their leadership hoped (wrongly, it turns out) that it was a kind of privatization that would generate business for their affiliates. There are also cultural considerations, such as subsidiarity in Germany, in which some social matters are considered too delicate to be monopolized by the state, and citizens must have the right to choose a trusted provider (e.g. one corresponding to their creed and locality). Subsidiarity is consistent both with conservative choices in purchasing (e.g. from incumbent church-run providers) and with a high degree of customer choice (e.g. vouchers) (Klenk 2015). Third are the doctrines of NPM and overall neoliberal bias in policymaking calling in-house production into question on grounds of cost, efficiency, and outcomes. As Davies (2008) shows in the UK context, even weak evaluation evidence can be used by governments to support privatization decisions. Fourth, there are legal considerations. Public purchasers in Germany, for example, reported in interviews being reluctant to carry out anything in-house that private actors could also do due to worries with compliance with the principles of European competition law. This, despite the fact that employment services can be exempted from procurement law and the EU Procurement Directive explicitly allows in-house production.[3] Fifth are considerations of "public value" (Hefetz and Warner

---

[3] These interviews were conducted before the implementation of the new European Procurement Directive became an issue in Germany.

2004), which explain why public-sector job centers retain an important role in the provision of services, and why the marketization process is sometimes reversed by moving work in-house. Services can be privatized, or privatization can also be reversed, in order to improve client outcomes or boost the organizational stability of in-house public-sector provision.

Whatever the context and stated justification of the make-or-buy decision, there are three main institutional paths through which a public authority might use external rather than in-house providers.

First, public services might be privatized. In this variant, services previously produced by the public authority are transferred to external providers. While this term conventionally refers to a transfer of a public asset—say a hospital or a factory—into private ownership, in employment services it refers to the transfer of a function. The staff previously engaged in producing these services may be transferred to a non-public provider, or the organizational unit in which they work may be spun off and converted to a private firm. This is what happened in the course of Britain's early New Deals, when the government created the firm Working Links as a private-sector joint venture and transferred public-sector workers into it. This was also the case in the countries that pioneered the marketization of employment services. The Netherlands and Australia created a market by transferring their public employment services to for-profit companies.

Second is that, due to historical precedence, services are purchased from an incumbent provider already carrying them out. One example is educational institutions (often affiliated with trade unions or employer associations) providing services for unemployed as formerly seen on a relatively large scale in Denmark and Germany. Even before national welfare states emerged and expanded their scope of activities, social services for vulnerable people were provided by charities, trade unions, or other forms of self-organization, or by municipalities. As public authorities gradually assumed responsibility for such services, and as these social groups became part of the clientele of job centers, these charities also became providers of externalized employment services. In Germany, in the wake of the compromise of 1648 that ended the Thirty Years' War, maintaining a balance between the Catholic Church and state-supported Lutheran churches became a precondition for the cohesion of the German nation-state. When the welfare state emerged centuries later, the subsidiarity principle was extended to grant the churches' affiliates a privileged status, independent of commercial considerations, as providers of social services. In legal principle, the state fulfils its responsibility for these services by subsidizing the activities of these charities (Sachße 1998).

Third is the co-production of new services with an incumbent provider of similar services. In this case, a potential market develops due to the extension of the scope of services that the public authority decides to buy from incumbent providers. This was common in all three countries before a centralized procurement function for employment services emerged. Public-sector bodies, especially municipalities, worked with local charities to devise schemes to train, advise, and organize make-work schemes for disadvantaged groups. Some of them were large well-established organizations run by churches or trade unions that added employment services to an existing portfolio of training, advice, and other social services. Others were more recent initiatives that evolved out of the so-called new social movements of the 1970s and 1980s, which were deemed to have better access than the public sector to the "hard-to-reach" groups that they were organizing. Finn (2015) describes this history in Britain and Seibel (1991) in Germany.

The resulting differences between transactions lead to differences in services that matter for clients. The transaction mode, for example, creates a difference in the importance of compulsion as opposed to choice in selecting services and providers. Under public purchasing the public authority decides; under vouchers the client decides. Depending on the degree to which the transaction creates resource constraints and uncertainty for providers, it can also lead to less time spent by clients with qualified staff. Depending on the coordination between funder and provider, front-line staff may use their discretion to resist sanctioning; this weakens in practice the element of compulsion built into policy. The transaction affects not only the quality and quantity of the service, but also the distribution of staff time. If payment by results is part of the price mechanism, for example, there is a strong possibility that clients far from the labor market will be neglected and resources will be focused on those close to the labor market.

For policymakers expecting that marketization will cause external providers to implement policies as intended, this gap between political intention and operational reality is not encouraging. It is well known from the literatures on implementation and street-level bureaucracy (see Brodkin and Marston 2013, as well as Rothstein 1998 for an insightful critique); but this literature has only begun to touch on the transactions used to govern services which, for externalized services, constitute this gap.

Elements of the Transaction

In this section we discuss two dimensions—who chooses the provider and whether or not procurement law applies—that are the defining features of the three transaction modes. Then we discuss four more dimensions that determine the degree to which transactions are marketized.

Choice of Provider

The notion of customer choice is a powerful one in public discourse and theories of public administration; but for most employment services it is not the client who chooses which service to use. In the work-first welfare state clients are referred to services and required to attend, a requirement that is backed up by sanctions. Typically it is the public authority that chooses the provider and not the client. In the exceptional case of vouchers, the service is an entitlement rather than a requirement, the client chooses, and the public authority pays.

Despite the principle of customer choice, it is a complicated matter who decides under voucher arrangements. Evaluations of the German training voucher system show that the number of vouchers reaching the provider is often insufficient to pay for courses, because clients are not finding courses to attend and are dropping out when they do find courses (Kruppe 2009). The literature on British training vouchers for young people during the 1990s showed that employers and public agencies used them to fund non-compulsory services to which they were referring clients, but that there was little scope for clients themselves to choose services (Unwin 1993). This research suggests, and our case studies confirm, that local voucher markets for specialized employment services can only function with informal non-market interventions, including recommendations from staff to clients—contrary to the policy of customer choice—that they contact a specific provider.

Under purchasing and grants the matter is more straightforward. It is the public authority that decides on the service, subject to certain constraints. For services funded through annual grants, the incumbent provider is almost always chosen; the funder has little choice because the service is continuous and capital-intensive, making change difficult and costly. For other kinds of grants the funder is usually limited to a small group of providers in a local network. In both cases the schemes in question tend to be voluntary for clients. For services purchased under procurement rules, there is wide variation in how open competition is—it can be limited to a hand-picked group or opened to all providers across Europe—but participation by clients is usually mandatory.

Can Procurement Law Apply?

When public authorities engage in purchasing a service, rather than merely allocating a money for an activity carried out by a provider, their actions are restricted by laws intended to promote free market exchange. The European Union's (EU) Procurement Directive (2014/24/EU) and the national laws that transpose it—in German it is part of the "Law against Market Barriers" (*Gesetz gegen Wettbewerbsbeschränkungen*)—have evolved with an eye to promoting open competition across Europe and a level playing field. While it imposes a complex set of requirements on public purchasers, as well as legal recourse for providers when there are violations, it is also flexible in many ways. Member states can exempt employment services from the rules of the directive as "social services of general interest." Contracts under certain size thresholds (€750,000 for social services) can be exempted because there is no "cross-border interest." The 2014 directive contains numerous passages emphasizing the importance of social and ecological criteria in public purchasing (criteria which were deliberately downplayed by the authors of the 2004 directive (Hartlapp et al. 2014: 88–91)).

The requirements of the directive can be illustrated by five procedures it spells out.[4]

1. Open procedure: any provider can participate, and the tendering exercise is advertised with selection criteria, normally with a time limit for receipt of bids of thirty-five days (art. 27).

2. Restricted procedure: similar to an open procedure, except that providers must submit a request to participate (art. 28).

3. Competitive procedure with negotiation: similar to the restricted procedure, except the outcome of the tendering exercise serves as the basis of a negotiation (art. 29). This is only allowed if "the needs of the contracting authority cannot be met without adaptation of readily available solutions; they include design or innovative solutions; the contract cannot be awarded without prior negotiations because of . . . the complexity or the legal and financial make-up or because of the risks attaching to them; [or] the technical specifications cannot be established with sufficient precision" (art. 26).

4. Competitive dialogue: similar to the competitive procedure with negotiation, but with a wider-ranging discussion of "the means best suited to satisfying [the public authority's] needs," including "all aspects ofthe procurement" (art. 30); restrictions to using it are the same (art. 26).

5. Negotiated procedure without prior publication: negotiation with a provider over the specification of the services without a public announcement of a tendering exercise. It can only be used if there were no "suitable responses" to a previous tendering exercise, where only a particular operator can provide the services, or under "extreme urgency"

---

[4] A sixth procedure, the "innovation partnership" also exists for large and complex information technology and public works projects. This procedure has not been used in employment services to our knowledge.

due to "unforeseen circumstances"; these contracts are limited to three years (art. 32).

This list shows that European procurement law explicitly recognizes the circumstances behind differing practices by allowing different procedures, some more marketized than others. Its rules about selecting procedures suggest that open competitive tendering may be inappropriate for innovative or complex services, those with legal and financial ramifications or an element of risk, or those that are difficult to specify a priori. Conversely, as para. 43 of the directive's preamble says, neither the competitive procedure with negotiation nor competitive dialogue should be used for "off-the-shelf services or supplies that can be provided by many different operators on the market."

But it does impose real constraints on the actions of purchasers. As one German purchaser told us,

> Procurement is an onerous burden. The reason for procurement is distrust that the purchaser makes truly independent decisions. I fundamentally reject the idea that employment services can be procured, because it is not about the manufacture of chairs but rather about the labor of people under very difficult conditions, and I am convinced that one may and should trust us as purchasers, and that we are able [even without procurement law] to make appropriate and efficient economic decisions.   (German purchaser 7)

What are the alternatives? Vouchers are exempt from European procurement law, along with other "customer choice" arrangements, on the grounds that they are "simple authorization schemes" to carry out a task, rather than public procurement, and grants are exempted on the grounds that they are "mere financing" (2014/24/EU sec. 5). In Germany—which does apply procurement law to a range of employment services explicitly in the legal framework defining the instruments of active labor market policy—there is an alternative legal framework governing grants and vouchers, namely *Zuwendungsrecht*, part of public budgetary law. Denmark has exempted employment services from procurement law, although European legal principles of equal treatment and transparency still apply; although Britain has not sought this exemption, subcontracting by Work Programme providers is exempt on the grounds that the private firms organizing the "supply chains" (the "prime contractors") are not public authorities. It is unclear what reforms to British procurement law will take place following Brexit.

Openness

One way to increase market competition is to increase the number of potential competitors. In manufacturing this is what globalization has done, with devastating consequences in most industrial areas in the global north. Built into EU treaties is a prerogative to reduce the barriers for the international mobility, not only of goods, but also of services, capital, and labor, i.e. to open markets within the EU. Most externalized public services—especially those purchased—are subject to statutory principles of transparency and equal treatment, and more detailed requirements if they are covered by the procurement directive. In employment services the most common form that market opening takes is the decision to allow private companies to bid for contracts once carried out exclusively by non-profit or public-sector providers and to subject those traditional providers to the same rules and procedures as private companies, in effect treating non-profit providers as if they were private companies. Introducing consumer choice over the provider is also a form of market opening.

There are limits to the openness of markets in our sample. First, accreditation is common, and was first introduced in 2004 in Germany for training providers wanting to participate in voucher schemes, later extended to providers wanting to participate in tendering for other schemes, and finally, and in 2012 to Germany's newly introduced activation voucher scheme. Non-accredited providers are excluded from the scheme to promote quality control. Second is prequalification for participating in tendering, as per the "restricted procedure" of EU procurement law. The largest example of this in our sample is Britain's framework for employment-related services that allowed providers to bid for the Work Programme and other schemes. Third, there is the use of criteria in the tendering process to disqualify bids from providers that have performed badly in the past or broken the law. Germany's procurement rules were recently amended to allow characteristics of the provider such as past performance (*bieterbezogene Qualitaetskriterien*), and the 2014 EU Procurement Directive contained new language encouraging social and environmental criteria in contracting. Fourth, public authorities might purchase new services from incumbent providers without competitive tendering, as per the "negotiated procedure without prior publication." In Denmark, which has exempted employment services from procurement law, this is taken further by allowing municipalities to extend an existing contract between a provider and a different municipality into their own territory without a tendering exercise. Fifth is the limiting of circulation of the call. While European procurement law requires advertising tenders above the threshold to potential bidders across the EU using the Commission's electronic system, smaller tenders may be advertised on a municipal purchasing website, along with unrelated tendering exercises for other goods and services, e.g. for public works. Sixth is the hand-picking of bidders prior to making the funding decisions. Such a "negotiated procedure without prior notice" is encouraged by EU procurement law for particularly complex kinds of contracts that the funder cannot specify in detail before talking to providers.

The overall trend in employment-services markets, however, is toward such *de jure* market opening, as local partnership arrangements have been replaced by more centralized and transparent purchasing and voucher arrangements. The consequence of this for providers has been increased uncertainty. But *de facto* opening in the form of an influx of new kinds of providers does not necessarily result. Although Germany has created an open market for employment services, international providers reported in interviews that participation on a large scale was not a lucrative proposition. The same could be observed in Denmark even in the period with national tendering and the largest market opening, where international providers without luck tried to establish themselves as market players in Denmark. Britain, by contrast, did create a new market segment with an eye to commercial considerations of providers; but the large scale of the contracts closed this segment off to most incumbent providers, which were too small, and led to a concentration of that segment. The effects of de jure market opening on the landscape of provision therefore depend on other features of the transaction.

Frequency

A feature of transactions commonly mentioned in interviews with providers is the length of contracts and the frequency with which it is necessary to submit tenders. Under competitive tendering for standardized goods, there can be contract cycles as short as six months (for some German schemes) or as long as five years (for the Work Programme); Danish contract length varies widely from municipality to municipality (from six months in some municipalities to three years in others and some partnership arrangements that are open-ended). Contract length may be set by annual budgeting consideration, by the length of the individual intervention, or more strategic considerations such as the avoidance of transaction costs or facilitating partnership with providers. Vouchers have extremely frequent transactions, since providers can redeem them on an ongoing basis whenever they have delivered a course or placed someone in a sustained job.

In all three countries, however, we observe some moves away from short-term contracting. One common mechanism is contract extension—i.e. renewal of a contract at the discretion of the purchaser without a new tendering procedure—which is allowed under European procurement law for "works or services consisting in the repetition of similar works or services." The German tendering system provides options for the renewal of contracts without tendering, thus creating longer periods of engagement for providers; this at the time of writing accounts for nearly half of the BA's purchasing budget, suggesting that the option is usually exercised. In Denmark, similarly, we visited a provider whose contract had been extended more than once, and workers we interviewed were not aware of any end date.

In the British Work Programme, we find a different mechanism—a long-term contract with prime contractors who face relatively little competitive pressure once they have been selected. The DWP mitigated the risk of funding cycles through a complex financial arrangement that included payment by results and calculating current spending amounts on the basis of predicted future savings (placing someone in a job in theory reduces spending on him or her by the government). This system is less competitive than a system in which the state actively orchestrates frequent and repeated competition. The purpose is to encourage private firms to enter the market by giving investors a longer time horizon to realize a return (Freud 2007).

While transactions have become more frequent in these markets over time, this trend is not unidirectional. Any move away from public-sector provision or grants that were automatically renewed, and toward time-bound contracts or voucher arrangements, represents a more dynamic market. Due to concerns about the overheads caused by frequent contracting and the disincentives that short time horizons create for private investors, however, public authorities using procurement have tended to reduce transaction frequency by increasing the length of contracts or introducing extension options.

Prescription

A third feature of transactions often mentioned by our interviewees was prescription, i.e. the detail with which the service was spelled out, for example in tendering documents, prior to being delivered. In employment services this is a controversial topic because of the complexity of the task and the changing environment in which it is carried out. Arguably, under these conditions providers should be constantly innovating and adapting services. On the other hand, many employment-services tasks, taken on their own, appear to be standardizable by their nature: German or English language classes for non-native speakers or vocational courses built around a national curriculum. Imposing standardization makes it more straightforward to compare the bid descriptions of service quality, making them more like commodities to be bought and sold.

In Germany part of the professionalization of the purchasing function has led to the creation of standard descriptions for the most commonly purchased services to facilitate the contracting process. Based on a description of a service in the law (*Instrumente*), the REZen (the regional purchasing bodies introduced in Chapter 2) provide more concrete descriptions of servicers (as *Produkte*), which they market to local job centers to purchase from a provider to implement (as "measures" or *Maßnahmen*). Representatives from the REZ point out that these off-the-shelf schemes reflect the kind of contracted-out work that is already carried out at the local level and making these descriptions reduces transaction costs by freeing local managers from the task of devising new courses that already exist elsewhere.

There are two main ways that public authorities in our sample purchase innovative services, both of which entail less marketization. The most common one is the experimental pilot project created by local government, witnessed in all three countries. Here, the processes, by design, evolve during the running time of the contract and therefore cannot be described in detail at the beginning of a tendering process. For these services public authorities use grant making or a form of purchasing in which there is little or no open competition, such as "hand-picked" procurement in Germany. This has tended to increase in recent years in Denmark, as Appendix A shows.

The second way of reducing prescription is through "black-box" contracting, as in Great Britain's Work Programme. In place of detailed prescriptions was an elaborate system of payment by results and checks on provider financial, managerial, and IT capacity. The services, however, were still in fact standardized. Because of a perception, articulated by numerous management interviewees that they knew "what works" based on the pilot projects in the years leading up to the Work Programme (GB manager 8), the prime contractors rolled out standardized delivery models across the country through a mixture of in-house and subcontracted provision. There was considerable similarity in the kinds of services that resulted and considerable frustration expressed by interviewees who wanted more innovation (GB umbrella 1). Exactly the same pattern was seen in Denmark when the now-abolished national tendering system was rolled out: the high autonomy for the providers to design services, in exchange for performance-related payment, was converted into standardized low-cost delivery models.

According to the principles of "market governance," providers should be free to innovate; the reality of marketized exchange, however, is that price-based exchange generates pressures to produce standardized—i.e. easily comparable in a competitive setting—services. This is the case in Germany where employment-services work has become more prescribed by the funder; but it is also the case in Britain where the task of standardization and prescription has shifted to primes. In Denmark municipalities take diverse approaches to the question of prescription.

Prices

A final issue is the price mechanism, which determines both the resources providers have and the cost of the service for the funder. Two features of the price mechanism matter here: how prices are set and the weighting of price versus quality in selecting providers. Prices that float according to supply and demand become important determinants in the selection of a provider and have a well-known danger: a "race to the bottom" in which downward price pressures create extreme resource scarcity among providers. In employment services, however, this kind of price setting is not universal.

The classic way for prices to be set in markets is to let them float according to supply and demand; in the quasi-markets we are discussing, price setting is not so simple. In the competitive tendering arrangements used by the DWP for the Work Programme and the REZ, the funder sets quality criteria and selects the provider on the basis of some mixture of cost and quality. But bids with low prices are disqualified if there are quality concerns (and with the Work Programme, "risk") with the services described in the bid; above that level, the cheapest one tends to succeed. The 2004 European Procurement Directive allowed tendering decisions to be made on the criterion of "lowest price" (2004/18/EC); German legislation requires that the decision should be the one that is most economical "taking into consideration all circumstances" (§ 18 Abs. 1 VOL/A). In a professional purchasing arrangement the only circumstances taken into account are those included in the tendering documents. Quality receives a certain weighting, but it is measured as "described quality" or the "lyrics of the bid"—as the manager of one struggling non-profit provider in Germany pointed out (German manager 4). In response to this criticism German procurement law has been amended to allow the purchaser to take past performance into account.

Prices can also be fixed or negotiated. Prices for German training vouchers are fixed on the basis of average hourly per-student costs calculated for particular kinds of courses; and for placement vouchers they are fixed by law. Fixed prices create less uncertainty for providers, but can be used to squeeze prices, as with German placement vouchers, whose nominal value has been frozen since 2002. Under grants and cost reimbursement, by contrast, prices are negotiated. As with most research grants, negotiations are informed by the principle of cost recovery, which recognizes providers' needs to cover salaries, overheads, and material costs. Under these conditions the choice is ultimately made based on the quality of the work described in the provider's bid, and the provider's reputation, rather than cost.

The price mechanism has become increasingly important both in the ratcheting down of unit costs and in the selection of providers. In the tendering process of the Work Programme, the largest provider won using a low-price strategy, and there are downward trends in the prices of several sub-segments in the German employment services, as we will show in the Appendices. Denmark experienced the same downward price pressures under the former national tendering system, but has become the exception here due to the increasing use of partnership relations.

The Diversity of Transactions

The transactions in our sample vary along these six dimensions. At the non-marketized end of the spectrum are grants, the traditional transaction mode, which we find under subsidiarity-type delegation. In our sample it is found notably in Germany's training centers for disabled youth (which have annual grants) and one-euro jobs (which have one-off project grants), and in Denmark those areas where marketization is not applied and where non-profit providers are favored (services for the disabled and wage subsidies). Grants are also a part of the British scene, funding workshops for disabled people and some municipal projects delivered by the voluntary sector.

There are two other transaction modes, both of which are typically more highly marketized. One is public purchasing, the most common transaction and found in all three countries. This includes "hard marketization" in the form of competitive tendering in Germany and Denmark; "soft marketization" in the form of hand-picked procurement in Germany and partnership contracting in Denmark; and "black-box" contracting as in Britain which combines elements of both. Another is vouchers, which in our sample is only found in Germany in the form of training and placement vouchers (and after our data collection was complete "activation" vouchers as well); Britain had a training voucher scheme in the 1990s, now defunct. Table 3.1 provides an overview.

Grants

The first transaction mode represents a funding situation prior to marketization, in which a function is delegated by the public authority to a service

Table 3.1. Transaction modes in employment services

	Grants	Vouchers	Purchasing
Examples	German training centers for disabled youth, one-euro jobs	German placement, training, activation	German competitive tendering, hand-picked procurement
	British municipal pilot projects, Remploy	British training vouchers for youth in the 1990s	British Work Programme
	Danish wage subsidies, services for the disabled		Danish competitive tendering and partnership contracting
Who decides?	Public authority	Client	Public authority
Can procurement law apply?	No	No	Yes
Openness	Low	High	Varies
Frequency	Varies	High	Varies
Prescription	Low	Varies	Varies
Price	Negotiated	Fixed	Varies, often supply and demand

provider, and that provider is paid to cover its costs. A price is negotiated and determined in principle by the cost of carrying out the service. The provider is not paid for outcomes or even particular services, but rather for a purpose. Providers' obligations vis-à-vis public authorities do not go beyond the deployment of financial means and statistical reporting about their clients, their conditions, and outcomes.

Under the "annual grant" the provider has a mandate from the public authority continually to deliver services undisrupted by the end of contracts. A choice of provider is made on an individual basis, whenever a client is referred—usually by a client in consultation with the referring agency—and the provider's role is not questioned. The provider is entitled to have costs reimbursed on the grounds of continually maintaining an infrastructure freely available to clients.

While such ongoing grants are unusual in employment services, we do see it in German vocational training schools for young disabled people,[5] and it is consistent with the German subsidiarity principle of delegating services for non-commercial reasons to particular non-profit providers. Prices are set through negotiations concerning which costs are eligible and to what extent increases in provider costs are taken into account. The more fundamental reason for maintaining this arrangement is that disruption of established, long-standing providers (*stehende Einrichtungen*) would be politically controversial and require changes to social law. When the funder takes a hard line in price negotiations over several rounds of negotiations, which is the accusation expressed by the association of providers (Robinson and Egert 2014), this transaction mode can lead to a long-term squeeze on the resources of providers.

A second variant is the one-off "project grant." Here, prospective grantees may compete, but the choice is not made on the basis of low price. Grants vary in their length: for small projects they can last a year or less, and for larger ones they can last three or more years. From the perspective of the public authority, project grants provide a high degree of flexibility. They allow it to earmark funds for a particular purpose by a particular provider of its own choosing, but without being locked into funding the provider. The funder may design a selection procedure that can be perceived as transparent and fair, possibly by involving outside experts; nevertheless, there is no recourse for providers against the rejection of applications.

---

[5] A similar mechanism was used until recently by the British government to fund Remploy, a nationwide state-owned enterprise with a long tradition of operating workshops for the disabled. After a 2012 government review it was broken up and a rump organization turned into a provider of services procured under the Work Programme and Work Choices. In the face of protests from trade unions and opposition politicians, the government closed fifty out of fifty-four Remploy factories (McGuinness and Dar 2014).

The largest example of this in our sample is the German one-euro job, a truncated make-work scheme, which increased in importance around the time of the Hartz reforms and has more recently been scaled back. While the name suggests that it is a subsidized job placement, it is not; unlike some past make-work schemes in Germany there is no employment contract and it also includes payments for support services for the client, including counseling and training. The application procedure is that providers approach job centers with proposals for projects, and job centers assess them internally. There are some selection criteria—most basically the work has to be additional to work already being done (*zusätzlich*), for the public good (*im öffentlichen Interesse*) and involve support services. The funding lasts as long as the project, typically one year, and participants are referred by the job center. This kind of work is dominated by non-profits, and the decline in the volume of work has put a strain on the finances of the non-profit sector.

Vouchers

Our second transaction mode, by its nature, creates a dynamic market situation, due to the high frequency of transactions. The voucher-holding client chooses the provider, procurement law does not apply, and providers have, unlike those operating under procurement law, no legal recourse against the decisions of clients. The only country in our sample that has them is Germany, which uses them to fund training, placement, and "activation" services.

In one way vouchers are non-marketized: prices cannot float according to supply and demand. But in other ways they can be highly marketized. Transactions are more frequent than under purchasing since the provider must work on an ongoing basis to receive vouchers from clients, which it can then redeem for cash from the funder. These markets are also very open, subject to the requirements of independent accreditation bodies. While competition does not take place based on which provider has the lowest price, there are still ongoing and intense pressures to keep costs down and, of course, to attract clients equipped with vouchers.

One area in which they vary is their prescriptiveness. Training vouchers specify very clearly a course defined under a national framework of vocational training. Placement vouchers, by contrast, say little about the way that the client will be found a job, aside from guidelines to prevent abuse (e.g. a firm claiming payment for placing jobseekers with an employer with which it shares some affiliation) (Hegele 2009).

The setting of prices is another important difference between the two schemes. Under placement vouchers, prices are set by law; they have been frozen since 2002 at around between 2,000 and 2,500 euros per placement sustained for twenty-six weeks, depending on the client's distance from the labor market. This resource squeeze is less severe under training vouchers, where prices are set as part of the accreditation process for courses and in principle are set according to the average cost of providing the service. In response to concerns about upward price drift, the BA has created a centralized procedure that can reject courses if they are above the prices set by the accreditation body and are not adequately justified (Bundesagentur für Arbeit 2012 and see Appendix C).

Public Purchasing

The most common and diverse transaction mode in our sample is public purchasing, where the public authority decides what the service will be and then buys it from the bidder on the basis of price and possibly quality. The public authority refers clients to the provider and the relationship is then managed with a formal contract that may be extended but eventually expires. Though covered by a single legal framework at the EU level, it is the most diverse of the four transaction modes. Competition can be open or restricted; contracts can be long or short; prices may or may not be determined by supply and demand; and there is scope for negotiating the specification of the work rather than prescribing it beforehand.

Our public purchasing transactions fall into three categories: "hard" marketization, "soft" marketization, and the "black box," which combines elements of the two.

Perhaps the hardest marketization in the sample is competitive tendering as organized by the REZ, the professionalized purchasing function created after the Hartz reforms to secure high quality and low prices, and to comply with the letter of procurement law and its main principles of equal treatment and transparency. Typically, prices are set by supply and demand, subject to quality thresholds; if a bid is below a threshold of quality points it is excluded, but it can also be excluded for being too expensive (see Appendix B). Our interviewees from the REZ reject any suggestion of low bids driving down quality and told us in interviews that they commonly excluded low bids on the grounds of quality. The REZ also monitors contracts, which typically run for twelve to twenty-four months, with an option held by the funder to extend by twelve months. For the REZ, the default procedure is open competitive tendering, but it can manage other procedures as well.

The REZ markets its services to local managers of job centers purchasing services, who are free to use other means such as municipal purchasing offices or purchase services in-house. While there is a very diverse range of services that can be purchased through the REZen, there are clear tendencies towards standardization. Part of the REZ's work is to create descriptions of commonly purchased services that can be purchased off the shelf, in an ever expanding "catalog" of upwards of forty "standard products." Another task of the REZ is to increase participation from bidders in tendering exercises, sometimes by contacting providers from neighboring areas when there are not enough bidders, "so that the prices do not get out of control" (German purchaser 4).

Similarly, in Denmark, competitive tendering is organized by some municipalities. After the abolition of the mandatory national tendering making the municipalities responsible, competitive tendering is often part of an overall municipal strategy of using non-public providers in services (e.g. based upon a political decision) or a result of defining the process of employment services as an end-to-end assignment. Competitive tendering is also used with services for clients classified as closer to the labor market and includes thereby often less complex services (as processing people through the system and making sure they are motivated and engaged in job-searching activities). This kind of competitive tendering is often very similar to the former national tendering with hard price competition and performance-related payment. The municipal purchaser is interested in making sure that the services are not too expensive, that a measurable number of services are offered (e.g. in relation to legislative obligations of interviews, job-searching activities, etc.), and that some effects can be documented. These contracts are typically two years long, but vary considerably between municipalities.

The "black box" is a British invention and refers to the kind of contracting used on the Work Programme, starting in 2011. The name comes from the wide discretion enjoyed by providers in designing services and a low degree of government oversight. In principle the government pays for results, i.e. sustained outcomes, and not for inputs, such as trained staff, buildings, and computers, which were specified in detail under previous DWP contracts. Prices in the Work Programme were set through a complex indicative price structure based on age and benefit claimed (JSA versus ESA), which serve as proxies for clients' distance from the labor market (Department for Work and Pensions 2010b), and by a discounting exercise that determined price scores in tendering. The DWP did take some steps to reassure investors that they could realize a return; in agreement with the treasury it eliminated the budget cap restricting the amounts that could be spent on outcome, sustainment, and incentive payments. Furthermore, while the DWP's direct contracting is governed by procurement law, subcontracting by private firms is not, which according to managers we interviewed at primes provides considerable flexibility in performance management.

The market that results is less competitive than the two cases of hard marketization. Access to the market is determined through a preferred bidder setup, in which firms bid to be part of a framework in one of eighteen "Contract Package Areas"; once they are "on the framework" then they can participate in tendering on the Work Programme and the smaller schemes that followed. In each area there were two or three primes delivering the Work Programme at once. The contracts are very long (five–seven years), and the funder's exit options are hardly used.

In both Denmark and Germany we also see "soft" marketization where purchasing is sometimes handled in a way that is less competitive and price-driven, usually to develop innovative services and to avoid disrupting non-profit networks of providers. German interviewees saw grants and hand-picked procurement as in some ways equivalent; however, grants are more difficult to administer because the granter has to monitor the spending of the grantee. Hand-picked procurement, by contrast, ends with a contract and a price which is paid provided the contract is fulfilled; the contractor does not have to provide proof how the contract sum was spent.

We asked the same German interviewees quoted above on the burden of procurement rules if grant making under *Zuwendungsrecht* would be preferable: "I have no opinion, to be honest. Zuwendungsrecht is much more complicated to reimburse. If I had to choose I would say: as simple as possible." When we asked if hand-picked procurement would be better, the interviewees answered in unison, "Yes" (German purchaser 7).

In Denmark this is called partnership contracting. Municipalities commonly use it for services for what our interviewees called "heavy" groups, for parts of the process and not for end-to-end services. There are multiple ways to establish this type of partnership. It can be initiated through an identified need for specific services not present in the municipalities (e.g. in relation to certain target groups) where providers and municipalities jointly develop services and programs. It can also be a result of providers specialized in specific target groups of clients or specialized services such as rehabilitation, health care, physical training, or stress management. Seen from the municipal purchaser such transactions often produce more expensive but also higher quality services. As the relation is trust-based (with open or short time contracts sometimes), and with the possibility to adapt services for municipal needs, this makes it easier to obtain deep knowledge of and influence on services at the providers. The providers will typically have the municipalities as regular customers rather than a fixed contract for a specified period and a certain number of clients. This market has many non-profit providers, but more and more for-profit providers have entered it.

Seen from the provider's side this kind of transaction entails some advantages. Price competition is less intense than under competitive tendering, and it is possible (or even demanded) to invest in higher-quality services (also escaping from the image problem inherent in the former national tendering). The staff also becomes more specialized with professional skills and psychologists, psychiatrists, doctors, etc. become members of staff. Some of the major players in the former national tendering have been through this type of organizational transition. As explained in interviews, they prefer this new way of engaging with the public purchaser as they often then will be involved very early in the designing of the services (instead of making a bid for already designed services described in tender documents). It is furthermore possible for the provider to keep relative high prices and high quality. The risk in this process is well described by a director of one of the for-profit providers, saying that it now "is more necessary to have lunch with executives in the job center" implying that the network and the purchaser's knowledge of the provider's services become more important (German manager 9).

In Germany partnership is based upon hand-picked procurement. Procurement law allows a "limited call for tender" and "hand-picked procurement" (*freihändige Vergabe*). In the first case, the call for tender is made known only to a limited number of providers (a minimum of three) because the service in question is very special and all operators who could perform it are known to the respective public authority. In the second case, the public purchaser approaches just one provider in order to negotiate a contract. The possible justifications for these are identical to those in the EU Procurement Directive, and because they are governed by procurement law, it can be contested by operators not considered and therefore justifications for the choice of the procedure must be meticulously documented in detail. Because it is subject to complex legal regulations, the REZ can only use hand-picked procurement with the approval of BA headquarters' in-house counsel.

Hand-picked procurement is used for purchasing bespoke services, as foreseen in procurement law. One example mentioned by interviewees was an experimental model project in which the BA together with a particular provider wanted to test an innovative approach. In another, there was only one provider in the area with the necessary equipment to carry out a scheme for young people trying out different occupations (metalworking, woodworking, bricklaying, and gardening) accompanied by social workers. In another example, the BA was co-financing a scheme with regional governments and municipalities where at least 50 percent is tied to the use of particular providers. In these examples, the public purchaser must collaborate in designing something innovative and unique, where of course the distribution of the workload between the two negotiating parties may vary. Prices must be justified by plausible calculations, but in the absence of direct competition and often a regional quasi-monopoly of the contractor there is no price squeeze. Justifying a "hand-picked" procedure and negotiating details with a particular provider is in many ways more cumbersome than spelling out a standard description and letting the market decide.

Conclusion

In this chapter we have spelled out in broad outline differences and similarities in how transactions are organized in employment services. The focus has been on laying out their main characteristics and variations, in order to define what marketization is. We have not said much about the policy reasons for choosing or moving away from them, or the consequences that we encountered in our visits to the providers. These issues will be covered in the subsequent chapters, and more detail on the transactions themselves will be provided in the Appendices.

What is striking is that transactions cannot be explained by the nature of the task. Transaction-cost economics does this by claiming that the governance of transactions is essentially a search for efficiency. While it is not difficult to find examples of public authorities attempting to reduce their transaction costs, there are also examples of public authorities building up expensive procurement machinery for similar services, where cost savings are unclear.

Social-policy literature on contractualism similarly focuses on a functional fit between marketization and two other trends: NPM and work-first social policy. But we have observed a wide range of transactions for a similar task. For German job centers vocational training courses can be organized via vouchers or procurement. Furthermore, the same services purchased separately in one place may be purchased together in a different place. German job centers and some Danish municipalities favor small contracts for services defined narrowly by function and client group; the British DWP and other Danish municipalities purchase the same services as large end-to-end contracts.

By studying the effects of marketization on government-funded services we are in effect reversing the lines of causality typically used. This would be implausible if the market and the transactions that structure it were overdetermined by better-known and more often-studied phenomena, such as the nature of the task or the features of the national "regime." But we find that this is not the case. Marketization at the level of the transaction has causal powers that managers, workers, and clients in front-line service provision tell us about in interviews; and it is a general awareness that the transaction has these effects that makes funders want to engage in marketization in the first place, and then roll it back in subtle or not-so-subtle ways. The next three chapters will describe these processes.

Contracting by Danish Municipalities

This appendix presents some of the main results of the Danish national survey referred to throughout the book. As we described in Chapter 2, the Danish national tendering model promoted strong price competition but was abolished in 2011. With the abolition of the requirement to use market-based providers for certain target groups, employment services contracting became a matter for the municipalities to decide. One consequence of municipalization was that national statistics on the employment-services market were no longer collected.

The Danish team decided to conduct a national survey among the purchasers in the ninety-eight municipalities in Denmark in winter 2013–14. A wide range of questions was asked including to what extent and in what way public purchasers in municipalities make use of non-public providers[1] in the PES and their views on the development of the market. The survey therefore makes it possible to identify the current (at the time of writing) local approach to involving non-public providers in employment services. The survey was web-based. The response rate was 65 percent (for some of the questions) and the sample is representative for the ninety-eight Danish municipalities when it comes to important characteristics, such as size and political landscape.

The majority of the municipal purchasers (86 percent) state that they make use of non-public providers in employment services (Table A.1), but the number of clients transferred to providers tends to be low (Table A.2). Only 12 percent of the municipalities use non-public providers to a high extent, i.e. for more than 35 percent of the unemployed. On the other hand, 25 percent of the municipalities state that fewer than 5 percent of the unemployed receive employment services from non-public providers. The extent of non-public providers used in the employment services therefore varies from municipality to municipality.

When looking at the public purchasers' views on the development of the market (Table A.3) we see that the majority of the municipalities agree (strongly or partly) with the statements that the use of non-public providers has decreased considerably in recent years and that the abolition of national tendering has reduced the use of non-public providers. More than 50 percent of the municipal purchasers also agree that non-public providers are more used for specialized tasks for weaker unemployed compared to generalized services for stronger clients. Furthermore, the majority of

---

[1] We use the terms "other actors" and "non-public providers" interchangeably.

Table A.1. The use of non-public providers (%)

	Yes	No	N
Does the municipality use non-public providers in the employment services?	86	14	66

Table A.2. The share of unemployed receiving employment services from non-public providers (%)

	Under 5%	5–10%	11–20%	21–35%	36–50%	Over 50%	Don't know	N
How large a share of all unemployed are in employment services from non-public providers?	25	17	25	15	2	10	6	52

Table A.3. Danish municipalities' views on the development of the market (%)

	Strongly agree	Partly agree	Neither agree nor disagree	Partly disagree	Strongly disagree	Don't know
The use of other actors have decreased considerably	50	34	5	5	0	6
The abolition of the national tendering reduces the use of other actors	30	38	7	14	4	7
The use of (competitive) tendering has decreased	32	32	14	5	4	13
Other actors are used more for specialized tasks for weaker unemployed compared to generalized services for stronger clients	21	36	11	16	9	7
The involvement of other actors has been more partnership-based and less tendering- and contract-based	16	30	25	16	2	11

N=56

respondents agree with the statement that the use of competitive tendering has decreased, and 46 percent (strongly or partly) agree with the statement that the involvement of non-public providers has become more partnership-based and less tendering- and contract-based. 25 percent of purchasers neither agree nor disagree with this statement. However, the results from the survey also indicate that competitive tendering is still the most used instrument for purchasing (table not included) and as shown in Table A.4, many of the municipalities use (or partly use) the same model as used in the abolished national tendering model—a national regulated competitive tendering system.

Table A.4. Use of the national tendering model (%)

	Yes	Partly	No	Don't know	N
Do you use the same model as used in the national tendering model (for example pay model, criteria, monitoring, etc.)?	22	33	39	6	49

Table A.5. Danish municipalities' views on why non-public providers are used (%)

	Strongly agree	Partly agree	Neither agree nor disagree	Partly disagree	Strongly disagree	Don't know
Other actors are used...						
for specialized tasks	31	48	15	2	4	0
as a capacity buffer	29	46	8	13	2	2
as an alternative for own services and for higher quality	29	35	15	6	13	2
for reducing expenses	10	25	29	15	19	2
for better effects	6	38	31	13	13	0
because it's a political priority in the Municipal Council	4	21	35	21	17	2
for getting better contact to companies	2	13	25	33	25	2
because they have another approach when meeting with clients	0	19	29	23	29	0
for lowering administration costs and bureaucracy	0	6	25	25	42	2
N=48						

Municipal purchasers' views on the development of the market provide a picture of how much has happened in the period from 2010/2011 to 2013/2014. The purchaser–provider relationship appears to have become more based on local partnerships and less based on contract relations formed by procurement; because it is locally driven it varies widely between locales.

Purchasers' views on why non-public providers are used (Table A.5) bring further details into this development and the new situation in the market of employment services in Denmark. Hence, most purchasers in the municipalities agree (strongly or partly) with the statement that non-public providers are used for specialized tasks, for providing a capacity buffer, and to improve quality (compared to in-house services). Non-public providers in most municipalities are not used mainly to reduce expenses of the services or reduce bureaucracy, and better effects are only stated among a smaller group of purchasers. The results thus demonstrate local variations in the arguments for using non-public providers.

When looking at the selection criteria and monitoring parameters of the purchasers in the Danish municipalities (Table A.6) it is striking that purchasers care most about quality, price, and past results, and less about the quality of jobs and opinions of clients.

Table A.6. Selection criteria and monitoring parameters of Danish municipalities (%)

	Very high extent	High extent	Some extent	Low Extent	Very low extent	Don't know
To what extent are the following criteria important when you conclude a contract with another actor?						
Quality	59	37	4	0	0	0
Past results and experience	31	47	20	2	0	0
Price	31	45	24	0	0	0
Local anchoring	22	18	29	20	8	2
Staff, e.g. educational background	16	29	37	12	0	6
Working conditions at provider	4	8	37	33	8	10
Network/relation to provider	4	22	37	16	14	6
To what extent are the following parameters used in your monitoring of providers?						
Assessment of quality	41	41	8	0	2	8
Performance goals (e.g. timeliness, level of activation, etc.)	39	33	16	2	4	6
User goals	6	39	24	16	2	12
Number of complaints	6	10	39	22	12	10
N=45						

Table A.7. Expectations of future market development: Is it your assessment that the use of "other actors" in the coming years will . . . ? (%)

	Increase	Be unchanged	Drop	Don't know	N
Insured unemployed	5	45	39	11	57
Social-assistance recipients	9	47	35	9	57

This applies to both selection and monitoring parameters. Past results and experience are also of crucial importance.

Finally, municipal purchasers expect that in the coming years the use of non-public providers will decrease for both insured unemployed and social-assistance recipients (Table A.7). In 2008 municipal purchasers were asked the same question in a national survey, and 59 percent answered that the use of non-public providers would increase. Five years later the figure was 5 percent or 9 percent, depending on the client group.

Contracting on Britain's Work Programme

with Lisa Schulte

In this appendix we present the working of the British employment-services market, using the example of the Work Programme, which in its early stages accounted for about half of spending on contracted-out employment services by the British government (see Chapter 2). We provide a detailed description of the transaction that underpins the "black box," including the mechanics of the tendering process, its outcome, and the monitoring of providers. The description is based on the tendering documents for the Work Programme (issued in late 2010), two major reports on it from the National Audit Office (National Audit Office 2012, 2014), three DWP-funded evaluations (Lane et al. 2013; Foster et al. 2014; Simmonds 2015), and data provided by the DWP on contract scores in response to a Freedom of Information Act request.

The Coalition Government moved quickly after taking power in May 2010 to cancel nearly all contracted-out employment-services schemes, including the Flexible New Deal, Pathways to Work, and Employment Zones. It bought out 230 contracts concluded by the previous government at a cost of at least £62 million (National Audit Office 2012: 8). The new contracts for the Work Programme included end-to-end provision for JSA claimants aged 25 and over (25+) unemployed for at least twelve months, JSA claimants aged 18–24 (18–24) unemployed for at least nine months, as well as several other groups, most of them in receipt of ESA. For the vast majority of clients, including the first two JSA groups, the scheme was mandatory and backed up by sanctions. In administrative parlance, clients were called "customers" but "mandated onto" the scheme.

In October 2010 the DWP invited bids for the "Framework for the provision of employment related services," which divided Great Britain into eighteen geographical "contract package areas," and announced results in November. These were assessed primarily on the financial and management capacity to deliver large contracts. In December the DWP invited tenders for the Work Programme, which was divided into forty contracts, with two or three covering the entirety of each contract package area. In February 2011 the results of the tendering exercised were announced and in June Jobcentre Plus began referring clients onto the scheme (for a fuller chronology see <http://workprogramme.co.uk/news>).

The contracts were large. Geographically they covered the countries of Scotland and Wales, entire English regions such as the East Midlands and Northeast, and several other geographies (e.g. Yorkshire was divided in three, London in two). The indicative annual value of contracts, according to the data provided by the DWP in our Freedom of Information Act request, for the forty successful bids was just under £500 million or an average of £12.5 million per contract. The indicative volumes of clients provided in the Invitation to Tender for Work Programme bidders foresaw a total of 2.17 million clients over the five-year scheme, on average 10,885 per year per contract. The largest groups were JSA 25+ (averaging 6,795 clients per year) and JSA 18–24 (1,633).

The contracts were also long-lasting. Clients are referred onto the Work Programme for five years, and the scheme lasts two years for each client. This means that the providers remain responsible for clients from June 2011 to May 2018. The funder has exit options built into the contract, including contract cancelation; there was also an option called "market shift" in which referrals of clients would be shifted from poorly performing providers to better performing providers.

Cost and quality were the two principal selection criteria, followed by a more difficult-to-interpret risk assessment.

Prices were determined through a complex structure, which formed the basis of discounts written into bids. This structure is presented in Table B.1. There were four payments. First were up-front payments called attachment fees to ensure that providers had a cash flow at the beginning of the scheme. Second were job-outcome payments made when a job was sustained twenty-six or thirteen weeks depending on the client group. Third were sustainment payments made every four weeks thereafter for up to eighteen months. Fourth were "incentive payments" for good performance for three client groups: the two large JSA groups and new ESA claimants assessed as work-ready, known as "ESA flow." Good performance was defined as "non-intervention plus 30%" (this was not achieved by any contractors). Payments were differentiated by client group. For the two large JSA groups the payments were lower than for former claimants of Incapacity Benefit and present claimants of its replacement ESA. These declined over time. Attachment fees disappeared in years 4 and 5, and job-outcome payments declined as well for the two large JSA groups and ESA flow.

Points for "cost" were calculated using discounts separately for the first two and last three years of the contract. Bids received one price point per percentage increase in their overall discount up to 20 percent; after that they received one point for two additional percentage increases in their discounts. To give an example, in two of its bids Deloitte Ingeus won a price score of 40. 20 points came from the first 20 percent of discount, and 20 points came from the following 40 percent of the discount; it is unclear how much of this discount came from the first two years as opposed to the last three.

The term "black box" refers to the service itself: namely, it is not prescribed in detail by the purchaser. The *Invitation to Tender* contained detailed information about the process of tendering, administration, and payment, among other things, but said very little about the kind of training, advice, and other support that clients should receive. Instead, under "Work Programme Delivery Model" (6) the basic principle of provider discretion is articulated:

> Providers will have considerable freedom to determine what activities each customer will undertake in order to help them into, and to sustain, employment. Specialist delivery partners from the public, private and voluntary sectors are best placed to identify the best ways of getting people back to work, and will be allowed the freedom to do so without

Table B.1. Work Programme price structure: indicative prices

Customer group		JSA 25 +	JSA 18–24	JSA Early Access	JSA Ex-IB	ESA Flow	ESA Ex-IB	ESA Volunteer
Attachment fee (£, by year)	1	400	400	400	400	600	600	400
	2	300	300	300	300	450	450	300
	3	200	200	200	200	300	300	200
	4 & 5	0	0	0	0	0	0	0
Max job-outcome payment (£, by year)	1	1,200	1,200	1,200	1,200	1,200	3,500	1,000
	2	1,200	1,200	1,200	1,200	1,200	3,500	1,000
	3	1,080	1,080	1,200	1,200	1,080	3,500	1,000
	4	960	960	1,200	1,200	960	3,500	1,000
	5	840	840	1,200	1,200	840	3,500	1,000
Job-outcome payment— qualifying number of weeks		26	26	13	13	13	13	13
Four-weekly sustainment rate (applicable to all years)		215	170	250	250	235	370	115
Sustainment: max number of four-weekly payments		13	13	20	20	20	26	20
Incentive payment		1,000	1,000	0	0	1,000	0	0
Max possible payment, client referred in year 1		5,395	4,810	6,600	6,600	7,500	13,720	3,700

Source: Work Programme, Invitation to Tender, Pricing Proposal Guidance: 44

detailed prescription from central government. We will specify some minimum requirements (for example around data security) but these will be minimized. During implementation and when the WP is in live running we will look for light touch methods to assure delivery of the proposals and standards, as set out in the bids and to minimize the burden on Providers.

The *Instructions for Bidders* (24–36) spell out how quality points were awarded for descriptions of: "service requirement" including minimum services to which clients would be entitled (20 percent), "supply chain management" (20 percent) including subcontracting, "resources & TUPE" (15 percent) including human-resource management issues, "stakeholder engagement" including work with employers and other local providers (15 percent), expected "performance" in terms of job outcomes (10 percent), and "implementation" including the mitigation of expected risks (15 percent).

There were 176 bids, forty of which were successful. Figure B.1 displays the bids' cost and quality scores based on data supplied by the DWP. Gray dots represent unsuccessful bids; black dots and the name of the firm in black represent successful bids. The vast majority of successful bids received close to the maximum number of quality points. Among those bids with high quality scores there was a very wide variation in cost scores. Figure B.1 shows that there was a range of approaches to bidding. At one end of the spectrum were SERCO and MAXIMUS, which offered little in the way of discounts; SERCO won two out of nine of its tenders. At the other end were Ingeus and Seetec which discounted aggressively; Ingeus won seven out of eleven.

As Figure B.2 shows, the decisions were not made purely on the basis of adding up cost and quality points. In seventeen out of eighteen areas the top scorer was one of the

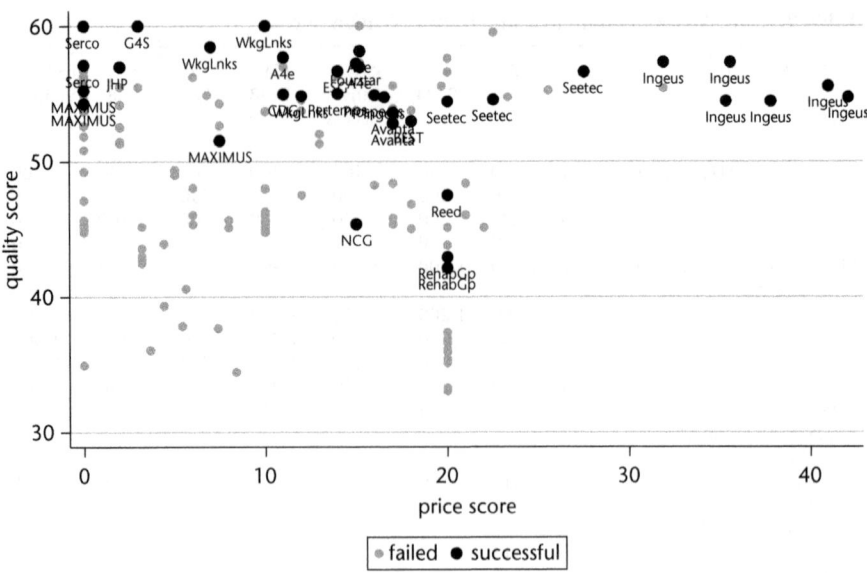

Figure B.1. Work Programme bids and providers

two aggressive discounters, Ingeus or Seetec. In six of those cases one of those firms did not win the contract despite having the top score. According to the *Instructions for Bidders* there is a "risk-assurance rating" that reflects discrepancies that staff identify between the qualitative and cost parts of the bids (39). These scores were not provided by the DWP, but the steps after assessing cost and quality scores allowed the funder to reduce somewhat the concentration of the market.

The DWP downplayed the concentration of the market in its evaluations; evaluators called it a "competitive oligopoly," in which five prime contractors controlled just over half of the market. Rather than comparing the market to its past structure of that of other countries' more fragmented employment-services markets, researchers compared it to the more concentrated electricity and supermarket sectors (Foster et al. 2014).

Over the course of the contract, the black box in principle used the incentive structure built into the above-mentioned payments as its main lever to improve performance. But there were other forms of regulation as well.

The main potential weakness of the Work Programme was the flexibility it gave providers to neglect clients; building "minimum service delivery" standards into the bids was the main means to mitigate this problem. It was a description of the services to which each client would be entitled to and accounted for 10 percent of the quality points (according to the *Instructions for Bidders*). The DWP then published these descriptions online, including the name of the provider, the number of the contract package area, and the provider's description of a minimum service delivery. These varied widely and included:

- vague promises, such as "we will keep in regular contact with you" (Ingeus) or "all customers will have access to a rapid return service if they drop out of work" (Working Links);

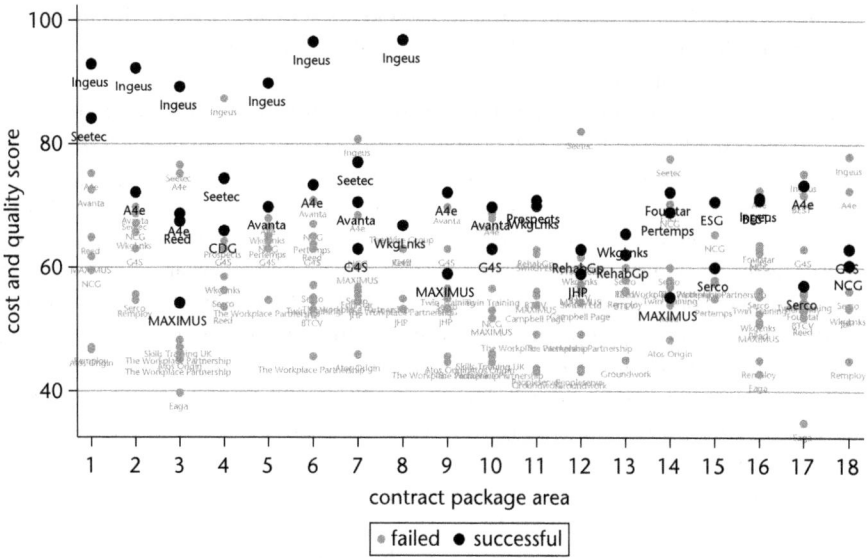

Figure B.2. Scores and funding decisions by area

Source: DWP response to Freedom of Information Act request, own calculations

- descriptions of the provider's processes, such as a timeline for induction and assessment (G4S, Working Links) or the full "customer journey" (Maximus, CDG); and

- concrete pledges such as a "named advisor" (A4e), monthly meetings with advisors (CDG), "contact" fortnightly (Maximus) or monthly (A4e), or "a service that is accessible to all on public transport within 30–45 minutes" (A4e).

The National Audit Office (2014: 34) criticized this approach, arguing that these differing standards—fourteen out of eighteen of which do not even differentiate between client groups—cannot be used for monitoring the level of support. Although the DWP reviews standardized quality indicators for 1,000 randomly selected case files every month, the NAO concludes that they cannot detect parking because the indicators do not differentiate between client groups. The NAO's summary of the data, however, is consistent with the claim made by other evaluators that parking was taking place: 46 percent of clients had had no contact with their provider in the past two months, and average caseloads fluctuated between 117 and 154 depending on overall numbers of clients on the scheme.

A second potential problem for the Work Programme was the abuse of subcontractors, especially non-profits. These contracts are risky, since they may be ended for poor performance and since they often use payment by results without guaranteed numbers of clients. Foster et al. (2014) find in a survey of subcontractors that, among those operating under payment by results, 78 percent described their contract as "slightly or extremely commercially unattractive" (141). With two exceptions, this subcontracting segment is where the non-profits were located, as we see in Chapter 4. The "Merlin Standard" was introduced "to ensure excellent sub contractual relationships between the top-tier and high performing third sector and other organizations," through mandatory accreditation and the possibility of mediation in disputes between primes and subcontractors (Simmonds 2015: 11).

Evaluation evidence on Merlin was lukewarm. Two waves of accreditation of primes showed improving contracting practice (although the report was not specific about the nature of these improvements), and in some areas, such as its efficiency, rigor, and conduciveness to improved practice, it received positive reviews. Non-profit subcontractors, however, were highly critical of its effectiveness in protecting them. When asked, "is the assessment process sufficient assurance that providers are compliant with the standard?" only 33 percent answered positively (Simmonds 2015: 64); and the mediation procedure was only used five times, with one anonymous provider telling the evaluator, "I feel to invoke the Merlin mediation process would be hugely damaging to my relationship with a Prime" (Simmonds 2015: 22). Foster et al. (2014) find a 66 percent satisfaction rate among subcontractors with the terms of payment, but note that this may be because those "facing financial difficulties had then left supply chains, which in turn made the programme more viable for remaining organizations in receipt of redistributed referrals" (33).

The main intended outcome of the Work Programme was to place participants in sustained jobs. "Non-intervention" levels were used as a baseline for judging the Work Programme and they represent the DWP's assessment of job outcomes without the scheme; "minimum performance levels" were this figure plus 10 percent and represented the DWP's assessment of the performance of past schemes. The latter were calculated for three groups: JSA 18–24, JSA 25+, and ESA Flow.

Using the DWP's benchmarks, the scheme performed well below expectations for ESA claimants, and at about the minimum performance level (i.e. levels similar to previous schemes) for JSA claimants. Through an analysis of contracts, the NAO shows a decline in spending for "harder-to-help" groups compared to figures provided in bids and, on average, only £630 spent by primes per ESA client compared to £870 per JSA client (National Audit Office 2014: 24–5, 31–2). The latter point is important for understanding the discretion prime providers enjoyed within the black box; it included the freedom to spend less than they had promised in their bids.

The DWP works closely with prime contractors to improve performance, e.g. through a "partnership forum," but it also has sanctions for poorly performing prime contractors. The first is the "market-share shift" that took place in August 2013 and affected ten out of eighteen areas. The principle is that 5 percent of client referrals are shifted away from poorly performing providers and towards weakly performing providers, with the intention of intensifying competition. The evaluation evidence suggests that this has not had much of an effect in practice due to its small scale and the overall context of declining referrals (Foster et al. 2014: 103–4). The second is contract termination for poor performance. This has happened in one of forty contracts, namely one run by NCG, which had one contract with the DWP. While the DWP did not find that the provider had "breached its contract and failed to meet minimum performance levels," it "issued its notice of termination under the voluntary break clause in the contract" (National Audit Office 2014: 33).

Vouchers and Contracting in Germany

In this appendix we present the technical details of the three German markets for employment services, namely procurement through competitive tendering, the training voucher scheme, and vouchers for private job-placement services.[1] The description is based on content analysis of a sample drawn from the tendering documents issued by the Federal Employment Agency (BA) between January 2013 and April 2014; an interview at one of the Regional Purchasing Centers (REZen) with the regional director and the director of the national purchasing unit; public presentations by the latter; interviews in one local employment agency and two local job centers; interviews with providers operating under the different transaction regimes; analysis of the relevant legal documents; and analysis of the BA's spending on external services 2008–13.[2]

In the aftermath of the 2008 financial crisis, spending on employment services peaked; figures presented here do not include short-time working allowances (which are a wage replacement, not a service). Since then, overall spending has declined. In part, this can be justified by decreasing unemployment numbers. As a result, the measure of public spending on ALMP measures as a percentage of GDP fell from 1 percent (2009) to 0.67 percent (2013), according to the OECD database.[3] However, the decline in spending has been overproportional to the decline of unemployment. Make-work schemes (which are subsidized via grants) were reduced most radically. Likewise, services purchased directly without tendering (mostly youth-training schemes for school leavers not finding an apprenticeship) were reduced. As a result, the share of

---

[1] In 2012, "activation" measures were added to the catalogue of legally defined instruments, and joined with placement vouchers under the heading of "activation and placement." However, activation (but not placement) can also be purchased via competitive tendering where it has meanwhile become the dominant category of purchasing. If implemented via vouchers, the mechanism is the same as for training vouchers. Rules for placement vouchers remained largely unchanged and are still different from training and activation vouchers.

[2] The source used, actually the most detailed and consistent one over time, is the "Eingliederungsbilanzen" downloaded from http://statistik.arbeitsagentur.de/Navigation/Statistik/Statistik-nach-Themen/Eingliederungsbilanzen/zu-den-Daten/zu-den-Daten-Nav.html. Because of data missing from the fully municipalized job centers, the analysis had to be restricted to spending by the joint job centers as far as services for recipients of minimum income benefits are concerned. This is straightforward insofar as only the joint job centers may use the services of the REZ which follow the procedures described here. No comprehensive evidence is available on the transactions between fully municipalized job centers and providers.

[3] http://stats.oecd.org/Index.aspx?DatasetCode=LMPEXP, retrieved on February 28, 2016.

fully marketized schemes grew considerably. The financial volume of vouchers remained rather stable (with the exception of larger volumes in 2009 and 2010), whereas the volume of competitive tendering increased as more and more schemes were subjected to compulsory tendering as a consequence of legal amendments. The financial volume of placement vouchers is marginal. Figure 2.1 shows these figures.

The German approach to externalized employment services contrasts sharply with the British "black box" approach. By tradition related to the semi-autonomous nature of the BA as a social-insurance body, the kinds of measures to be used are meticulously described in legislation in terms of target groups, durations, percentages of subsidy where applicable, and, since 2002, the transaction mode to be used in procuring the service. In 2013, spending statistics used for calculating the size of the market in Chapter 2 comprised twenty-one different schemes; this does not include yet another fourteen schemes where some sort of payment goes directly to the client or to a private employer, not a service provider. The legal specification of interventions structures the transaction mode (grant, procurement, or voucher) and lots purchased.

The law also spells out conditions for participating in employment-services markets. Providers wanting to participate in tendering or in voucher schemes must undergo accreditation by an independent agency. These agencies, in turn, are accredited and supervised by a central body of accreditation accompanied by a consultative board in which the social partners, the three levels of government, and the associations of providers are represented.

There are two separate accreditation procedures: one for the provider and one for the service. In the provider accreditation, process, financial stability, professional profiles of core staff, human-resource development, and quality management are considered. By contrast, service accreditation is more focused on didactical concepts and their orientation towards labor-market needs. Vocational training courses must comply with a larger number of criteria than activation measures. Private job-placement services need only provider accreditation, not service accreditation; i.e. within the very narrow scope of legally defined fees for successful placements, providers can operate as they wish. Accreditation fees and—arguably even more—lack of familiarity with accreditation procedures as such are the key barriers to market entry of new providers. These accreditations must be renewed at intervals between three and five years.

Competitive Tendering

The public purchaser role is more decentralized than in Britain but has more central oversight than Denmark (at the time of our study). The technical process of tendering and of evaluating bids is concentrated since 2007 in five REZen set up by the BA. They correspond to the regional division of the BA at its middle tier into ten regional directorates, except that some REZen serve more than one directorate. At the local level, there are three types of organizations that purchase external employment services, either in cooperation with the respective REZ or on their own account:

- 156 Arbeitsagenturen (local branches of the BA) serving the general public and jobseekers with contribution-based claims to unemployment benefits *must* use the services of their respective REZ for purchasing;

- 303 "joint" job centers, i.e. joint ventures of a municipality (city or county) and the Arbeitsagentur responsible for that area, serve the working-age and able-to-work recipients of means-tested minimum income benefits and their families; they *should* use the services of their respective REZ but, by virtue of their nature as legally independent bodies, may also run their own procurement services or use municipal facilities usually tendering construction or utility contracts;
- 105 fully municipalized job centers in which the municipality serves the clientele and *may not* use the REZ but must conduct their own tendering procedures.

Purchasing procedures via the REZ are initialized by Arbeitsagenturen or job centers, whose managers define the services for a particular group of their clients. They can choose from a catalog of more than forty pre-defined services listed and frequently updated by the BA headquarters' Purchasing Coordination Centre. They may request modifications of these "standard products," define "individual products" not found in the catalog, or modify standard products to their needs. Individual products that prove successful in practice may later be added to the catalog. However, the expanding catalog of "standard products" leads to standardization tendencies not least because of the effort of defining new services.

Since each lot put out for tender is defined in terms of locale (jurisdiction of the respective employment agency or job center), target group (e.g. single mothers with migrant backgrounds), and type of intervention (e.g. group coaching with assistance in writing CVs, job interview training, and organized internships), contracts are comparably small. The duration of the contract is usually identical with the duration of individual participation; only where individual participation is very short term, contracts may envisage higher numbers of participants to be rotated through the scheme over a longer period of time. Often the contract includes an option for renewal without tendering; in 2012, the financial volume of contract renewals equaled that of contracts awarded after tendering (Köngeter 2013). Contract renewal spares both the purchaser and the provider transaction costs but does not reduce uncertainty since there is no guarantee. Renewal also provides more continuity than repeated tendering and allows a seamless service over a longer period of time.

Client groups referred to a provider under a particular contract are intended to be rather homogeneous, though providers often complain that they do not get the kinds of clients specified in their contract. There is no scope for differential payment schemes within one and the same contract; rather, differentiation according to client groups occurs between contracts. For the same reason, the scope for "creaming and parking" is much more limited than in a black-box model with heterogeneous client groups. Furthermore, outcome-related payment schemes are rare, and where they are used the outcome fee only comes on top of a larger participation fee.

For activation courses with clients very distant from the labor market and from any organized activity, the provider may receive an attendance bonus that remunerates the extra effort of picking clients up at home and getting them out of bed. Some contracts include fees for particular services some clients may need and others not, like debt counseling, or for completing defined stages, like profiling of competencies or drawing up an action plan. Some contracts include the reimbursement of extra costs incurred for some clients, like fork-lift truck licenses, so as not to "punish" the provider for organizing individualized support.

There are different models in use for sharing, between the purchaser and the provider, the risk that the numbers of clients envisaged for referral are not available; this is contested territory. One solution foresees a split between a guaranteed fee for participation "places" (including the availability of professional staff) and an additional fee per participant actually referred to the provider. Such a model can put the provider in a position where it cannot fully recover wage costs for staff it is obliged to pay. On the other hand, participant numbers above what is expected may force the provider to hire additional staff on a freelance basis in order to cope with the workload. The provider always operates in a squeeze between demonstrating professional quality and stability on the one hand and responding to demands on flexibility on the other.

The process of tendering is rather complex. After the local unit has defined the service in terms of target group, objectives, inputs, numbers, and timing, the REZ draws up and publishes the call for tender. They receive bids through an online portal and check the completeness of the documents and eligibility of bidders on the grounds of valid accreditations. The bids are then sent out for evaluation by the local Arbeitsagentur or job center that is purchasing the service. Local evaluators know which organization is the bidder but they do not know the price of the bid.

Evaluators use a strictly formalized grid that feeds into a decision algorithm (elucidated in Ferber 2015). Evaluators have to grade bids by allotting points in a large number of predefined dimensions on a range of 0 (poor) to 3 (outstanding). Choices at one of the two extremes must be justified in writing, whereas grades 1 and 2 need not be explained. Dimensions defined as "key criteria" work as knockout criteria: a grade of 0 in any one of these leads to exclusion from further consideration.

After all bids have received their evaluation scores, those with an overall score of less than 85 percent of "good" will be excluded as well. The benchmark here is the overall score that would be achieved with grading "2" throughout. Figure C.1 provides an illustrative example. We assume that grade "2" in all dimensions would add up to a score of 100 and a grade of "3" in all dimensions would add up to a score of 150 (the maximum value of the y axis); the 85 percent threshold is represented by the dotted horizontal line. Bids A and B fall below this line and are therefore excluded from further consideration; B is actually the cheapest bid.

Next, the "value-for-money" ratio (evaluation score divided by price[4]) is calculated for the remaining bids. The bid with the highest "value-for-money" ratio defines a benchmark corridor which is 10 percent wide (this is according to Ferber a common practice although it can be wider or narrower). In Figure C.1 the benchmark setter, the bid with the highest value-for-money ratio, is F. The solid line between bid F and the diagram's point of origin represents all of the points with the same value-for-money ratio. The dashed line represents a 10 percent lower value-for-money ratio than that of

---

[4] In figure C.1 the x axis has deliberately not been given a scale since neither the currency nor the orders of magnitude of prices matter for our example. Note, however, that X is a metric scale whereas Y, based on qualitative evaluations, is actually an ordinal scale, though metric operations must be performed with the scores in order to make the formula work.

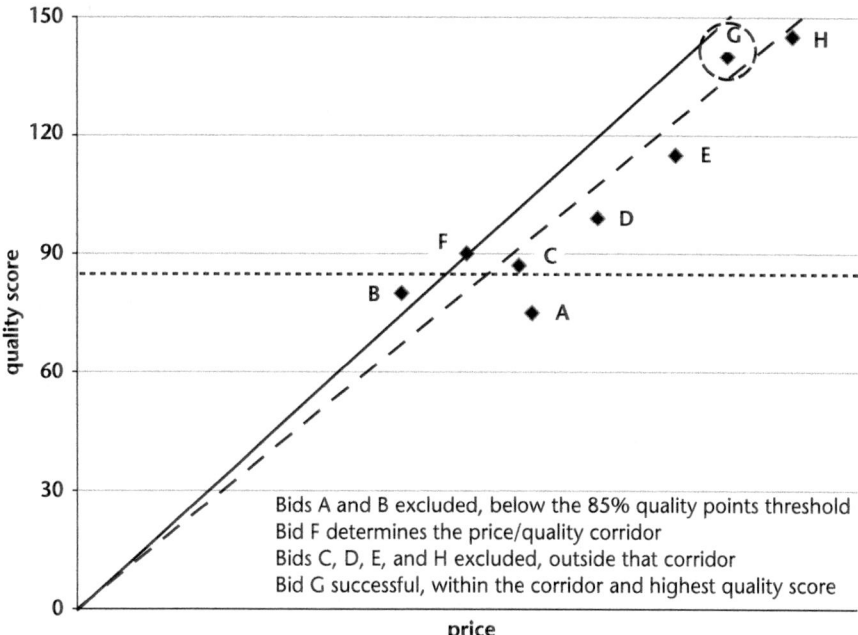

Figure C.1. Price and quality points in a hypothetical BA purchasing decision

bid F. The space between the solid and the dashed line is the corridor of consideration, and bids C, D, E, and H are excluded because they lie outside this corridor. Within this corridor the bid with the highest quality score wins. If no other competing bids were within the corridor, F would win; here, bid G wins, because it is within the corridor but has a higher quality score.

This procedure allows the BA to claim that "it is rare that the cheapest bidder wins" (German centralized purchaser, second interview, 2013). In theory, the formula prioritizes quality over price, and so does the BA in its public presentations of the scheme. The BA also emphasizes that average prices per month and client have not deteriorated over the years for some standard products that remained stable enough to allow longitudinal comparison—which can be confirmed on the basis of the BA's spending and participant statistics.

The bidder with superior quality rating has a price margin between 12 and 30 percent over the corridor leader. However, during the tendering process, nobody knows the parameters of the corridor that will emerge, so knowing this theoretical margin does not help. Providers say in interviews that they are losing out because of price; this goes both for non-profits and for for-profits. In Figure C.1, this would be true for bid H, which has the highest-quality score but its high price puts it outside of the corridor.

One factor that reinforces perceptions of price dumping is the inherent difficulty of assessing quality on the basis of descriptions of services written into bids. Experienced bid writers say in interviews that, as they gain more experience with this procedure, their descriptions of the work (i.e. the "lyrics of the bid") become more similar to those of their competitors. The incentive for evaluators to avoid extreme ratings (which must be justified in writing) has the same effect. If quality scores become more similar, price scores become increasingly important in the final decision.

The BA does not disclose data that would allow us to assess the relative weighting of price and quality in practice, namely

- which percentage of bids is actually excluded because of substandard quality,
- which percentage of contracts is awarded to the bidder with the highest "value-for-money" ratio,
- and which percentage is awarded to bidders with higher quality and higher price by virtue of the corridor rule.

Service descriptions submitted by bidders are not published, so it is not possible to discuss how quality is evaluated in the process. Providers operating in more than one local area reported submitting identical bids for identical products in different areas, with different outcomes. Such results are inherent in the decentralized nature of the process. Since evaluation of the bids is done by staff in the respective local units, the same text may be evaluated differently in different locales, depending on professional culture or local labor market conditions. Even in the unlikely case of identical evaluations, outcomes will depend on the competing bids submitted for a particular local tender. It can be easily demonstrated in Figure C.1 how just one bid missing or one additional bid can radically change the outcome.

Ferber (2015) compares thirteen assessment methods used in public purchasing. Of those that actually claim to optimize between quality and price, BA appears to have the most sophisticated procedure. But because price and quality cannot be made commensurable, he argues, there is no optimum mixture. For example, the funder could honor quality more by widening the corridor to 15 percent, which would make bid H the winner. But even with a wider corridor a funder may be compelled by the procedure to accept a cheap and mediocre bid, depending on the distribution of bids received on the graph.

Training Vouchers

Vocational training traditionally plays a major role in the portfolio of active labor-market policies in Germany. This reflects the structure of the German labor market which is highly professionalized and structured by certificates, offering only scant opportunities for jobseekers without any formal vocational qualification. Only around 13 percent of the employed workforce have no formal qualification, and only around 16 percent of notified vacancies do not require a formal qualification. But 46 percent of the unemployed do not have a formal qualification.

Since 2003, direct contracting between employment agencies[5] and providers has been replaced by issuing vouchers to clients who then choose the provider themselves. For finding a training provider, clients may use the website KURSNET on which all courses accessible with training vouchers are listed with the contact details of providers.

---

[5] Job centers as a second tier of the German PES only came into existence in 2005.

Clients with less web literacy may use leaflets local providers are allowed to place for pick-up on the premises of employment agencies or job centers.

Since 2012, job centers have an alternative option to purchase training courses via competitive tendering for clients who would have difficulty using vouchers and making choices on the provider market. Little use has been made of this option in practice. This is probably due to the fact that the use of vouchers entails less work for the local job center than running a tendering procedure as described above. Another possible explanation would be that job-center staff themselves are skeptical of the more radical marketization implied in tendering as compared to vouchers.

Possibilities to study vouchers were narrower than for competitive tendering since there is no publicly available source of information on the content of training vouchers. Providers list the courses they offer under voucher schemes on a national website;[6] but this does not tell which courses actually attract sufficient vouchers to take place or what is written on a voucher. Therefore, the following description is primarily based on interviews with providers operating under voucher schemes and information the BA gives to providers on its website.

Vouchers are issued to clients for whom participation in vocational training is regarded as necessary for finding a job. The voucher stipulates the training objective (e.g. chainsaw license; flight attendant; certified logistics manager) and the duration. There is a maximum duration of two years for a full vocational degree for which young apprentices would need two and a half or three years. The maximum duration of validity of the training voucher is three months, which implies that courses must start three months after the voucher was issued.

To accept and redeem vouchers, a training provider must be accredited as an organization and must also have accreditation for the specific course stipulated on the voucher. Accreditation includes approval of prices per participant and hour which, since 2012, must be checked by the accreditation agency against a list of average prices published annually by the BA. Prices differ widely between €4.54 for home economics and €10.77 in informatics (prices for 2014), reflecting different cost levels for technical equipment and sectoral wage differentials which influence the salaries of instructors proficient in different vocational fields. Averages are calculated on the basis of accredited courses, so there is a circular and price-dampening mechanism in place. Courses submitted for accreditation may not "unreasonably" exceed the average of the respective category, and averages are based on accredited courses. Nevertheless, average prices are slowly rising (Barton-Ziemann 2012), which is also reflected in the BA's overall average spending for vocational training per participant and month. If the provider seeks approval for a price above the applicable average, e.g. because technical instruction is to be combined with practical language training for newly arrived migrants, the application must undergo a special appeals procedure on the grounds of extra effort justified by the particular labor-market policy value of the course. Between April 2012 and November 2013, only about 45 percent of accreditations submitted for appeal were finally approved. Providers interviewed argued that sophisticated concepts are

---

[6] <http://kursnet-finden.arbeitsagentur.de/kurs/>.

rejected on the grounds that they exceed average prices, and that this is detrimental to innovation.

Once a provider has started a vocational training course with participants who submitted their training vouchers, the provider will receive monthly payments. In order to achieve this, the provider has to complete a short questionnaire for each and every participant, stating the voucher number. Activation vouchers follow largely the same mechanisms, except that where placement is part of the provider's task, an outcome-based component identical to that of placement vouchers (see the next section) may be part of the voucher.

Placement Vouchers

Placement vouchers were introduced in 2002 in reaction to what was framed as a "job-placement scandal." Unemployed jobseekers with contribution-based entitlements to unemployment benefits are entitled to receive a placement voucher after six weeks. Otherwise, issuing a placement voucher is a discretionary decision of front-line workers in employment agencies and job centers. Finding a private job-placement agency is more difficult than for training vouchers, since no database exists for them. Providers are supposed to do their own marketing in order to attract customers.

With only around 40,000 placements through vouchers and a total spending of just over €20 million in 2014 this is a very small proportion of spending on active measures, which was €4.8 billion that year.

The fee attached to a placement voucher in case of successful placement is normally €2,000 and can be raised to €2,500 in the case of long-term unemployed or disabled jobseekers. Of this fee, €1,000 is paid after job durations of six weeks and the rest after job durations of six months. Since the introduction of a statutory minimum wage as of January 2015, placement in a job that pays below the minimum wage rate does not count unless the worker falls under one of the exceptions to the minimum wage.

4

Employment-Services Sectors under Resource Scarcity and Uncertainty

The funding practices discussed in Chapter 3 create the market and determine the pressures on management. It was common for managers at non-public providers we interviewed to describe their task in terms of organizational survival. They reported a resource squeeze due to lower prices and increased administrative demands and uncertainty due to the cyclicality and increasing openness of contracting. While governments intended these changes as a means to steer or even re-engineer the landscape of provision, we found the reality of management coping strategies rather complex and hard to predict.

In this chapter we examine the pressures that marketization exerts on management and the measures they take to mitigate them. We focus on the sector level, in the landscape of organizations funded by, but external to, the PESs to implement the policies of the work-first welfare state. This excludes labor-market intermediaries not funded by PESs, such as temporary labor agencies; services funded by PESs that are not ALMPs, such as sheltered employment for the disabled or outsourced back-office functions; and the in-house services of the PESs. Here we look at the sector level; Chapter 5 will focus on the organization level.

While very few studies consider employment services as a sector, there are a number of related studies that we draw on for our depiction. Literatures exist on management in the kinds of organizations that are in this sector, but which focus on larger overlapping groups of providers, such as those employing social workers (e.g. Blank and Schulz 2015) and non-profits (e.g. Bode 2003; Cunningham and James 2011). Related German studies focus on social workers as a profession (Stolz-Willig and Christoforidis 2011), on services focused on the school-to-work transition (employment services for just one age and target group—Rosendahl 2013), or on adult education as a sector that overlaps with employment services (Dobischat et al. 2009; Rosendahl 2013). Studies focused specifically on the marketization of employment services tend to focus on state policy rather than providers (e.g. Van Berkel and Van der Aa 2005; Zimmermann et al. 2014; Wiggan 2015). Where providers are the object of investigation, it is in terms of their internal practices rather than collective activities as a sector (e.g. Considine 2001; Bredgaard and Larsen 2006; Rees et al. 2014). Only in Britain, where the sector has developed self-awareness, are there studies on it as a sector, such as Davies' (2008) account of their lobbying or Rees et al.'s (2013) comparison of non-profit and for-profit providers on the Work Programme.

These studies raise several important issues facing managers at the providers we studied, including both the pressures and management capacity to cope with them, which we will use to structure our discussion:

(1) *Uncertainty* is present in any kind of market, but in these markets is structured in varying ways. This variation includes uncertainty over whether or not contracts are won, clients referred, and payment received, as well as the market structure itself, including swings in the volume of work and the rules of the market.

(2) *Resource scarcity* can result from a squeeze on prices, reduced payments, or reduced volumes of work, as well as the increasing administrative burden of tendering, reporting, and accreditation.

(3) Providers have *strategies to mitigate these pressures*. Uncertainty can be mitigated by managing it as calculable risk and shifting it onto staff and/or subcontractors; or in large organizations it can be mitigated by redeploying staff. Resource scarcity can be mitigated through reduced investment, hiring, and service levels, prioritizing more lucrative activities (e.g. creaming and parking), or lobbying and negotiating with the funder to increase prices.

(4) *Power dynamics* include the varying roles of public, private, and non-profit providers operating under contract with the public employment services as well as the degree of fragmentation (i.e. whether providers see themselves as part of a single sector).

(5) *Influence* includes the channels of communication between funder and provider, including the role of umbrella bodies.

The main finding of this chapter is that by creating a market structure, the public authority distributes power, within the sector and between provider and funder. This gives providers varying options to mitigate resource scarcity and uncertainty. While the British market creates a concentrated structure of prime contractors with a high level of discretion, the German market reinforces the fragmentation of the sector and tightly controls the operations of providers. Denmark is in the middle, with providers fragmented at the national level and facing deep uncertainty over the rules and structure of the market, but without such a consistent or strict squeeze on prices.

State structure is of central importance to the way the market is structured and the landscape of provision that results. In both Denmark and Germany, municipalities have strong constitutionally anchored roles in the provision of service. In Denmark episodes of centralization are temporary, leading to flux in the market; and in Germany centralization tendencies—are checked by the constitutional court, the political system, and the administrative autonomy of the BA. The result is that Denmark and Germany have heterogeneous markets for employment services. In Great Britain, by contrast, centralization tendencies have been unchecked by such institutional constraints and government rhetoric promoting "localism" and the "big society" has not prevented the rise of a centralized employment-services market in the hands of a few large firms.

This chapter discusses each country case in turn, followed by a comparative analysis.

Denmark

Denmark is a case of deep uncertainty and a weak provider landscape. The problem facing Danish providers is less a squeeze on prices than extreme fluctuations in the overall volume and kind of work. As mentioned in Chapter 2, Denmark has gone through three waves of marketization, with fluctuation in the degree of marketization, the amount of funds available for externalized employment services, and the make-or-buy decision of municipalities.

While the providers operated by trade unions were pushed to the margins in the first and second wave of marketization, the for-profit sector was deeply challenged under the third wave of marketization. The two key moments for the sector were the removal of incentives for municipalities to use non-public providers for employment services in 2010 by a conservative government and the abolition of national tendering and requirements to use market-based providers for certain target groups were dissolved in 2011 by a social-democratic government. As we show in Appendix A the result was an extensive decentralization of the market for employment services. According to the spokesman of the umbrella organization of private job providers, the consequence of the dissolved national tendering system has been a diverse landscape of some few large and several small providers with relatively little power and the size and number of providers decreased during the years (Danish umbrella, second interview). However, the changing market structures are not seen as purely negative by the providers, and some have benefited.

In Denmark, *uncertainty* is deeper than in the other two countries, in part because it extends to the rules of competition and the volume of work, in part because change is not unidirectional. The imposition of mandatory tendering of certain services under centralized procurement in 2005 and payment by results tended initially to favor private providers and undermine non-profit provision by the social partners. During the first and second waves of marketization there was substantial profiteering, which the funder later reduced by stipulating maximum prices. Nevertheless, there was uncertainty associated with winning tenders, with the volume of referrals once the tender is won, and with payment by results (in which 75 percent of payments were for jobs sustained for up to fifteen months). Denmark's providers were here facing the same kinds of uncertainty as their counterparts in Germany and Great Britain.

After the change in government in 2011, however, uncertainty was compounded by the dissolving of national tendering and the elimination of requirements to externalize work. The abolition of national tendering was described by our Danish for-profit sector interviewee as "Black November," while a civil servant in another interviewee ironically described it as "letting the market decide". It gave municipalities—which already had considerable taxation and budgeting autonomy—more flexibility in make-or-buy decisions and in purchasing. Interviewees suggest, and our national survey confirms, that when municipalities were no longer obliged to use competitive tendering, many found non-market alternatives and an "insourcing" of external work took place and more partnership- or network-based relations between the municipal purchasers and providers have emerged. The latter include negotiated partnership agreements with incumbent providers, the extension of existing contracting relationships from one municipality to another (so-called frameworks), and a shift from using the non-public providers for generalized services to using them for more specialized services.

The underlying rationales behind the insourcing of external work are, according to one of the municipal purchasers we interviewed, that it is difficult to attract private providers that meet their expectations on results and quality due to a lack of experience and professionalism. Also the for-profit providers we interviewed are well aware that quality (since 2011) has become a more crucial parameter from a municipal perspective than previously: "If you do not make quality you cannot earn any money" (DK manager 1).

Furthermore, the shift from national to local tendering has, according to some of the providers and purchasers we interviewed, led in some municipalities to very small contracts. This is particularly the case in the municipalities with more partnership- or network-based relations between the municipal purchasers and providers. However where practices remain similar to the former national tendering system, the contracts are running for a longer period (around three years) and the number of participants is higher. The national survey demonstrates large national variation where the lengths of the contracts depend on the target group (social assistance receivers, receivers of unemployment benefit, sickness benefit, etc.). Thus, changes in the structure of the market had a direct effect on the likelihood that work would be subject to competitive tendering or externalized.

In spite of this uncertainty under the third wave of marketization the for-profit providers we interviewed also agreed that they have benefited from the recent changes:

> If you look at the whole industry of private providers after the "Black November night" and subsequent negative media campaign (November 2011), then I think it has been positive for the whole industry. Before (2010) the public jobcenters knew that the services they received from us have been very cheap and they get something that is very bad. (DK manager 1)

Resource scarcity took the form of a decline in the volume of work and less a squeeze on prices. Providers complained less about prices being squeezed than in the other countries, but it had been an issue under the first two waves of marketization. The result had been more standardized services and quality reduction as the providers realized that investments in services didn't pay off in the performance-related payment and lowering costs for services was the most important method to increase the competitiveness of the providers and the profitability. Since 2010 the volume of work and price competition has been reduced with less tendering and more specialized tasks for private providers; but, as we see in Appendix A, 86 percent of the municipalities confirm they still use non-public providers.

Recent changes in municipal procurement practices are not seen as solely negative by the providers. Even though many of the providers were earning big money in the previous system (a director at one of the for-profit providers called this "quick and dirty money" earned by just processing the primarily easy-to-place unemployed through the system) they also point at the problems with balancing low prices and high quality and they would in general prefer to compete around quality rather than purely prices. The expectation from the providers is that more specialized services for the more hard-to-place unemployed also will make the prices go up. The tendency towards a more partnership-based model is seen by most of the providers as positive for the organizations and for service quality.

One director for a for-profit provider describes how such new relations are developing:

> If we talk about quality we can see something positive is happening for the moment. This is a result of many years' development, where we have come to know some of these jobcenters very well. We now have relations to jobcenters where they just phone us and say: We do have a problem with this specific target group can we put our heads together and find out what to do? And then we do the project with them. The project will not be put to tender, because the procurement

rules are changed so they don't need to announce the project. Else we jointly can make a pilot-project and then put it to tender. We build up projects jointly... I have nothing against services being subject to competition or put to tender, but it is really fun to be part of the initial and developing phase of a project together with the municipality. And luckily some jobcenters think the same, because we have a longstanding relationship. (DK manager 2)

Since 2011 extracting price concessions has not been a priority for the national decision makers. The interviewee from the national labor market authority expressed an accepting view of private profit making and denied that the high profit levels during the early phases of marketization were considered scandalous in Denmark, even if the state did respond by reducing prices (AMS interview 1). There were complaints from providers about the administrative burden, especially associated with claiming payments for sustained job placements. But it is expected by some of our interviewees that prices will increase under the emerging local partnership relations.

Danish providers as a sector have had little capacity for *mitigating these changing market structures*, and they have had little influence in the decisions that have reshaped the market. Under the second wave of marketization, when the dominant kind of transaction was competitive tendering (i.e. hard marketization) providers were hit by reduced spending on employment services. Under the third wave of marketization, since 2011, non-public providers are more often used by the municipalities for specialized tasks to disadvantaged unemployed rather than generalized interventions for insured and highly educated unemployed people as a capacity buffer. Some providers report overhauling their business models, by hiring staff with professional qualifications, such as social workers or psychologists, and improving the quality of their services. But such professionalization presupposes higher prices. Other providers have invented entirely new business models where the entire staff has been replaced; one manager we interviewed reported making the transition from a training provider to a welfare-to-work generalist almost overnight.

The *power relations* in the sector disadvantage external providers. According to a spokesman of the umbrella organization of providers, fifteen large companies existed with more than 100 employees at the peak of the market, along with many other smaller firms including numerous one–two-person operations (umbrella interview 1, 2013). According to the former chairwomen of the umbrella organization of private job providers, there have been large fluctuations in the number of members in the umbrella organization due to the rapid changes in the market. In 2004 the umbrella organization had nine members; in 2011, thirty-four; and in 2015, thirteen (Christina Grøntved presentation, April 23, 2014).

Some of these firms were started by former public-sector workers who saw an opportunity, had a new idea, and started a firm. It is common for a firm to live for two to five years off of a particular piece of work and then to collapse, and as our survey shows municipal public purchasers report having this "flexibility buffer" as an important reason for using private suppliers. The smallest firms are therefore highly vulnerable to the end of contracts, while the larger ones are more likely to adapt to changes in demand. In addition to private firms, there are also social enterprises and a smaller sector provider which traditionally has focused on the so-called "heavy" clients (sometimes referred to as non-profit social economic companies), usually not under payment by results. However, in recent years the larger firms have also been more concerned with these groups and more specialized services due to the changing market structures.

Multinationals are not involved in the Danish market, with the exception of the largest player, a Denmark-based multinational that also operates in Norway. One Dutch-owned multinational provider (Agens) tried to set up a company in Denmark, but had to give up after a failure with a huge experiment in one municipality (Koege), where half of the clients stayed at the public service and the other half was transferred to Agens.

Employment-services providers are in a weak position to *influence* the development of the market. This is in part because of low membership in the umbrella body. The weakness of providers is also a function of the strength of trade unions, who have mobilized their members to campaign against the use of private providers, with considerable success in public discourse. Union providers have largely abandoned the employment-services market, managers interviewed still see unions as their adversaries in the political sphere.

In Danish employment services the funder dominates, but its identity and approach changes. Part of the reason is the complex political and administrative dynamics governing employment services, including municipalization and the loss of faith in the market by policymakers at the national level. Employment-services providers have an association, but its membership is small, especially when compared with its chief political opponent, the trade union movement. The weakness of the sector is also due to the same Denmark-specific market turbulence that marginalized the social partners; although the for-profit sector has survived it is weakened.

Great Britain

In Great Britain there is real uncertainty and resource scarcity, but without such dramatic fluctuations in market rules and volumes as in Denmark. Large private-sector providers have a much stronger capacity to mitigate these problems because of the discretion they have in the design of services and management of supply chains under "black-box" contracting. These providers have contributed substantially to the development of this design, and their power to do so has flowed from their scale as organizations, their concentrated resources, and the dependence of governments on them. These strong capacities do not exist in the much smaller subcontractors that constitute the vast majority of organizations involved.

Uncertainty is built into Britain's welfare-to-work schemes via a government policy of risk shifting. Aside from the risks of not winning contracts and programs being reconfigured due to turnover in governments, providers face the financial risks of payment by results. Providers saw the Work Programme as unnecessarily risky: one international provider pointed to Australia as a case where contracts do not automatically come to an end, even under conditions of poor performance that is not the fault of the provider (GB manager 3).

The risks entailed have to do with the lack of guarantees of participant numbers referred to providers, and payment by results shifts an increasing share of the payment into sustainment fees over the course of the contract. In addition, because each area has two or three providers, the government can shift the percentage of referrals from poor performers to good performers (i.e. the summer 2013 "market-share shift"), or terminate a contract (which it did with NCG). On the other hand, the government compensates by eliminating spending limits on potential outcome payments and through a contract with a long running time. The promise of rich rewards would, according to policymakers, draw capital from the financial sector (Freud 2007; DWP 2008). The risks would lead to a shakeout of the sector, as one senior manager told us in an interview, as poor-performing prime providers failed and their numbers declined (GB purchaser 6). Our interviewees report the financial sector balked due to the excessive risk (as did some potential bidders (GB manager 6)). For most prime contractors, the necessary investment came from the internal resources or from business partners rather from the financial sector as was the original plan (GB managers 1–4). These risks are designed at a national level to be calculated and managed by large for-profit companies with access to capital and strong management capacity.

Resource scarcity also exists under Britain's welfare-to-work schemes. Due to weak employer hiring, payment by results has automatically translated into reduced spending on welfare-to-work programs. Second, there is a decline in the overall maximum payment over the course of the contract. All unit prices therefore decline over the term of the contract. Third, providers report a massive administrative burden associated with managing the large contracts and claiming outcome payments up to twenty-four months after the client has moved into work. Finally, the DWP asked for discounts during the Work Programme procurement exercise, and a provider that was—as our interviewees argued and our analysis of DWP data confirmed—one of the more aggressive discounters, Deloitte Ingeus, won the largest share of contracts.

These problems are exacerbated by cuts to related specialized services to which providers could refer their clients, especially training, advice, and health interventions delivered by local government or the non-profit sector, often targeted at particular client groups (single mothers, disabled people, and particular age groups or ethnicities). One provider we visited had planned to refer services to "partners" but was finding this difficult due to demands for payment (GB manager 3). This broad resource squeeze in British public services forces providers to fund such services using their internal resources or not provide them at all. Our interviews with front-line staff show that resource scarcity was a problem for the quality of services.

Compared to the other two countries, however, the prime contractors are very well placed to *mitigate these problems*. The surprising health of the prime providers can be seen in the fact that the concentration process predicted by the funder has taken place only to a limited extent: prime providers have been acquired by firms wanting to enter the market (Ingeus, A4e, and Best) and merged with subcontractors (the CDG merger with Shaw Trust). In addition, interviews gave us examples of generous bonuses distributed to senior staff and dividends distributed to owners in the first stages of the Work Programme when the government began paying up-front "attachment" fees. At that time payments of £11 million to A4E director Emma Harrison were reported in the media (Boffey and Helm 2012). After the phasing out of attachment fees, there was considerable concern about the viability of the sector, but the way that concentration took place demonstrated the continued viability of these firms. When the largest provider, Deloitte Ingeus, announced that it was looking for a buyer, the sector was concerned; but it was purchased by the American firm Provident Services Corporation, in a deal in which Ingeus' owners received an up-front payment of US $225 million, plus up to US $135 million in potential payments under an "earn-out" agreement (Plimmer 2014).

How can there be profits to distribute under these apparently hostile market conditions? First, there are countervailing internal management practices—choices about investment, performance management, and employment relations—that allow management to cut costs. Work Programme providers reported in one survey reducing spending per ESA claimant well below the amount stipulated in their bids (see Appendix B); they cut overall spending by 12 percent (National Audit Office 2014; we will discuss in-house management practices in Chapter 5). Second, there is a longer-term possibility of increased payment. When low-wage employers increase their hiring, providers might expect an increased number of job placements and hence outcome payments. Third, there is the bigger picture of primes gaining expertise and relationships that they can use to win other kinds of work, most notably according to our interviewees in the prison sector (GB managers 3 and 4). Fourth, prime contractors shift risks onto subcontractors—indeed, the 2014 National Audit

Office (NAO) report shows that subcontractors were used by primes as a capacity buffer, since the decline in spending by providers on subcontractors was much greater than the overall figure.

These conditions of profitability all presuppose a particular set of *power relations* that favors large prime contractors. This core of large organizations contracting directly with the government—their roles institutionalized as preferred bidders under the ERSS Framework—contrasts with a periphery of hundreds of smaller organizations that serve as subcontractors. The core is made up predominately of multinational corporations, which have a market share of 75 percent in the prime contractor segment of the Work Programme.

Table 4.1 lists all Work Programme prime contractors, all but three of which are for-profit. It shows the share of work they carry out and the number of contracts, based on data supplied to us by the DWP under a Freedom of Information Act request. The top four providers, accounting for more than 50 percent of the market, are for-profit corporations that operate on a multi-national scale. This shows that, while the largest providers are welfare-to-work specialists, there are other big players that are generalist providers of privatized public services that manage a range of security, back-office, and social-service contracts, among others. Since the Work Programme tender, Table 4.1 shows that there has been restructuring: out of eighteen primes, eight have been purchased (two by multinational companies based abroad), three have taken over or merged with providers working as subcontractors, and one has lost its contract. There are now fifteen primes.

The sector has a dualized structure, with a core of prime providers managing a periphery of "tier 1" and "tier 2" subcontractors. The periphery includes small private firms and non-profits, as well as educational institutions and units of local government working as subcontractors. There are just over 800 organizations working as subcontractors for the Work Programme, the vast majority with one or two contracts. The composition of this periphery reflects the landscape of providers that grew up under the old regime of employment-services contracting, with the DWP and its predecessors as funders alongside municipalities and regional funders of training and economic development schemes.

Two contracting models have been described in our interviews. Prime providers that rely on a 100 percent subcontracted supply chain (e.g. the generalist outsourcing companies SERCO and G4S) have a tight performance-management system, while prime providers that rely on both in-house provision and subcontracted provision (e.g. the welfare-to-work specialists A4e and Working Links) are perceived to work with a less tight monitoring of their supply chain. Foster et al. (2014) find that 100 percent contracted-out provision tends to involve more competition and more contract cancelation than a mixed model.

Table 4.1. Prime contractors on the Work Programme

	Work Programme bids		Market share	For-profit or non-profit	Multinational company	Country of origin	Welfare-to-work specialist	Notes
	Won	Lost						
Ingeus Deloitte	7	4	0.216	Fp	y	US-Australia	y	Bought by Provident (US)
A4e	5	7	0.13	Fp	y	UK	y	Bought by Staffline
Working Links	3	6	0.097	Fp	y	UK	y	
MAXIMUS	3	6	0.093	Fp	y	US	n	Took over Remploy
Avanta	3	4	0.083	Fp	n		y	Bought by Staffline
Seetec	3	5	0.065	Fp	n		y	
G4S	3	8	0.056	Fp	y	UK	n	
Rehab Group	2	1	0.038	Np	y	Ireland	y	
Serco	2	9	0.034	Fp	y	UK	n	
CDG	1	0	0.029	Np	n		y	Merged with Shaw Trust
Pertemps	1	3	0.027	Fp	n		y	Bought by APM (AUS)
Fourstar	1	3	0.027	Fp	y	UK-NL	n	Bought by Staffline
Reed	1	8	0.021	Fp	y	UK	n	
ESG	1	1	0.021	Fp	n		y	Bought by Interserve
BEST	1	1	0.019	Fp	n		n	Bought by Interserve
JHP Group	1	7	0.016	Fp	n		y	Merged with Learndirect
Prospects	1	2	0.015	Fp	n		y	
NCG	1	11	0.012	Np	n		y	Work Programme contract canceled

Source: Work Programme bid data from DWP, own calculations; company information from firm websites and <http://www.workprogramme.co.uk/news>

While the selection of subcontractors is not at all transparent, it does differ from the direct procurement by the DWP. As private companies the prime contractors are not bound to EU procurement and state aid rules and therefore have more flexibility. They do not have to advertise tenders—indeed, much of their supply chain was put together as part of the Work Programme tendering process—and unlike the DWP they use the organization's past performance as a criterion in selecting contractors (GB manager 4 and purchaser 6). Compared to the Work Programme, there is considerable fluctuation of subcontractors, including public-sector ones.

Table 4.2. "Churn" of tier 1 Work Programme contracts January 2012–September 2013, by sector

	Public	Private	Voluntary	Primes	Total
Total January 2012	61	158	168	28	387
Contracts lost	21	47	66	3	134
(share Jan 2012)	0.34	0.30	0.39	0.11	0.35
Contracts held	40	111	102	25	253
(share Jan 2012)	0.66	0.70	0.61	0.89	0.65
Contracts gained	6	26	23	4	55
(share Jan 2012)	0.10	0.16	0.14	0.14	0.14
Total September 2013	46	137	125	29	308
(share Jan 2012)	0.75	0.87	0.74	1.04	0.80

Note: Rows do not add up because prime contractors are a subset of the private and voluntary-sector providers.

Source: DWP subcontractor lists, own calculations

Britain's employment-services periphery is fluid and volatile, as our analysis of tier 1 contracts (Table 4.2) shows. Under a so-called tier 1 contract a "prime" subcontracts the complete service (known as end-to-end) for a specific group of clients (a tier 2 contract, by contrast, is for more specialized services). Tier 1 contracts are less numerous, but more important for the individual service provider, since they are larger and more likely to require investment that is specific to the Work Programme. Out of 387 of these contracts listed in January 2013, 134 were not listed in 2014, a loss of one third, less for private organizations and more for public and voluntary-sector bodies. The private sector was also more successful in terms of holding contracts and winning new ones than the public and voluntary sectors, with a 13 percent net decline in the number of contracts, as opposed to a decline of 25 percent for the public and voluntary sectors. Prime contractors experienced a small net increase in tier 1 contracts.

A striking feature of Britain's employment-services sector is the subordinate role of local government. Its work is not governed by a written constitution (as in Germany) or public-sector performance management (as in Denmark), but rather by the supply chain management of the for-profit firms for which they act as subcontractors. Local government works alongside hundreds of for-profit and non-profit organizations in that capacity, and the survival of their services for jobseekers becomes increasingly dependent on their success as subcontractors.

The volatility of this subcontracting sector, which extends to its public-sector players, reflects a power imbalance within the sector. As one DWP representative told us, unequal relations in contracting were to be expected, so safeguards were in place:

> To be blunt about it you don't have a supply chain other than to squeeze it a bit really, so our response to that is, well firstly if they go beyond squeezing their supply chain to trashing it they won't deliver, that's what they've got to manage well otherwise they don't make any money out of the contract. Secondly we've put

protection into that because we have something called the MERLIN standard which is something which is very novel and it's a sort of accreditation in the supply chain standards. (GB purchaser 6)

The effects of these safeguards are unclear. One prime provider admitted a number of widespread bad practices in the bidding process, in which eager subcontractors were included in bids but not informed until afterwards about the terms of payment; this was a deliberate strategy to shift risk (GB manager 2). Regarding the "Merlin Standard," a DWP-funded evaluation found a widespread perception among subcontractors that it was not protecting them from unfair contracting practices (Simmonds 2015). Interviewees reported that inspections were taking place in close consultation with the prime contractor and did not punish supply-chain management practices that deviate from the Work Programme bids. The complaints procedure is rarely used because, as one subcontractor told us, "if I went to Merlin, we'd never get work again . . . You don't bite the hand that feeds you" (GB manager 12).

The sector's core firms have a strong *influence* on public policy, with the aid of the think tank Inclusion and the lobbying body ERSA and a usually responsive group of senior civil servants and cabinet ministers. Policymakers in the government and the opposition both recognized that the private sector will only participate in this market if it can expect to make a profit; this was the premise of DWP's commissioning policies in the final years of Labour (Freud 2007) and continued under the Conservatives. Our management interviewees spoke quite openly about lobbying in the run up to the Work Programme tendering exercise:

We had two years effectively of market shaping . . . That's where you talk to the market about how they can deliver more effective, efficient services and in the process create the opportunity for you to bid into the contracts that result from that dialogue. [Interviewer: Talk to the market, you mean talk to the Department of Work and Pensions?] The Department of Work and Pensions, think tanks, the providers, the public. (GB manager 2)

Large providers are highly visible in the policymaking process. (Small providers are marginal, and few can afford membership in ERSA.) They participate in policymaking not only via ERSA's lobbying activities, but also directly, with senior executives. These interactions take the form of regularized exchanges with senior civil servants (such as the "Work Programme Partnership Forum"), exchanges with ministers and opposition politicians (including extensive lobbying in the design phase of the Work Programme), and testimony before parliamentary committees. This close relationship was temporarily interrupted during the period after Work Programme tenders were issued, which according to our private-sector interviewees, put DWP management in "lock-down mode" and to the bidders' consternation temporarily shut down communications with the funder. This, however, was an exception to the rule.

One open question is how providers use their influence to cope with payment problems. This is a sensitive topic, since the government does not want to be accused of bailing out failing for-profit providers, especially after the expensive buyout of contracts for previous schemes. The 2014 collapse of a large contract with Atos Healthcare to assess disabled claimants gave the government an opportunity to claim that it was not paying badly performing contractors (Siddique 2014). Nevertheless, the prime providers' influence matters, since the government depends on a small group of large organizations for the success of its welfare-to-work programs, and since prime contractors depend on government agencies to refer clients.

In one case mentioned by a management interviewee, contractors collectively threatened to withdraw a particular scheme (not the Work Programme) if they did not receive more referrals. This proved an effective way to force changes to the way that clients were referred (GB manager 12). While many of our management interviewees expressed concern about the economic viability of the Work Programme, there has been no renegotiation of the contract.

Britain's employment-services sector has the strongest capacity for collective action in our sample. This can be seen beyond its influence in policy and administration, at the grass roots of provision. It has initiated a professional body, the Institute for Employment Professionals (IEP), to cope with human-resource challenges. IEP was officially launched in 2012, with strong support from senior management in several of the prime contractors and Inclusion. Its main function is to "professionalize" the sector by turning front-line employment services into a recognized profession with formal qualifications, clear career progression, and overall recognition as a profession. It has created three courses of training for employment advisors, recruitment consultants, and tutors. It sponsors networking events and organizes training, and in September 2013 it reported 3,853 members. Membership fees are for most members paid by the employer, and membership appears to be more common among front-line managers than among front-line staff. IEP plans to extend its membership and services into the in-house Jobcentre Plus workforce (Foster et al. 2013).

British employment services has developed over the past decade into a centralized and dualized sector. While the funding mechanism of the Work Programme creates resource scarcity and uncertainty across the sector, prime contractors and subcontractors have different abilities to mitigate it. Prime contractors not only have sophisticated systems and high levels of discretion in-house, but they also have a very strong lobbying capacity and corresponding influence in politics and administration. Subcontractors have few of these capacities, and their vulnerability can be seen in their loss of contracts with primes and interviewees' reports of them exiting the sector or becoming insolvent.

Germany: Funder Dominance

The German provider landscape is a collection of non-profit and for-profit organizations with much smaller and shorter contracts than those in Britain and an ongoing squeeze on prices. The funder in Germany is far more complex than that in Britain, with a higher degree of local autonomy and variation in the way that funding is managed, as well as a lower degree of centralized control by politicians. The structure of the external providers is also more complex, with less self-awareness by providers as a "sector" and a large number of overlapping umbrella organizations. This reflects the diverse orientations and historical origins of the providers and the diversity of statutory underpinnings and funding. The resulting fragmentation tends to empower the funder over providers, and the influence of providers in German public policy is purely technical and from a position of weakness.

Uncertainty in German employment services takes different forms depending on the transaction mode, but the risks are not as readily calculable as in Great Britain. For measures funded by procurement the critical form of uncertainty is the tendering outcome. Because contracts last twelve–twenty-four months, the funder has frequent exit options from contracting relationships that it can exercise by default. While there has been an increase of options to extend contracts for a year without a need to re-tender, this represents the removal of a requirement to exercise exit options rather than encouragement for long-term relational contracting. There is also uncertainty as to the number of clients in many of these programs, although it is common for the funder to guarantee 50–85 percent of the announced volume of work.

For organizations operating under voucher arrangements, the main form of uncertainty has to do with the number of customers who come through the doors.

> So I would say that the process on the whole is in principle economical. I say "in principle" because we have to calculate 15 participants ... In practice we hardly ever get this many, just because the education voucher business has a broad supply structure, which has the consequence that each [provider offering a certain course in a particular local market] gets five training vouchers and none can start a scheme because it is simply not sufficient to get started on an economical basis.
>
> (German manager 2, second interview)

For training providers reimbursement is per participant and hour of course, and providers can only afford to provide a certain course if they have enough participants, while job centers often decided to provide vouchers for a specific course that could then be used by customers at several providers. While the number of vouchers issued might be enough to cover the costs of a course, it would be divided between all the providers offering that course. Immediately after the Hartz reforms this had the result that none of the providers reached a sufficient number of participants and had to cancel the offered courses, contributing to a wave of bankruptcies.

For placement vouchers uncertainty is different. It does not only include the number of job seekers who approach the provider, but also has to do with the amount of employer hiring and the employability of voucher holders.

Resource scarcity has numerous sources. For measures funded by procurement it has to do with prices; the procurement offices allow prices to float according to supply and demand. There is variation in the effects of this practice on prices, but for a standardized service that can be provided by many different organizations our interviewees argue that it is an effective way for the funder to keep down costs.

For measures funded by vouchers the mechanism of cost containment is different. The value of placement vouchers is fixed by law, and can only be increased by lawmakers. Consequently, since their introduction the nominal value of placement vouchers has not changed.

A third mechanism for resource scarcity has been cuts to make-work schemes, such as the so-called one-euro jobs. While this was once a large source of income for non-profit providers, because the schemes included both payments for "flanking" support services and a subsidy for "public-benefit" work, the number of these has declined dramatically since 2010.

A fourth dynamic contributing to resource scarcity has to do with a general increase in the administrative burden. The introduction of accreditation for providers and their courses or services incurred substantial costs for the small firms involved, and providers interviewed also report an increase in requirements to report activity. The latter is a direct result of the standardization of the work by the funder, with detailed descriptions of work used in procurement leading to more work by front-line staff documenting this work.

The *mitigation of these problems* is more difficult in Germany than in Britain, for a number of reasons. Unlike Great Britain, where the black box gives providers discretion in how it deploys staff and invest in premises, staffing levels and infrastructure for BA contractors are specified in detail in tendering documents and contracts. Non-profits cope with this by sweating their own assets, i.e. employing low-paid but qualified staff and by owning buildings. Some providers still live off the fixed assets acquired before marketization was rolled out, but it is only a matter of time until such resources will be exhausted.

One strategy for managing uncertainty under the training voucher regime is the modularization of courses. Reminiscent of nineteenth-century schoolhouses, providers put participants of different funded courses in the same sessions.

We start with only one participant, and since the whole measure is pulled apart, modularized and then an additional educational justification is sought, and it's said, "It is better for people who are at different skill levels, then they can support each other." We create heterogeneous groups. They start every three months, and then if possible in four different professions ... We pile them in a room and modularize the measure, pull out the common content and teach together and split the groups only in phases where different content [is needed].   (German manager 10)

Large providers can, furthermore, cross-subsidize their employment-services activities, although we encountered other examples of providers creating a subsidiary for a particularly troubled business area and then shutting it down for business reasons and making staff redundant (German manager 15). Small providers did not have this option.

They also possess strong relationships with local managers of the job centers, who to some extent could work around contracting rules to design programs of work with incumbent providers in mind, especially if they were procured via local channels rather than the REZ.

The providers have remained the same [as those whom we contracted before tendering became mandatory], because they are really good ... The fact that we must explain how it is that over 8, 9, 10 years the same provider does the same work, I think has something perfidious. This question should not really be asked. It is asked when someone says "Well, something is not right!" Exactly the opposite is the case. There is something, namely the quality. But then they come back with: "What's there? Certainly corruption?"   (German purchaser 4)

If we believe this measure is so special that it can be carried out in this place by only one [provider] and we therefore use hand-picked procurement, then of course we talk about this scheme with the provider beforehand. Could they do it, do they have the capacity, then we decide to do it with them. If we use competitive tendering we do not discuss it with the provider ... Though, we do not do that, in a way that allows the provider to dictate how the substance of the contracts should be; we are the ones who do that ... And the planned price has to be right, of course. We plan a price in advance and if then the only supplier who could do that particular job that he cannot make it at that price, then we need to rethink that again, whether we are planning a higher price or we let it be.   (German purchaser 6)

Providers in Germany also mitigate resource scarcity through a variety of within-organization practices, as we will see in Chapter 5. For example, both for-profits and non-profits tend to employ staff on a temporary basis. One small private placement firm we visited had extremely tight performance management of staff, like Work Programme providers, and relied heavily on temporary contracts. Other job-placement firms are one-person firms whose income can be topped up by the benefits system as *Aufstocker* if it falls below the level of ALGII. Another small training firm we visited reported hedging risks through short-term rental agreements and the extensive use of freelancers as trainers. But providers' abilities to carry this out depends crucially on the kind of funding: most purchasing by the BA prescribes staff numbers and qualifications as part of its definition of tasks.

The *power relations* of the sector favor the funder. While British policymakers emphasize the strong voice of the sector, German administrators in interviews emphasize their disdain for looking after the sector (*Landschaftspflege*) and their orientation toward making "schemes for clients and not for providers." There is wide local variation in the mix of providers employed and wide diversity in the providers themselves. The sector is far more difficult to define than that in Britain. Non-profits are numerically dominant in Germany but do not have the power of Britain's large firms. While at least two of the large providers that operate in Britain have attempted to take hold in Germany, one has exited the market, and the German-based turnover of the other remains quite small.

The range of umbrella associations provides some indication of the sector's fragmentation (Table 4.3). Within the non-profit sector, for example, most providers are affiliated with a "welfare association" defined by political or confessional orientation. As groupings of employers, these are among Germany's largest employers, with Caritas employing more than 500,000 staff, and they cover welfare services ranging from hospitals to social work to employment services. These umbrella bodies organize training and information exchange, carry out lobbying, and also organize industrial relations matters. Caritas and Diakonie, in analogy to the churches with which they are affiliated and which enjoy constitutional privileges, have their own collective agreements, employee representation, and labor law.

There are also numerous other umbrella associations defined by function. These include several whose names begin with *Bundesarbeitsgemeinschaft* (BAG)—meaning literally "federal-level working party"—and are defined in terms of the legal framework of their members' work. Examples include BAG Arbeit that represents providers of job training and subsidized work schemes for the unemployed covered by the two main laws governing social protection against un(der)employment (SGBII and III) and BAG Berufsbildungswerke that represents providers of vocational training for the disabled covered by a different statute. Other associations include a number of small associations for private job-placement agencies that use placement vouchers (most of these have, according to one interviewee, disappeared or become moribund) and various groupings of organizations that deliver training, supported employment, or make-work schemes. There is considerable duplication of services and functions, and it is common for larger providers to belong to more than one umbrella body, often a confessional welfare association and a functional BAG.

Table 4.3. The associational landscape in Germany

Welfare associations	Deutscher Caritasverband	Catholic
	Arbeiterwohlfahrt	Social Democratic
	Volkssolidaritaet	German Democratic Republic Heritage
	Deutscher Paritätische Wohlfahrtsverband	
	Diakonie Deutschland	Independent secular Protestant
	Deutsches Rotes Kreuz	
Subsectoral associations and professional associations	BAG Arbeit	Make-work
	BAG Wohnungslosenhilfe	Homelessness
	BAG örtlich regionaler Träger der Jugendsozialarbeit	Youth work Occupational training
	BAG beruflicher Trainingszentren	Occupational training
	BAG der Berufsbildungswerke	Make-work
	BAG Kathosliche Jugendsozialarbeit	Catholic youth work
Other functional organizations	Katholische Bundesarbeitsgemeinschaft "Integration durch Arbeit"	Catholic make-work
	Evangelischer Fachverband für Arbeit und soziale Integration e.V.	Protestant make-work
	Wuppertaler Kreis e.V.—Bundesverband betriebliche Weiterbildung	Business-affiliated training
	Stiftung Bildung und Handwerk	SME-affiliated training
	Bundesverband der Träger beruflicher Bildung	Union-affiliated training
	Kooperationsverbund Jugendsozialarbeit	Youth work
	Verband der Personaldienstleister und Arbeitsvermittler; Ring der Arbeitsvermittler e.V.; Fachverband Personal- und Arbeitsvermittler e.V.; Bundesverband für Verbände privater Arbeitsvermittler; Bund privater Arbeitsvermittler	Private job placement Umbrellas

The sector's fragmentation can also be seen in the politics of the statutory minimum wage introduced in the sector in 2011. One difficulty was that there were sharp differences of opinion over whether it was desirable. While a group of training providers close to the trade unions (*Bundesverband der Träger beruflicher Bildung*) supported and sponsored it, an employer-oriented group of providers (the *Wuppertaler Kreis*) opposed it. A second difficulty concerned the definition of the sector covered by the new rule. It did not include every organization delivering employment services for the BA; instead, it covered 22,000 employees in "establishments or independent parts of establishments that predominately carry out training and further education" under the statutory framework that governs the funder. A representative from the largest trade union in the sector, the united services union

(Vereinte Dienstleistungsgewerkchaft—ver.di) discusses the work with the smaller union for education and science (Gewerkschaft Erziehung und Wissenschaft—GEW) to establish the sectoral minimum wage.

> There was no employers association ... in 2005 an employers association was formed, in the form that some members of an interest group of educational institutions (in the Bildungsverband) formed a single-purpose association (Zweck-gemeinschaft) that should act on the employer side as collective bargaining agent. After initially tough negotiations with inexperienced representatives of the Zweck-gemeinschaft we dropped the idea of a sectoral agreement in 2007, and moved towards a minimum wage. Employers also came along immediately, because they wanted, just like us unions, collective bargaining rules to deal with the companies engaging in wage dumping. In order to complete the collective agreement for the sectoral minimum wage, we had to first get things on track in the political sphere, by getting the training sector into the relevant law, the worker-posting law ... The prerequisite for this was the proof that the members of the said Zweckge-meinschaft employ a total of as many employees that the collective agreement for the industry (more precisely, the teaching staff and financed by SGB II and SGB III continuing training bodies) can be considered representative. Now we have then a long dispute with another group of employers who opposed any collective agree-ment for the sector, including against a minimum wage collective agreement ... We as trade unions working in this phase closely with the members of the Zweckge-meinschaft to provide ... the proof of representativeness of our planned minimum wage collective agreement. That was a very tedious process and the opponents have also been very diligent and have opinions written that should prove that the Zeckgemeinschaft covers only a small part of the industry and therefore the planned minimum wage collective agreement cannot claim representativeness ... We think that they want to use dumping practices and corresponding low wages, not only to defend their market share, but also to expand it ... The group of opponents are predominantly those educational institutions that are close to the German employers' associations. (German trade union 1)

The dominant actor in this sector is the public purchaser. Under procurement and grant making, it is local management (the director of the job center or *Arbeitsagentur*, depending on the client group), usually with strong input from the regional purchasing center (the REZen) though with the possibility for job centers (not the *Arbeitsagenturen*) to use municipal procurement offices or to set up their own procurement units (under vouchers there is a more mechan-ical process determined by law and decree). The REZen are noteworthy not only for developing a strong professionalized procurement function, but also for support they provide to local public-sector managers in the design of programs of work to procure.

Providers do have some *influence*, despite their evident weakness. There is frequent contact between providers' representatives and the BA, the REZ directors are important representatives, and according to our interviews with both sides, some of the providers' concerns are taken on board. From attending public meetings in which there was debate between funder and providers (including our own final workshop in April 2014), it was evident that there is a kind of lively welfare corporatism. It is not a matter of bargaining with the funder or lobbying politicians, but rather a kind of technical feedback, in which these associations are treated as representatives of their clients' interests rather than their self-interest as organizations. In public administration there was widespread skepticism about whether non-profits distinguished themselves in a meaningful way from for-profits, but at the same time there was a distaste for the idea of distributing profits to the owners of contractors. Our interviewees in the responsible ministry told us, "there is no non-profit"; and then when told about profit making in British employment services they responded, "but that is public money!".

Perhaps the clearest example of the weakness of providers in this structure comes from our questioning of international providers about their efforts to expand market share. One problem they reported was low prices and small contracts, which made it difficult to justify new up-front investments or develop new and innovative provision. A second problem was the difficulty of building relationships with purchasers, which were not national-level politicians or senior civil servants in Berlin or Nuremburg, but rather the local managers of job centers and *Arbeitsagenturen*. There was thus little scope for lobbying as a strategy to shape the actions of the funder.

> It is the case that you have more influence through centralized structures. My management told me for years: just go to the minister, talk to him, then you'll get the contracts. I had to reply that the principle of subsidiarity applies in Germany and so it doesn't work that way here. I can talk to a lot of people, but I don't get any contracts that way. Meetings at the Federal Ministry of Labor bring nothing, when it comes to contracts. That's a huge difference. Elsewhere you simply meet with ministers, etc. We even had meetings in the Chancellor's office—but it brings nothing.   (German manager 9)

Given localized contracting and little to offer in the way of potential profits, multinationals had made little progress in taking over the large German market.

Discussion

This chapter has discussed employment services from the perspective of the management of providers, including both pressures from funding arrangements and consequences at the sectoral level. In Great Britain contracting practices have allowed a concentrated market to emerge with strong organizational capacity as well as a strong ability to mitigate pressures of uncertainty and resource scarcity. In Germany contracting practices have had almost the opposite effect: the fragmentation of the sector, making it vulnerable to the squeeze on resources that takes place under all three of the main transaction modes. Denmark is like Germany with the employment-services sector in a weak and fragmented position, although this is more due to volatility in market structure and volume than it is due to a squeeze on prices. In each country the state has created a market structure with specific power relations, and these power relations determine the way that firms mitigate market pressures.

Uncertainty exists in all three countries. Cyclical contracting with automatic expiration is a source of uncertainty for providers in all three countries. In Britain it is designed by the funder as a form of calculable risk associated by payment by results which the large contractors are generally effective at managing, often by shifting them onto subcontractors. In Germany uncertainty takes different forms under the different transaction modes and has become a routine part of business for the providers that have survived: tendering outcomes under procurement and volumes of clients trained or placed in jobs under vouchers. In Denmark uncertainty is deepest, because it has not only to do with the outcomes of tendering or the claiming of outcome-based payments, but because it also has to do with the changes in market structure itself, including the reversal of marketization decisions by some municipal funders.

Resource scarcity is also severe in all three countries. Increasing administrative requirements are cited by interviewees in all three countries as draining resources away from provision. In Britain it is due to a decline in outcome-based payments due to lower than predicted numbers of referrals and poor performance by providers. This is compounded by deep cuts to more specialized services to which providers could refer clients with particular needs. In Germany it takes the form of a price squeeze due to competition in procurement, a nominal price freeze in placement vouchers set by statute, and, in effect, a cap on prices for training vouchers, but also a reduction in funding for once lucrative (and non-marketized) make-work schemes. In Denmark the decline in the volume of work has been more of a problem than prices, which in some municipalities have become more generous.

Where providers differ is in their capacity to mitigate these pressures. In Britain these pressures are severe, but providers have the discretion and scale needed to mitigate them, i.e. by targeting their investments in a way that reap performance-related payments, while passing costs and uncertainty onto the workforce and the supply chain. In Germany providers face similar constraints, but lack the discretion to mitigate them, with strict requirements placed on staff, services, and infrastructure. In Denmark, providers have tried to adapt to the changing market structures among others by focusing more on specialized services targeted at "heavy groups" rather than more generalized services. In all three countries managers shift risks onto employees through insecure jobs.

These three employment-services sectors vary in terms of the distribution of power and influence. The British government has encouraged a sector to form with a clear identity and a strong associational capacity, whose collective activities extend beyond lobbying to include improving the sector's human-resource practices and stabilizing the labor market. Among the dark sides of this arrangement are the treatment of large multinational firms as potentially too big to fail, and the marginalization of non-profits and municipalities as sub-contractors. The diversity of German funding practices and statutory instruments has created a sector that is fragmented along many dimensions (most notably task and sector), cannot be captured statistically with any satisfactory degree of accuracy, lacks a clear identity, and has a weak associational capacity despite—or exactly because of—the multiplicity of associations. The conflict within the sector over the statutory sectoral minimum wage and the peculiarities of its design and enforcement illustrates this problem. In Denmark, rapid fluctuations in the nature of the market have weakened both the providers run by the social partners and private providers. Neither Germany nor Denmark has an employment-services sector with the power, influence, and clear sense of identity approaching that of Britain's sector.

Chapter 5 explores further how providers react to these market pressures in their internal workings, with more detail provided on employment relations and work organization.

5

Employment Relations and Labor Process

Institutional Disorganization
and Management Control

with Graham Symon and Johannes Kirsch

In this chapter we examine the internal workings of service providers. Chapters 2 and 3 examined the policy and administrative dynamics that generate and constitute marketization; Chapter 4 discussed the organizational landscape that emerged as a result and introduced the pressures on providers caused by marketization. This chapter presents our data on the institutional regulation and subjective experience of work for front-line employees. We give some indication of the effects of marketization—or more precisely management's responses to marketization—both on staff and the character of services.

In this chapter we examine two effects of marketization within providers. The first is the disorganization of employment-relations institutions (Doellgast and Greer 2007), in which the rules that protected workers in the past—such as collective bargaining or co-determination rules—cease to apply or to carry out their intended function. We examine this institutional change in terms of worker voice, pay determination, and job insecurity. The second is the assertion of managerial control in the labor process (Clarke and Newman 1997), including the tightening of performance management, the undermining of professional autonomy, and changes in the quality, quantity, and distribution of staff–client interactions. We show within each market segment how particular dynamics of resource scarcity and uncertainty shape each outcome.

The findings in this section have to be taken as indicative. The number of providers is many times larger than the number of funders, and in some cases employment-services providers do not see themselves as part of the same sector, making it difficult to paint a comprehensive picture. Publicly available statistics are rare on basic issues, such as employment numbers, union membership, or collective bargaining coverage. Instead, we have some estimates from umbrella bodies, policymakers, and union representatives, who themselves have limited information, as well as studies and statistics. These are all country-specific, with a different focus from ours. We also have qualitative assessments from our interviewees, whom we have selected to represent the diversity of the market (e.g. different transaction modes), the different interests (e.g. management, labor, and government), different levels of authority (e.g. front-line workers, strategic and operational management, local and national policymakers, purchasing specialists, umbrella bodies, workplace-level worker representatives, and regional and/or national union staff). Given the diversity of our interviewees and organizations, ours is a plausible depiction of employment-services workplaces in the three countries.

This chapter begins with a preliminary discussion of how, in light of the literature, marketization might affect public-service employment. It sets out the dimensions of employment relations and the labor process and presents our findings from the three countries organized along these dimensions, including within-country variation between market segments operating under different transaction modes. In the comparative discussion we show how these dynamics vary across the different national contexts.

Marketization and Employment in Public Services

The scholarly consensus is that the tendencies associated with NPM have altered the nature, scope, and climate of institutional industrial relations and employment conditions across the public services (see Bach and Bordogna 2011; Gold and Veersma 2011). Public-sector reform has taken place at varying speeds and in varying ways—whether through privatization or internal reform—but the reform of labor has been a highly salient issue in every European country (Lethbridge et al. 2014). One intention of NPM is to make services both responsive and flexible by confronting the "vested interests" of public-sector workers (Bach and Bordogna 2011), and this intention is explicit in quasi-markets theory (Le Grand 2006). The reality of many privatized and contracted-out workplaces is that pay is lower, unions weaker, and work more intense; and this finding is not specific to Anglophone countries (Doellgast 2012; Hermann and Flecker 2012).

Comparative employment-relations researchers typically treat the non-market institutions regulating the workplaces as overdetermining the effects of market dynamics. Labor laws, unionization, collective bargaining frameworks, organizational function, and ethos (Gold and Veersma 2011), as well as social regulation built into public-sector purchasing itself aimed at propping up these institutions (Jaehrling 2015) are all present in our sample and, to varying degrees, shape employer behavior. Their effects, however, are made more complex by broader shifts in the political economy, including various forms of disruption brought on by intensified competition (Greer and Doellgast 2013) and path-dependent institutional changes with other causes (Thelen 2014). Workplaces therefore vary within countries in ways that standard national-institutional explanations cannot account for.

The effects of marketization may be contingent on the way that funding is organized, i.e. how competitive it is (Greer et al. 2011, 2013) or whether contracts have safeguards in place for workers (Jaehrling 2015; Grimshaw et al. 2012). Our argument is that market structures explain much of the variation in employment outcomes because they distribute scarcity and uncertainty in ways that reshape organizations and workplaces. In Chapter 4 we made this case for the landscape of provision as a whole. In this chapter we apply it to the internal workings of providers.

Our analysis focuses on three dimensions of organized employment relations and three dimensions of the labor process (Table 5.1). For clarity they are framed here in a simplified way; in the remainder of the chapter we will see how these dynamics differ between the countries and their relationship with the degree of resource squeeze and uncertainty created by the particular kind of market in each country.

Employment relations scholars examining externalized public services typically focus on privatization rather than (what we call) marketization, and for some good reasons. Moving work into the private or non-profit sectors can be a challenge to public-sector unions, because private-sector providers may be non-union or have different unions. This can lead to differences in pay systems, job security, and the labor process, since this difference in worker representation leads to, and reflects, differences in the institutional regulation of work. These differences include challenges to frameworks of collective negotiations and worker participation (Doellgast 2012; Hermann and Flecker 2012).

The study of marketization will force us to dig deeper into why privatization often has these effects. What is it about the way that non-public providers are funded that drives change and differences within the group of non-public providers? There is considerable evidence that government contractors are being squeezed by funders and that this is affecting a wide range of employment outcomes (e.g. Cunningham et al. 2013 on Britain and Dobischat et al. 2009 and 2010 on Germany). In this chapter we will select a few that are particularly important in the organizations we are studying to identify some of the mechanisms through which these changes take place as well as factors that might mitigate this squeeze.

Table 5.1. Workplace dynamics under marketization: dimensions

Disorganization of employment relations	Erosion of worker voice	Declining coverage and functioning of unions and works councils
	Individualization of pay-setting	Declining coverage of collective bargaining, rise of non-covered competitors, performance-related bonuses, and other incentives
	Job insecurity	Non-standard work, coming and going of contracts; dismissals as a form of discipline
Intensification of management control	Tight performance management	Monitoring and self-monitoring of staff using IT systems
	Devaluing of professions	Exit of skilled workers, workforce with diverse occupational background
	Deterioration of staff–client interaction	Speedup, decline in time with clients, and personalization, rise of "creaming and parking"

There are several mechanisms through which marketization could undermine formal collective worker voice.[1] First, the coverage of unions and works councils may decline because the opening of the market to commercial providers allows for the emergence of new competitors that do not have unions or works councils. Second, the functioning of worker voice may be compromised because it is weakened by management in response to cost pressures or the uncertainty of contracting; employers may take the issue of pay out of collective bargaining with the union. The erosion of formal worker voice may be mitigated somewhat if incumbent providers with existing traditions of worker participation succeed in protecting their market share, or if they are in a country like Denmark where union membership is still widespread and taken for granted.

A second change is to pay determination. Under marketization, incumbent providers covered by collective bargaining may lose market share to lower-cost firms that are not covered by collective bargaining. Second, incentives for management to hit targets may be passed on to workers in terms of performance-related bonuses or pay packages for top performers above the rest. This may be mitigated by pay minima set by statute (as with the German sectoral minimum wage) or by collective agreements that are encompassing or serve as a reference point for the highly unionized provider landscape as a whole (as in Denmark). In these latter cases the institutional regulation of pay includes a wide variety of workplaces, making it difficult for employers to find loopholes in worker protections through "institutional avoidance" (Doellgast et al. 2009; Jaehrling and Méhaut 2013).

The third change is to job security. Marketization creates risks which providers can shift onto staff in three main ways. The first is non-standard work.

---

[1] This analysis could be extended to informal, individual, and/or management-initiated channels of worker voice. Because of difficulties with comparison we have excluded these here.

This may take the form of temporary contracts timed to correspond with contracting cycles or freelance contracts that can also give employers loopholes in terms of employment rights, making it easier to reduce staffing when there is a downturn in business. A second is punitive dismissals: staff lose their jobs due to poor individual performance as determined by management. A third is redundancies caused merely by the coming and going of contracts or a decline in the volume of work. The latter form of job insecurity may be mitigated somewhat from an employee's perspective where transfers of undertaking rules apply to changes between contractors, strengthening employees' employment security in lieu of protecting their jobs (e.g. Cooke et al. 2004).

There are, in addition, three changes to the labor process that matter for the quality of services. First is performance management. While marketization might be motivated by a desire for a more efficient organization of work, the practical consequences for, and responses of, management vary. There may be very detailed performance management with the aid of IT systems and quantitative targets to focus staff attention on the job outcome. This may not only facilitate the monitoring of staff by management and the standardization of processes, but may also contribute to self-monitoring, in which staff compare their performance with their targets and their colleagues. This kind of tight management control has been studied in studies of call center work (e.g. Batt et al. 2005) but is also increasingly observed in public administration (Carter et al. 2011) and has been observed in US public services for the unemployed (Esbenshade et al. 2016).

Marketization is closely related to deskilling. There is a strong argument for employing trained social workers and teachers given the complexity of the employment-services task and needs of clients. But new performance-management techniques might lead to a devaluing of skills and qualifications and an exit of professionals from employment-services work (Ranald 1999). Non-commercial providers that employ workers with formal social-work qualifications may drop out of the market because they fail to win in tendering. Employers may favor "results-oriented" staff with a diverse range of backgrounds, including former clients with certain soft skills or workers with a background in human-resource management, sales, or recruitment. As one report by the British welfare-to-work industry's think tank Inclusion put it, "there is a challenge that asks whether it is necessary to introduce industry standards or qualification levels when there is a concrete and easily identified indicator of success and quality." The authors then quote one manager: "the best performing [front-line advisor] may not be the most 'well qualified'" (Crawford and Perry 2010: 20).

These changes affect staff–client interactions. The intention is indeed that marketization should make services more responsive and flexible; but the result may be the opposite. The first problem is the amount of interaction. The resource scarcity brought about by squeezing prices and siphoning resources through profiteering and transaction costs may lead to work intensification and reduce the amount of time staff have to interact with clients.

The second problem is the kind of staff–client interaction. It could be purely to process individuals through the system and provide basic job-search assistance, or it could also provide more detailed services that address what are considered barriers to work such as a lack of professional qualifications, health problems of various kinds, and personal circumstances such as caring responsibilities or difficulties accessing transportation. As Baines (2004) points out, there is an affinity between quantitative performance management, the speeding up of work, and the refocusing of the work around targets.

The third issue is the distribution of this interaction. Under conditions of numerical targets, staff tend to sort clients and prioritize those who are easiest to help, in order to hit targets; this is a finding from Lipsky's (1980) discussion of street-level bureaucrats responding to quantitative targets. It has been observed in privatized public services, such as schools, health insurance, and employment services. Paugam (2003) finds in French employment services two kinds of sorting: employability (i.e. identifying clients who are a good fit for available jobs) and opportunity (i.e. identifying clients whose needs correspond to available services). Under the mixture of uncertainty and resource scarcity manufactured by some payment-by-results arrangements, the pressure to carry out sorting for employability is intensified, and the scope for providing other services to address barriers to employment are reduced. The Work Programme is a well-known example of this (Rees et al. 2013).

Resource scarcity can affect all of the above variables: management may respond to lower prices by engaging less with unions and works councils, squeezing or individualizing workers' wages, reducing the number of workers, rolling out detailed performance-management systems, hiring staff on the basis of results orientation as opposed to professional qualifications, reducing the length of staff–client meetings, refocusing these meetings on outcomes that are remunerated, or refocusing staff attention on clients who have the highest potential to produce those outcomes. The uncertainty associated with the end of contracts or the vicissitudes of voucher markets intensifies pressure on several of these fronts, especially those that reduce job and income security of workers, intensify performance management, and refocus the service towards those activities that are remunerated. However, there are a few ways in which these trends can be mitigated, either through particular changes to the transaction (e.g. specifying staffing numbers and qualifications or working conditions in contracts) or through non-market institutions that shape the workplaces in ways unrelated to the transaction (e.g. strong, well-organized trade unions).

Denmark

Denmark is known in the comparative employment-relations literature as a case of strong unions and weak job security, and our case studies confirm this. Under these conditions it has been possible for a mass-processing model of provision to emerge with strong management control and in some instances poor quality of interaction with clients. However, because marketization has been a rather volatile phenomenon which has assumed many forms and which has been altered, promoted, and re-regulated by national policymakers over the years, there is a wide diversity of practice in employment services. As we show in Appendix A, funders give price, quality, and local presence higher priority than staff working conditions, and only a minority of municipalities take working conditions at providers very seriously in the selection of contractors (see Table A.6).

Voice

The role of trade unions varies between providers but we have not observed a weakening of worker voice. There is a difference, however, in union density between the public and private sectors, with union density being lower in the private sector than in the public and according to the head of the umbrella organizations even lower among the private providers, especially when the market was highly competitive under the second wave of marketization.

There are also differences in the attitudes to the active role of unions in the private employment-services sector, maybe because unions are affected by privatization and marketization in different ways. Hence, the view of HK (the National Union of Commercial and Clerical Employees), representing employees with low levels of formal qualifications was much more negative than our respondent from the Danish Association of Social Workers (Dansk Socialrådgiverforening—DS). This may reflect a difference in the categories of workers that they are representing. The former is more exposed to marketization, and since the 2011 abolition of the national tendering system, some of the private providers on the market have changed strategy by offering more specialized services towards more vulnerable unemployed people. Because of the shift towards partnership contracting for more specialized services, providers have become more interested in recruiting high-skilled social workers, who would be DS members. As our DS respondent points out, not many social workers are employed by private companies mainly offering interviews and job-search activities, but rather companies providing individualized services to the clients (DK unions, 1 and 2).

Pay Determination

Similarly, marketization has only to a very limited extent changed pay determination in Denmark. Collective bargaining norms still apply to many of the staff who have been transferred out of the public sector into external providers.

Although there is little to suggest wage dumping by private providers, there is much evidence of the individualization of pay. Private providers do to some degree use performance-related wages (additional to a basic wage) and we have observed a growing use of bonuses in wages. According to one of the public providers we visited, 95 percent of the salary is base pay while 5 percent is performance-related bonuses (DK manager 2). The limited use of performance bonuses was confirmed by the front-line workers. One worker we interviewed—a university graduate with extensive management experience—had been recruited by a non-profit provider from the for-profit sector on superior terms and conditions, reflecting conditions for her job classification. Her view was that it was non-profit providers, and not for-profit providers, who were engaging in "wage dumping," that the private sector paid better, and that wage differentials were reinforced by a lack of knowledge by workers about conditions in other parts of the sector (SK front-line worker 1). While this suggests that pay is individualized, our Danish interviewees could not say whether the more significant variation was upward or downward or how much variation there was.

Job Insecurity

When assessing whether marketization increases uncertainty one has to take into account that job security in Denmark in general is low. However, we have observed some differences between the public sector and the for-profit sector when it comes to employment contracts. Employees within the public job centers are mainly employed on permanent contracts, while the for-profit sector has much more scope for external contracts. Privatization has made a difference for job insecurity.

The picture becomes sharper when we look at external providers. Here, employment contracts are a mixture of permanent and temporary, with a moderate use of freelance contracts. "Permanent" means a maximum of a six-month notice, and while freelancers have no notice period, they can be more expensive. According to one of the private providers we visited 80 percent of the staff were on permanent contracts and 20 percent were freelancers (DK manager 2). A different private provider reported reluctance in hiring freelancers due to lack of loyalty and commitment to the workplace. Staff on permanent contracts was preferable (DK manager 4).

While some Danish providers use non-standard employment contracts, they pay a price.

Our interviewees provide two reasons why Danish providers might need such flexibility. First, many municipalities use private providers as a capacity buffer, i.e. in order to cope with fluctuations in caseloads without themselves having to hire or fire. The funder was thus passing uncertainty onto providers by changing the number of referrals from time to time, which was then being passed onto staff.

Second is the fluctuation of the market itself, which forces providers to replace their staff. When the national framework for tendering was established in 2005, providers had to shift toward providing services with a very strong focus on the job placement. One manager recounted at our final project workshop that this entailed, more or less overnight, making all of the front-line staff delivering training courses redundant and hiring a different workforce to focus on job placements. When the national framework was abolished, providers had to adapt again to changing demand which varied by municipality (Christina Grøntved presentation, April 23, 2014).

Performance Management

Due to marketization management has exerted strong control over work organization in the for-profit sector. Front-line staff within the for-profit sector is not only subject to the general requirements from the law on active labor market policy (for example, requirements about repeated activation participation) but also subject to quality specification of tenders, tight management control, and performance-related payment models. Especially under the second wave of marketization in Denmark, when the national competitive tendering system dominated the market, this had practical consequences for how the private providers organized their services. Since the abolition of the national tendering framework in 2010 the picture has become more varied and depends on the particular local arrangements worked out between provider and municipal purchaser. As we will show in Chapter 6, it was in particular the performance-related payment models which had an impact on the quality of services which resulted in mass-processing models of provision.

One common theme across the interviews was the increase in data entry in order to report to the funder, which our front-line staff interviewees reported as using up 25 percent to 50 percent of their time. This could take the form of documenting activities for the funder, tracking clients, and/or reporting job-placement outcomes; in-house staff at job centers are facing the same challenges in Denmark.

According to one of the front-line workers we interviewed the performance-related payment models between funder and provider have a direct impact on her work and interactions with clients—in particular the detailed requirements about staff-to-client ratios and activity rates set up by the public purchasers (front-line worker 3). Also the targets set up by the private companies have an impact. Every week performance measurement is used by the private providers to measure whether the targets have been reached and in order to report to the public purchaser. In some circumstances economic bonuses are paid by the private company if an economic profit is yielded.

In a different establishment we visited—which was providing end-to-end services for people deemed very distant from the labor market—management control was somewhat looser. While staff and management referred to pressure for performance and hitting targets and a need to be oriented towards producing results, what they meant concretely was drawing up reports for the funder. There was an important financial logic to this, but it was related to winning repeat business rather than securing job placements:

> It's all in relation to the social worker in the job center. And of course if they can see that there's some progression and changes, and we're writing a lot of reports to the job center. It's really tricky. For us it's business. If they're coming back, that's more business for us . . . We're aggressive with more contracts—trying to get more hours, more money. So it's always a fine line between business and ethics.
>
> (DK front-line worker 1)

When we pressed our interviewees to discuss numbers of job placements it became clear that among their clientele it was rather rare to place anyone in a sustained job, although they did use brief placements with employers to provide work experience. Our two front-line interviewees at this organization could name an example of a client who found a job, but none of them (including management) could tell us for certain how many job outcomes had been achieved. One responded to our question by arguing that job placements are an inappropriate metric for evaluating a service for people who are hardly job-ready and that this service could just as easily be defined as a health service as an employment service (DK front-line worker 2).

Professions

Most front-line workers in private providers are not required to have a specific professional qualification or background, although this depends on the business models of providers and the service they are offering. As we showed in Chapter 2, during the first and second wave of marketization in Denmark the providers were mainly offering generalist services such as interviews and job-search courses towards unemployed people with a higher education. Consequently the recruitment to the private sector became rather broad and included staff with a background in the military, university graduates with a very wide range of degrees, and people with competences within communication or sales and knowledge of the local labor market. Important to our management interviewees were "energy," interpersonal skills, and orientation toward "results."

Managers at the private providers we interviewed noted problems with professional social workers—they "registered everything" and had difficulty "thinking outside of the box"—but that their use of psychologists depended on the kind of work (manager 4). Another told us that psychologists, social workers, and teachers were "no-go" when it came to hiring (manager 2). A representative of the umbrella body told us that it was common to employ social workers, and that social workers were increasingly results-oriented (umbrella body 1). The specialized provider we visited was a good example of the kinds of services that expanded in wave 3: it employed large numbers of psychologists and social workers as well as graduates with various university degrees, and had previously had physicians on staff (manager 5).

While marketization may have had some effect on the role of formal qualifications at external providers, there has been a clear shift away from social work in public-sector job centers. They, too, recruit a broad spectrum of employees with a very varied professional background in response to demands that they become more results-oriented. Consequently, the number of social workers within the public sector has decreased (Baadsgaard et al. 2014) and the management in some public job centers express that they are reluctant to hire social workers because of their professional ethos (Breidahl and Seemann 2009). However, the attitudes towards employing trained social workers vary widely between job centers.

Interaction with Clients

Generally seen, marketization has not made services in Denmark more responsive or flexible, especially in the very competitive market in the second wave of marketization. Resource scarcity and detailed requirements about interactions with clients seemed to have a negative impact on the quality of services. Hence, because of price and performance pressures, combined with a lack of firm definitions of what such activities could be, provision became highly standardized. It took the form of meetings to process people through the system and job-search activities. Consequently, we observed a lower quality in the content of the interaction. It was (and still is) an important target for the public purchasers that the amount of interaction with clients is maintained to a certain level. Therefore, marketization has not had a direct impact on the quantity of service, and the staff–client interaction is in many places rather intensive.

Even though we have not directly observed creaming and parking in our empirical material the assertion of managerial control seems to have had an impact on the capacity of front-line workers to cope with complex needs. This reflects demands under payment by results that tried to keep expenses for services low.

Because of change over time it has since 2011 become more difficult to say anything definitive about the impact of marketization on the interaction with clients. However, the more partner-based way has created space for a more professionalized and specialized service and thereby room for a more flexible and responsible service. This is clarified and discussed more deeply in Chapter 6.

To summarize, the Danish case exhibits a high degree of within-country variation and change. Presently there is a divide between providers continuing to carry out standardized mass-processing services and those that carry out more specialized professionalized kinds of work. In both cases pay is individualized but kept in check by high union membership. But they seem to differ in terms of the degree of management control as opposed to professional autonomy, and the quality and quantity of service.

Great Britain

In Britain we observe disorganized employment relations and tight managerial control over work organization at the for-profit prime providers, but wide variation at the subcontractors. While most public-sector subcontractors recognize trade unions and set pay through collective bargaining, all primes except for one lack union structures or collective bargaining; non-profits are highly varied. Other forms of professional autonomy are absent, and managerial opinion is divided as to whether formal qualifications are of use in such a results-driven sector. Most striking, however, are the highly sophisticated performance-management systems that lead to tight managerial control, that standardize very quick processes, and that facilitate in most cases creaming and parking.

Worker Voice

The role of trade unions varies between providers. In public-sector subcontractors there is still traditional trade unionism with strong workplace structures and collective bargaining arrangements, albeit under pressure due to government policies to limit pay increases. Outside of the public sector the

117

trade union function is seldom to negotiate a framework of rules to govern the workplace; instead it is usually to resolve disputes and assist workers in employment law cases or negotiate over particular issues (such as redundancies or increasing pay at the bottom of the scale). To do this effectively without activist structures in workplaces is time consuming for trade union full-time officials and taxing on union resources (GB union 3).

Trade union representation is strong in the public sector and absent or weak in the voluntary sector and most private-sector providers. The large public-sector union UNISON and the general union UNITE had recognition in the municipalities we visited, reflecting more the overall framework of industrial relations in local government. The Public and Commercial Services Union (PCS), which is the largest civil-service union, has members in some of the large commercial organizations, concentrated in one large provider, as well as strongholds in a few providers of outsourced back-office information technology services. Union members were reported by PCS staff across the sector, but they were scattered. Efforts to organize workplace structures and secure recognition from employers were ongoing but difficult. There was, for example, a group of young enthusiastic workers attempting to build a union at one of the large providers, but this campaign fizzled out. Management hostility to unions and worker fear was widespread, according to PCS staff: "they (the employers) just won't talk to us and won't let us near their staff...We have people (activists) working in these places, but they are afraid for their jobs and...under pressure" (GB union 2).

At the one commercial provider where PCS was recognized and membership density was 50 percent, activists reported a hollowing out of workplace structures. This was explained by activists principally due to the high turnover of staff due to the turnover of contracts; this made it difficult to sustain union structures. Activists would leave the employer, not to be replaced by new ones, creating an immense workload for those union representatives who remained (GB union 3). Another problem was a dilemma faced by the union between its political work and its members' material interests in contracted-out providers. While the union criticized private provision as a matter of principle, its members' jobs in the commercial sector depended on privatization. In outsourced back-office services, for example, more than 100 jobs were being destroyed by insourcing, and PCS members were going on strike for improved redundancy payments (GB union 5). In another case, a provider of contracted-out health assessments was targeted by welfare claimants groups, and PCS activists within that provider criticized the national union for discussing with these groups coalition work to reverse attacks on the social-security system (GB union 6). Multiple interviewees reported an unresolved question of how to structure the union in the commercial sector in a way that would take advantage of nearby union strongholds in job centers.

Pay Determination

Wages at these providers were, like the public sector, stagnant; but they were also individualized. While collective bargaining sets pay in public-sector providers, private-sector and voluntary-sector pay is determined largely through "benchmarking" organized originally by private consultancy firms and now by ERSA. One large provider we visited at the outset of the Work Programme reported an extremely wide range of pay scales due to staff transfers from seven different organizations (in the contract that covered the region where we collected interviews). These ranged from £16,000 to £25,000 per annum. In 2014 the same organization reported having brought salaries at the bottom up to ERSA's estimated industry average,[2] bringing the bottom of the scale up to £20,000. At two other DWP contractors (not on the Work Programme), PCS representatives reported a successful living wage campaign that had brought up wages at the bottom in the face of overall wage stagnation, although they also report overall management unilateralism in the setting of pay and being poorly informed about pay (GB union 3). In the private sector, performance-related bonuses for front-line staff are widespread, though not universal; they are apparently less common in the voluntary sector, where pay is generally lower. Pay overall in the private sector is individualized but close on average to that in the public sector, with strong downward pressures in both.

Job Insecurity

In Britain, where we saw a mixture of permanent and fixed-term employment, insecurity was universal. The majority of employees we spoke to had permanent contracts, but these were precarious due to the turnover of contracts and the possibility of using the threat of dismissal as a disciplinary mechanism. Non-standard employment was also observed: one non-profit employer operated a system of six-month rolling contracts, with only two weeks' notice being given as to whether contracts would be renewed.

An important reason for insecurity was the turnover of contracts, which was fresh in interviewees' minds in 2011–12 when the site visits took place. TUPE (Transfers of Undertakings and Protection of Employment) rules featured prominently in the interviews, unlike in Germany and Denmark. They are supposed to protect workers being transferred in the context of a change in contractor, but our interviews with management, trade unionists, and front-line staff pointed to numerous problems. The principle of TUPE is that workers' terms and conditions of employment and their jobs are protected if their work is transferred from one organization to another. Under the evolving

---

[2] ERSA carries out a pay survey but would not share this data with us.

regime of employment-services contracting, however, its applicability is unclear, since the work changes from one contract to another. In one example involving back-office services, government insourcing of work did not trigger TUPE, because the DWP was shifting an outsourced task onto existing employees. In two examples we examined where TUPE did apply in the context of work being shifted from incumbent providers to the new prime contractors, employees lost their jobs in the transfer because the personnel requirements of the new contract were lower than those of the old contract (GB unions 1 and 3). Two front-line workers pointed out that they and all of their colleagues in the establishment had had to reapply for their own jobs twice in eighteen months, as part of a TUPE-governed transfer, and be subjected to rather intensive assessment processes (front-line workers 4 and 5).

The issue of using dismissal as a disciplinary mechanism to root out poor performers was sensitive, and usually came up when discussing other employers. One manager at a non-profit told us that he had left his job at a for-profit provider and moved to his present employer because, "I don't believe in sacking people for not hitting their targets" (manager 5). But there was at least one example of a front-line worker pointing to it as present in the workplace. In one of the private-sector primes without a recognized union, interviewees reported that while relations with managers were cordial enough, the line manager did not tolerate dissent: "[He] is a good guy; you can have a laugh with him. But if you said anything [complained] you'd be out the door [dismissed]" (front-line worker 3).

The flip-side of insecurity is voluntary turnover, including both movement within and out of the sector. This is an important concern of management (Crawford and Perry 2010), and our interviewees provided numerous examples of both. Many had voluntarily moved between the public, private, and voluntary sectors often due to a preference for one sector over another. In addition, many interviewees, when we asked them about their career plans, suggested that they did not plan to remain in the welfare-to-work sector. Reasons for exiting the sector included feeling overqualified for the job (e.g. front-line workers 4 and 11) and disapproval of performance-management practices (e.g. front-line worker 3).

Professions

In Britain there is no sign of strong professional autonomy or high value placed on formal qualifications. Unlike Germany and Denmark, qualifications for staff are not written into tendering documents, and this reflects a widespread view that formal qualifications do not capture what is needed to be effective as a front-line worker in the sector. One manager puts this view succinctly: "There's one [front-line operative] in one of our branches who hasn't a qualification to her name; in fact she's barely literate herself [sic.]. Yet she is consistently the best performer in getting results" (GB manager 4). But managers expressed differences in opinion in this area and there were some moves toward professionalization.

Our interviewees had backgrounds in high-street recruitment or sales and more traditional welfare-to-work providers in local authorities, the civil service, social work, charities or private contractors. Others were recruited shortly after graduating from university or had come into the sector as clients. While this variation reflects the changing nature of work and management, including increasing requirements to achieve job-placement targets, it also has several disadvantages for management and workers. Two of the qualified social workers we met reported dissatisfaction due to underutilization of skills (front-line workers 5 and 11). Both workers and managers reported problems with a lack of clear career progression, a problem highlighted as well by the umbrella body (Crawford and Perry 2010).

A common qualification in the sector is Information, Advice, and Guidance (NVQ level 3), which is equivalent to two A-levels, i.e. at the level of secondary school. At one municipality we visited it was regarded as mandatory for operatives to enroll in the training in order to work in employment services. Front-line workers we interviewed were generally positive about the qualification, appearing to value both the educational value and the fact that an employer was investing in their human capital, giving them a sense of security even in the face of fixed-term contracts (GB front-line workers 13 and 15). However, beyond this fairly low qualification there was no incremental continuation of formal qualification that might support a career structure.

As discussed in Chapter 4, one management response to this problem was to create a new professional body, IEP. IEP was officially launched in 2012, with strong support from senior management in several of the prime contractors and the sector's think tank Centre for Economic and Social Inclusion, later renamed Inclusion. Its main function is to "professionalize" the sector by turning front-line employment-services work into a recognized profession with formal qualifications, clear career progression, and overall recognition as a profession. It has created three courses of training (up to NVQ Level 3) for employment advisors, recruitment consultants, and tutors. It sponsors networking events and organizes training, and in September 2013 it reported 3,853 members. Membership costs £90 per year, which for most is paid by the employer, and membership appears to be more common among front-line managers than among front-line staff. IEP plans to extend its membership and services to the in-house Jobcentre Plus workforce (Foster et al. 2013). The efforts of IEP and other parties interested in establishing a greater degree of professionalism and career structure in the industry were somewhat undermined by the refusal of some key providers to support the framework. When

IEP sought to engage with the providers in question they were rebuffed by the response that the providers had perfectly adequate in-house training schemes and career paths (GB umbrella).

Performance Management

The management systems of prime providers played an important role in the assignment of quality points in Work Programme bids. These systems are mentioned in most of the prime contractors' own descriptions of their "minimum service delivery" as providing access to information about job opportunities and e-learning opportunities, and they are also commonly used for assessing clients. Contractors we interviewed had, in addition, call centers that maintained contact with clients after the job placement; and subcontractors' employees reported using the electronic systems of their primes. These systems were often mentioned in interviews as used to book appointments, collect information, assist clients with e-learning and identifying job vacancies, and monitoring the work and job outcomes realized by staff.

Using electronic systems to log activities is standard across the entire sample in all three countries; but the Work Programme providers had created much more sophisticated systems.

> [The office manager] can see everything on the "dashboard"; she sees all the graphs and figures and how everyone's doing. She'll be like, "oh! he [a colleague] is doing well this week; what's he taking in his tea!" or "come on, what's up with you this week" like she's just messing around. But really she's serious. You do get a bit worried about it.   (GB front-line worker 4)

In some providers comparisons between staff were used apparently in a spirit of good humor with no ostensible sanction for comparatively poor performance, and in one provider targets were collective for the whole location, reflecting the differences in the kinds of clients in the caseloads of the various advisors. At other providers these were taken very seriously by staff and managers; they were not only being used to monitor the quantitative performance of individual workers by managers but were also being used for self-monitoring by the workers themselves. This could be divisive in the workplace, as one front-line worker told us: "I always meet my targets. In fact, I go way past them. Then I'm looking at the guy next to me, who's messing about and doesn't care, and I'm thinking 'why should I bother?'" (GB front-line worker 3).

Interaction with Clients

While a sense of genuine empathy with clients was generally expressed by most of the front-line operatives we interviewed, many front-line workers expressed a sense that they were unable to give the levels of help and support that clients needed. This had a number of manifestations: time constraints due to high caseloads, a lack of specialized support to refer them to due to resource constraints, and creaming and parking due to targets.

When asked to give examples of particularly satisfying interactions with clients, most interviewees could readily recount such an episode. Typically this would be an individual who was experiencing considerable adversity, then through the help of the operative the individual would find stable employment. On the other hand, there were interviewees reporting feelings of frustration and even thinly disguised contempt for certain sections of their clientele. As one front-line worker told us, "I wouldn't recognize some of [my clients] if I passed them in the street. In fact there was one guy starts talking to me in the lift, then I realized that he was my next appointment" (GB front-line worker 3).

Another resource constraint on the relationships with clients was the inability to routinely prescribe interventions for clients that would provide investment in skills or intervention for a debilitating condition that might be inhibiting employment prospects, such as substance abuse or mental illness. There was some liaising with and "signposting" of services provided by external agencies such as the health services, further education colleges, and housing departments. The difficulty came when a service was potentially costly to the provider. With regard to finding training opportunities, one interviewee reported:

> There was this guy, an ex-serviceman; he'd been in Iraq; came home and couldn't find work. His marriage had broken down too. We really wanted to do our best for him, because he was such a nice guy. He'd done loads of stuff in the army as well. We tried to get him on an HGV [truck driving] course to get his license it would cost over £1,000. They [the managers] are simply not going to pay that. We felt like we'd let him down.   (GB manager 11)

Such ambivalence can perhaps be attributed to the punitive and coercive context within which the relationship between client and operative is configured. The service was work-first rather than holistic, and front-line staff were involved in sanctioning by raising "doubts" which then Jobcentre Plus would translate into sanctions, i.e. withdrawal of benefits, most commonly when clients missed meetings. At one establishment we visited staff reported that the process of sanctioning was extremely cumbersome, and one front-line worker reported spending time contacting Jobcentre Plus to ensure that the doubt translated into a sanction. Job centers in Britain have long been reported as a theater for confrontation and aggression (Bishop et al. 2005), so it is unsurprising that external employment-services providers should also experience flashpoints. Indeed, when we visited the premises of one provider the staff had been in the process of remedying the damage done to the reception area by an aggrieved client who had taken exception to being "sanctioned," as a result, by his reckoning, of being reported to Jobcentre Plus by the provider for non-engagement (front-line worker 12) and the incident had the entire staff on edge when we visited.

Perhaps the most striking aspect of the staff–client interaction, however, is the distribution of attention, i.e. creaming and parking, discussed in more detail in Chapter 6. Clients are quickly assessed and sorted with the aid of IT tools, sometimes guided by a member of staff, sometimes not. The classification tends to be three way: red (distant from the labor market), amber (some barriers to address), and green (close to the labor market). For clients deemed to be close to the labor market, there are focused job-search services, often with training, counseling, and group interviews with employers. At one location we visited these clients were allocated to advisors with small caseloads; at another location we visited, each advisor had to decide how to prioritize clients, in the context of a strong focus on individual quantitative targets.

For clients deemed to be distant from the labor market, by contrast, there are the minimum service standards, which according to our interviewees were typically some form of contact—phone, email, or in person—once per month or per fortnight. This understates the problem, since the National Audit Office's (2014) study of case files showed that just under half of Work Programme participants had not had any contact with their provider in the previous month. But even where clients were in contact, parking could be a problem. One manager described a feature of an office of a Work Programme provider that was ubiquitous in our sample, namely banks of computers where clients can search for jobs and take online courses without assistance from staff. His comment: "if that is not parking, I don't know what is" (GB manager 12).

To summarize, we were able to observe in-depth the transformation both of contracting and of the organizational landscape of contracting. The DWP's contracting practice very deliberately created risks for providers, a kind of uncertainty to form the basis of calculated management strategies, at the same time that the price was squeezed at the outset through discounts. Primes have rolled out systems on a large scale to carry out this contract in a way that is commercially viable, i.e. profitable, with little interference from the policy-makers or organized workers. The consequence is a standardized service delivered by a mixture of private, non-profit, and municipal providers, sped up and controlled using sophisticated IT systems, corresponding to the "work-first" motivation of policy, that systematically neglects clients deemed distant from the labor market.

Germany

Germany has the widest within-country diversity in work and employment relations in the field of employment services. Most non-profits we visited, large and small, were struggling to adapt to marketization, but some still had relatively organized industrial relations and strong professional control in the workplace. Where purchasing was in place, the funder had imposed strong price-based competition in procurement combined with very detailed prescription of the work and the way it was to be carried out. Private firms operating under placement vouchers were different: they combined disorganized employment relations, often in extreme form, with tight management control over the labor process. In the first case, employment relations and the labor process were changed in the short run marginally; while these were not the exemplars of organized employment relations, there was still a strong non-commercial professional and organizational ethos at work. In the second case, a fully disorganized employment-relations system had emerged enabling tight management control over the work. Other private firms operating under public procurement were somewhere in between: in the face of a general commercial approach the detailed specification of work often required them to hire the same kinds of staff as non-commercial providers.

Worker Voice

This is not a sector with a clear regulatory framework enabling workers to organize; to the contrary, there are several stark divides with regard to worker representation depending on the kind of work and organization. First, there is a peculiarity in German individual and collective labor law in that the Christian churches as well as their charitable organizations have their own statutes regarding representation at the workplace and pay determination (Kreß 2014). Whereas works councils can enforce their codetermination rights and veto positions in the labor court, employee representatives in church organizations cannot. The doctrine here is that cooperation in the Christian spirit is always consensual and does not require external enforcement of rights. Likewise, these organizations do not participate in collective bargaining; wages and working conditions are set by commissions made up of equal numbers of employer and employee representatives, but without the possibility for industrial action. Traditionally, these commissions more or less replicated successive public-sector collective agreements, which became less automatic when the public-sector bargaining system split in two in 2006. These church privileges are criticized even by theologians, especially where church-affiliated organizations operate almost exclusively on public money for social services (Hengsbach 2011). Pay and working conditions in the religious sector are relevant because, scattered among thousands of legally autonomous organizations, the churches and their affiliates employ 1.3 million people, the fourth largest "sector" after the metal and electrical industries, the public service, and retailing (Stefaniak 2011).

The second divide is between works councils with full and unrestricted rights and those operating in establishments that stand for specific attitudes or orientations, such as newspapers, political parties, employers' organizations, or trade unions. In the latter case, participation in the economic governance of the firm is restricted, and so is the works council's say in personnel issues as far as representatives of the organization's values and purposes (e.g. media editors, political advisors, PR spokesmen, etc.) are concerned. This divide is not exactly a question of non-profit or for-profit; nevertheless, non-profits are more likely than for-profits to be committed by their statutes to a certain cause that could justify such a restriction. Among the relevant causes are "charitable" and "educational purposes." The boundaries are not at all clear and must be contested for individual organizations by judicial action (Grambow 2013). Employment services funded from labor-market programs do not as such justify an organization's characteristic as carrying a specific attitude or orientation; however, since many providers of employment services engage in a much larger range of operations, some will qualify as "charitable" or "educational"[3] in the sense of the law.

The third divide is whether a works council has been elected at all. Legally, the election of one person is possible where there are normally at least five workers, and three representatives can be elected if there are at least twenty-one workers, five representatives from fifty-one workers, and so on. With an electorate of 200 workers, there will be nine works council members, one of whom is entitled to full exemption from work. Elections will be held following an initiative of workers or a trade union represented in the workplace; there is no public guarantee or supervision. In practice, works councils are very rare in organizations under fifty employees (Ellguth and Kohaut 2016), and many employment-services providers are in that size category. Furthermore, the existence of a works council, especially in smaller employers, depends very much on the encouragement, acceptance, discouragement, or outright obstruction of the employer and an organization's climate of opinion. So it does not come as a surprise that we found works councils in providers once founded in the context of civil society movements and by "social entrepreneurs"

---

[3] The German word here is *"Erziehung"* (child rearing, educational support for handicapped youngsters, pedagogical correction) as distinguished from *"Bildung"* and *"Ausbildung"* (general education, initial and continued vocational training), a differentiation impossible to translate into English. At any rate, the legal wording is not to say that the provision of vocational training or training in job-seeking techniques would allow an organization to curtail the voice of the works council.

and less in training providers closely affiliated to employers' organizations or economic chambers.

Even where there were active works councils respected by both workers and employers, their scope of action under marketization was very limited. They were very much aware that the issues they were grappling with—pay levels, types of contract, workloads, disregard of health and safety issues, deprofessionalization, downsizing of the workforce—were not inflicted on them by the employer's whim but by the state-made markets the organization had to operate in. As one told us, "It is not feasible. We know we would ruin the firm if we were to successfully demand that" (German works council 2). Rather than being able to make much of a difference in terms of outcomes for workers, these works councils were largely restricted to adding some legal and moral legitimacy to the decisions their employer had to make anyway and to give workers the feeling that their problems were at least recognized if they could not be remedied.

With regard to trade union membership, we are once again grappling with the lack of identity of employment services as a sector in Germany. The services union ver.di operates a working group, "continued adult education" (AG Weiterbildung), which claimed to represent around 17,000 members in 2014 (German union 1). However, continued education obviously extends far beyond what is financed as employment services, even though ver.di has a priority here. GEW, the union for school and university teachers, has significantly fewer members in the sector, but the demarcation between the jurisdiction of GEW and ver.di is unclear.

Pay Determination

Pay is a controversial topic in German employment services, because of strong downward pressures on remuneration of highly educated workers. One survey found that most workers for firms operating under BA funding were freelancers, and that most full-time freelancers had net monthly incomes of between €800 and €1,100 (Dobischat et al. 2010). Even where collective bargaining applies, pay is not high. The pay scales used by municipalities would stipulate a monthly salary for an entry-level social worker with a bachelor degree of around €2,650 from January 2017, which is €15.30 per hour; this increases with tenure. It is only marginally above the statutory minimum wage for training providers in the sector and less than the salary that would be paid under the collective agreement for agency temps (€2,800 to €2,900 per month).

As we saw in Chapter 5, employment services—or more specifically training providers—became one of the few sectors covered by statutory wage minima prior to the rollout of a national minimum wage. This is because the sector is covered by a patchwork of collective agreements, an unorganized sector that is subject to the statutory sectoral minimum wage that applies only to pedagogical staff (€14.60 per hour from 2017), a sector that is bound to the general statutory minimum (€8.84 from 2017), and a sector that uses freelancers whose contracts are not subject to these rights. The so-called "academic premium" attached to gaining a university degree is low in employment services; the minimum-wage regulation for the construction sector, for example, foresees €13.10 for a trained painter in West Germany.

The sectoral minimum wage is difficult to enforce. After taking legal advice, the BA decided against building enforcement of the minimum wage into its tendering procedures on the grounds that providers not covered cannot be excluded from participating in the tender (Bundesagentur für Arbeit 2016). A well-resourced public agency, Finanzkontrolle Schwarzarbeit, is charged with the detailed work of enforcement. Finanzkontrolle Schwarzarbeit staff told us that this is more difficult than in other sectors since in cases that come to be disputed it has to be determined whether the organization in question or an "economically independently operating department thereof" is covered. The test is whether or not it is "predominantly providing initial and further training under the legal framework of SGB II and SGB III." Organizations providing these training courses may also carry out other services, and disputing the independent operation of a unit focusing on such services can be a strategy to keep the organization as a whole free of coverage. Trade unions and works councils are of little help in enforcing the sectoral minimum wage since they tend not to be present in those organizations where wages fall below the minimum (German labor inspectorate). The sectoral minimum wage is more of a reference standard and last resort, and less an operational wage regulation.

Among those providers operating under placement vouchers, we saw no sign of collective wage determination, and individualization of pay was extreme. In one of the training providers we visited, freelancers were used extensively and often required to work at very short notice. Pay was negotiated individually and oriented on the professions from which the teachers came (German manager 2). Similarly, in the job-placement company, pay was negotiated on an individual basis, and it was highly variable by individual. Some had performance bonuses and others did not, and some interviewees complained about a lack of transparency and fairness in these arrangements (German front-line workers 5–8). The firm would periodically have weeks of action (Aktionswoche), in which staff would receive a bonus if they hit a particular target. The manager was a proponent of performance-related pay: "In the past I didn't use that, and people said, I get paid at the end of the month. If you're working on bonus you have to step on the gas [Gas geben] in order to get paid, in this and any other kind of work" (German manager 3, second interview).

Where collective bargaining did apply, the structure was eroding. A regional Catholic provider of adult education—including vocational training funded under labor-market programs—provides a particularly striking example of how providers react to market pressures. Traditionally, this provider was tied to the church-specific wage regulation described above, more or less emulating pay levels of the public sector. In 2007, this provider actually called in the Vatican central administration in order to get permission to leave the framework of church labor law and wage regulation and having their own in-house collective agreement instead. The issues at stake were not only pay levels but also the extended use of fixed-term contracts. Permission was finally granted by a papal special court set up in Aachen (Hengsbach 2011). The judgment provides succinct indication of downward pressures in the market in its acknowledgment that it is no longer possible to deliver social and educational services procured by public-sector organizations under pay, employment, and working conditions equivalent to those of the public sector.

Within large providers, pay structures were fragmenting. In another provider studied, three systems of wage regulation existed in parallel. Long-tenured employees had maintained their labor contracts which tied their wages to the old collective agreements of the public sector. When the public-sector bargaining system was broken up in 2006 into one for employees of the *Länder* and another for the municipalities and central government, the provider started tying new labor contracts to the latter. When marketization pressures increased, new hires were made via a temping agency created for that purpose, applying what was then the most favorable collective agreement in the temporary work sector. Meanwhile, however, pay rates in that temping agreement have outpaced those of the municipalities, so in 2016 the provider switched back to the municipal agreement for new hires (German manager 11, revisited in 2016 for another project). The municipal system still has a progression of salaries with tenure absent from the agreement for temporary agencies, so what is better for whom in which circumstances is a tricky question. This shows how this provider with all its fragmentation of wage structures was still very vulnerable to competition from those paying only the sectoral minimum wage, not to speak of competitors ignoring it or not being bound to it because employment services were only a margin of their business. In order to maintain economic viability, it was customary for this provider to do some very short-term assignments without any additional hiring, i.e. at hardly any extra cost, by temporarily increasing workloads and assigning multiple tasks (German works council 2).

Job Insecurity

Job insecurity was a serious problem across our German sample. There was widespread use of freelancers (especially by training providers) and fixed-term contracts (especially for recent hires). A common practice for new hires was a six-month contract, with possible renewal, for example if there was sufficient work and if performance was adequate. If downsizing of the workforce would become inevitable, there would be a clear ranking order: freelancers go first, next fixed-term contracts will not be renewed and assignments of temping workers will be terminated, finally the more recent hires of the provider as such would be dismissed, leaving the provider with very long-tenured older workers in the end. Since new hires may take longer than working on the new contract is allowed to wait, this is one of many sources of permanent overload for the existing workforce; absenteeism resulting from overload creates a spiral of overload (German works council 2). The largest organizations had far more scope for long-term employment because social workers could be redeployed internally to other services organized by the same provider, but even here we met newly hired workers on temporary contracts.

The job-placement firm we visited was highly aggressive in its use of fixed-term contracts and dismissals of staff. This partly reflected a decline in its business related to difficulties in finding employers with large numbers of job openings; this had led to the closing of offices and a substantial decline in employment numbers. Permanent staff complained that the company would hire staff on six-month contracts on low wages, these staff would underperform, and then their contracts would not be renewed. They also alleged that management sent threatening emails mentioning "arbeitsrechtliche Konsequenzen" (literally, labor-law consequences) for non-compliance (German front-line workers 5 and 6).

Professions

The devaluing of professions is a third serious problem in Germany. One peculiarity of Germany's "social occupations" is that the squeeze on prices by the funder keeps down wages by creating resource scarcity and reducing providers' ability to pay. This is even the case if there is a shortage of trained social workers, which is presently the case due to the expansion of services for the increasing numbers of refugees. This has two variants, depending on the market segment.

The first is the use of a results-oriented workforce which does not necessarily have professional qualifications. Private placement firms operating under vouchers employ staff without any specific professional profile. One manager expressed a strong aversion to the ethos of professional social work: he called social workers the "worst ever" employees because they were not sufficiently focused on job outcomes and preferred to have lengthy discussions with clients (German manager 3, first interview). The background of staff at this company was similar to that at Work Programme providers: they have worked in sales, in job centers, and in other employment-services providers, and some came into this work via their experiences as clients.

The second, more common variant, is that the traditional professions—in employment services the most common one is a social work qualification called *Sozialpädagogik* that requires a bachelor degree at a *Fachhoschule* or university—remain in place due to the requirements of the contract, but jobs become worse: lower paid, less secure, with more reporting work, and less time with clients (Enggruber and Mergner 2007). Under training vouchers and purchasing, formal qualifications and length of track records of vocational instructors and social workers are prescribed in detail in accreditation and tendering documents. At one commercial provider we visited, managers made it clear that the occupational background of staff depended on the contract (German manager 14); at another provider managers argued that it was unclear whether a contract using payment by results was financially sustainable given the requirement to hire staff whose occupational ethos favors detailed intervention (German manager 5).

This prescriptive approach allows the BA to wash its hands of the problems created for professionals by price pressures and uncertainty caused by contracting. But the latter make it increasingly difficult for providers to actually deploy the kind of staff formally required. As we will show, there are informal speedups caused by the administrative difficulties incurred by the uncertainty and resource squeeze of contracting.

Performance Management

On the face of it, performance management is ubiquitous across our German cases. In all providers operating under procurement there are detailed reporting requirements, and under vouchers there are strong material incentives for providers to attract customers and, in the case of placement firms, find them jobs. In the workplace, however, these pressures have diverse consequences. Some providers manage performance far more tightly than others.

Under the prescriptive approach of the BA described above, performance management is less about chasing outcomes than documenting inputs. Individual targets were rather unusual, even at the provider we visited that was running a job-placement scheme under which it was paid by results.

Under placement vouchers the situation is different. The IT system is similar to that of Work Programme contractors in that it enables very detailed individual-level monitoring of staff focused around the job outcome. One interviewee told us that 90 percent of the job could be monitored (German front-line worker 7) and another said that every time she said "hello" on the phone it was logged on the system (German front-line worker 8). But it also monitors whether staff have hit their individual quantitative targets, and was quite effective at focusing their attention on job outcomes.

Interaction with Clients

Across the sample there are very strong pressures on time, which speed up the work. Under contracting, problems with staff–client interaction are mitigated through the detailed specification of the amount of time to be spent with clients and the professional qualifications of staff. Under placement vouchers, by contrast, the service takes the form of a very quick job placement, with its own form of creaming and parking.

BA contracting squeezes resources, and hence staff time, in two ways. First, staff have to spend substantial amounts of time on reporting rather than in face-to-face interactions with clients. One instructor in a youth-training workshop, who was also a works councilor, described the tension between doing the job and documenting work, and how this sometimes spilled over into unpaid work during breaks:

> If one of our apprentices is not performing well and not improving I should advise and supervise him very closely for a while, but then I might not have the time to document it in the system, and if it is not in the system, is has not happened. However, if I spend my time at the computer I cannot help the apprentice. Some try to solve this contradiction by doing the documentation during their lunch breaks.   (German works council 2)

Second, despite requirements to hire certain numbers of staff, the reality of squeezed prices and job insecurity means that staff have to take on more tasks. Providers still do employ the staff with the qualifications promised in accreditation or tender documents, and they can present these employees in case of an audit by the BA, but these workers are not necessarily with those clients they are supposed to serve. They may be looking after other clients, servicing several courses simultaneously, or they may be on sick leave due to work and stress overload. Front-line staff reported in interviews how on ever more frequent "days of emergency" they find themselves teaching courses for vocations in which they are not qualified themselves, or in workshops the technology of which they do not know how to operate (German works council 2). In this way, the quality of the services that are actually produced in interaction with clients can deviate more and more from the written description of the service from the tendering exercise.

Placement vouchers are in some ways similar, since they place a severe resource squeeze on providers, forcing them to provide a quick service. Our interviewees reported that the process of job placement, from initial contact to signing the employment contract, typically took three days. There are no resources for additional coaching or training, an issue that may have been addressed with the 2012 rollout of "activation and placement vouchers." Many clients, however, are not appropriate for the available jobs, and sorting them is an important part of the task. One front-line worker told us that he had developed an intuitive "Bauchgefühl" (gut feeling) for finding the most job-ready clients after five minutes of small talk. Another separated the job-ready out through frank discussion of the difficult requirements of the job—usually the physically strenuous nature of it—which were potentially a problem for jobseekers with health problems (German front-line worker 5). The centrality of sorting for this firm was emphasized by the manager in telling a story about why his service was superior, from an employer's perspective, to that of the job center:

> HR managers from [the employer] sat here in our front room...There were 188 proposed applicants from the Arbeitsagentur. We had 80 people who showed up for interviews, the rest didn't come. The ones who showed up were in a catastrophic state. That means they could not fulfil the requirements of the job. They smelled of alcohol, didn't bring the application forms, were wearing jogging suits: that was a catastrophe. Out of this, 3 people were sent to job interviews. The boss said, OK, will hire them, and then we'll see...And the firm saw what kind of garbage [*Schrott*] comes from BA if you work directly with them...They would have received 188 suggestions from BA...and the huge task of processing them.
>
> (German manager 3, second interview)

The jobseekers who are not deemed job-ready—which he characterizes as "Schrott"—are sent back to the job center as a matter of course. While this skews attention towards the most job-ready clients, it is not technically creaming and parking, since no clients are "parked" on the caseload of the provider; the latter remain eligible for service from the job center, unlike their equivalents on the Work Programme. Instead, the provider engages in cherry picking, or as the German evaluation literature calls it "raising picking" (Bernhard and Kruppe 2010).

To summarize, there are clear cost pressures across the German organizations that do not compensate for the inputs demanded in the service or the transaction costs entailed in unsuccessful bids, accreditation for courses that do not materialize, documentation, and auditing, all of which create overheads to the service costs which cannot be officially reclaimed in calculations for bids or in course accreditations. Our interviewees tell consistent and detailed stories about the price squeeze and how providers cope with it, stories which, given the tradition and background of the non-profit providers, would not make sense in the absence of price pressures. Prescriptiveness of contracts and input-oriented documentation maintain a surface of quality and professionalism which is eroded by the organizational reality produced by the resource squeeze and short-termism of contracting.

Comparison and Conclusion

Employment services is an intriguing sector for studying work comparatively—both its institutional regulation and its lived reality—because of the within-country variation brought about by differing market structures. At one end of the spectrum were for-profit providers in Germany and Great Britain that have grown up under relatively marketized funding arrangements, with individualized pay, insecurity in employment, unclear occupational regulation, but with tight management-control systems and strong pressures for the creaming and parking of clients. At the other end were local units of large German charities contracting with the BA, which had developed initially under non-market subsidiarity principles, and coping with a marketization trend with functioning—but declining—worker representation, collective bargaining for pay, relatively secure employment, weak performance management, strong occupations, and a resulting resistance to pressures on the staff–client interaction. Table 5.2 summarizes our qualitative findings.

Most of the cases lie somewhere in between the two extremes. Danish organizations are difficult to categorize because of change over time, but in general the contracting landscape combines strong trade unionism and pay levels oriented around collective bargaining with job insecurity. The labor process varies widely depending on the contract, some of which specify specialized services delivered by qualified professionals, and others of

Table 5.2. Observed variation in workplace dynamics

	Denmark	Germany		Great Britain	
		vouchers	Purchasing	WP "primes"	WP "subs"
Disorganization of employment relations					
Weak/weakening worker voice	N	Y	N	Y	N
Individualized pay	N	Y	N	Y	N
Insecure jobs	Y	Y	Y	Y	Y/N
Management control in the labor process					
Tight performance management	Y	Y	Y/N	Y	Y/N
Devaluation of professions	Y/N	Y	Y/N	Y	Y
Deterioration of staff–client interaction	Y	Y	Y/N	Y	Y/N
Speedup	Y	Y	Y/N	Y	Y/N
Work-first	Y	Y	Y/N	Y	Y/N
Creaming and parking	N	Y	N	Y	Y/N

Note: Y = yes, N = no, Y/N = varied

which favor the standardized mass processing of clients. British public-sector organizations combined organized industrial relations with strong management control (sometimes via the IT systems of the primes for which they were subcontractors), and small German charities combined disorganized industrial relations with strong professional discretion. Even where there was weak management control built into work organization, there was not always strong professional autonomy. Workers faced extensive administrative work documenting their activities for the funder and in the British charities and municipalities formal qualifications played less of a role than in German charities.

Under conditions of marketization, we find that formal worker voice can be difficult to sustain and impossible to establish. In the form of trade union and works council structures it is largely absent from the for-profit sector of Germany and Great Britain. In Germany this is because the organizations are small; in Great Britain it is because they are anti-union. At the two providers that still recognize PCS, the functioning of worker representation has eroded as contracts have turned over and managers have marginalized them. In large German non-profits there is a history of worker representation, which is sustained; but this is in large part because these organizations are not only carrying out employment services but have broader integrated portfolios of social and health services. However, Danish trade unions have not been substantially weakened under conditions of marketization. Many workers have been voluntarily transferred from the public employment sector to the private for-profit sector and retained their union membership. The Danish private sector has higher union density than in the other two countries, although it is lower than the public sector.

Marketization also creates difficulties for establishing and maintaining compressed pay structures regulated by collective bargaining, although in each country there are exceptions. In Germany this problem is most extreme, with substantial numbers of freelancers at private firms on very low pay. While training providers for the BA have become one of the few areas of the economy with a sector-specific statutory minimum wage, this has been controversial in the sector. The exception to the disorganization trend is some of the large charities which include employment services in much larger frameworks of collective bargaining (or emulation of public-sector bargaining outcomes by consensual pay commissions in the church-affiliated charities); but even here there are parts of them that are escaping from the framework citing the financial pressures of contracting. Great Britain has dealt with it in a different way, through the living-wage campaigns of PCS and at some firms through the equalization of pay for employees transferred from contractors prior to the Work Programme. Nevertheless, there is no move towards a sectoral framework to govern pay, and where pay is linked to public-sector collective bargaining this has meant over the past five years nominal pay stagnation. Great Britain's public-sector providers are still integrated into the broader framework of collective bargaining of local government. Denmark represents a final exception where the encompassing collective bargaining system has been quite resilient, due to the possibility for local and individual bargaining as features of the system. Hence, a smaller part of the salary in the for-profit sector is based upon performance-related payment. A final practice that some managers in all countries report is using higher pay for some new recruits in order to increase quality; how widespread this is and its overall effects on the distribution of income is unclear.

Job insecurity is a third aspect of disorganization of employment relations. In Germany, this is extreme, with widespread use of freelancers and short-term contracts; the rationale for this is clear—firms and non-profits cannot afford the risk of hiring permanent staff if the funding is temporary, or if there are rapid and unpredictable swings in work. In Great Britain contractual status is less of an issue, but insecurity is, not only due to the coming and going of contracts, but also due to the power of firms to fire poor performers. TUPE protects workers to some degree by protecting their wages and working conditions, but its applicability is hampered by differences between older contracts and newer ones, in particular the reduction in staffing due to a reduction in prices. In Denmark, despite the weakness of employment protection for core workers, many providers use freelancers because of the rapid changes that can take place in contracts and volumes of work, although this is expensive, risky, and some providers have a policy against using freelancers.

Our cases also differ in terms of management control over the labor process. The tightest forms of management control can be found in for-profit primes in Britain, but analogous systems can be found, on a smaller scale, in some providers in Denmark and Germany. We also saw, however, non-commercial approaches to providing employment services in all three countries, at other providers where management control was weaker.

One aspect of this organizational shift was the devaluing of professions and formal professional qualifications. The backgrounds of staff were extremely diverse in all of the countries—staff were recruited from corporate management, the civil service, the non-profit sector, commercial welfare-to-work organizations, temporary agencies, retail sales, and from the clientele. Formal qualifications were equally diverse—from few formal qualifications to seemingly unrelated university degrees to obviously relevant professional qualifications in advice, guidance, teaching, or social work.

Germany and Denmark were diverse, with some German firms operating under voucher arrangements able to avoid hiring staff with a strong professional ethos, but generally with a strong presence of qualified social workers and professional instructors due to requirements set by the funder. However, under the veil of the BA's qualitative prescriptiveness, the professional quality actually produced for clients is eroding due to pressure on prices and wages, skills shortages, short-termism, and the discouragement of the professional spirit. In Germany professional regulation is especially weak under the placement voucher scheme and in Denmark under mass-processing services using payment by results. Great Britain has the weakest professional regulation, with social workers a small part of a workforce that is very diverse in terms of both background and formal qualifications. While some managers see this as an advantage, others see it as a problem, and commercial providers have responded collectively by creating a professional body and a new framework of qualifications. The continued salience of formal professions depends on the work as it is defined by the funder; where providers have the discretion to reap payments for job outcomes—as at Work Programme providers and under placement vouchers—high-level professional qualifications are devalued and professionals replaced by diverse workers deemed by management to be sufficiently results-oriented.

Performance management is a second aspect of management control. In Germany the outcome-based management of work in providers is obstructed by the prescriptiveness of contracts and the professional ethos of staff. The exception is private placement firms where these barriers are absent, but this is a minor exception because this market segment is small. In Great Britain management of work within providers is generally very tight. Providers use sophisticated IT systems and individualized human-resource practices with no need to negotiate over them with staff and few regulatory barriers from the funder. Denmark is varied, with some very tight management control and some very loose depending on the nature of the work and the contract. Perhaps the main divide here was between non-commercial providers that were closely watched by the funder and were therefore subject to time-consuming data-entry requirements and commercial providers that had systems that were more clearly focused on producing and reporting job outcomes. In the first case they document inputs; in the other they chase outcomes.

These differences in work organization shape staff interactions with clients. Where the BA tightly regulates work, German managers have little ability to reduce the frequency of contact or to encourage creaming and parking. At private placement agencies, by contrast, staff were quick and efficient in sorting clients and placing the job-ready in whatever jobs were available. In Great Britain, there are strict limits to the amount of time staff can spend with clients, strong pressures from management for creaming and parking, and a work-first focus that determines the substance of these interactions. This is enabled by a mixture of payment by results and loose regulation. Finally, in Denmark we witnessed similar tendencies under the second wave of marketization, but more by staff just processing people through the system with low spending in services rather than creaming and parking. In the third wave, this turned into a more local decision between local job centers and providers. Where it takes the form of partnership contracting, the funder creates a more professionalized and specialized task, in which clients must be handled in a more responsive way.

Marketization at the level of the transaction affects both the institutional regulation and the lived experience of work. We have argued that this is due to management responses to the intensification of resource scarcity and uncertainty. These employment factors are closely related to the character of the service: the quantity, quality, and distribution of time staff spend with clients. In Chapter 6 we explore the consequences of these findings for governance.

6

Governance Implications

Dilemmas and Tradeoffs

Marketization in this book refers to features of transactions determined by policymakers. These decisions reflect a range of intentions embedded in the overall principles of governance. Policymakers use markets in the hope of reducing public regulation and bureaucracy, while improving services in terms of quality, price, effects (job outcomes), and possibly customer choice as well. Incentives built into market rules do have a powerful effect on the behavior of workers and management, but given the failure of marketization to live up to its promises and expectations the real effects are different from the intended ones (Bredgaard and Larsen 2008; Breidahl and Larsen 2015; Larsen and Wright 2014).

The resulting difficulties for public authorities, managers of providers, and front-line staff have been the subject of the previous chapters. In Chapters 2 and 3 we explored these problems in our discussion of public authorities' efforts to manage external providers using different transaction modes (grants, vouchers, or purchasing) with differing degrees of marketization. We showed the choices entailed in marketization from the perspective of the funder. Chapters 4 and 5 discussed the problems from a different angle, by looking at the management responses within providers and the consequences for front-line staff. We showed the consequences of these decisions for providers in terms of the resulting resource scarcity and uncertainty, as well as providers' responses both collectively as a sector and individually within organizations. In this chapter we discuss how these difficulties in workplaces affect the overall principles that animate the activities of the state in the area of active labor market policies—what we call governance.

Rather than offering solutions to these difficulties or merely criticizing the outcomes, we discuss them as dilemmas and tradeoffs inescapably associated with the use of market mechanisms by public purchasers. While choices may not be difficult for policymakers to justify, they do entail tradeoffs in terms of policy goods. For example, how can a purchaser:

- define quality and extract cost savings while giving providers the space to invent new methods as a competitive advantage?
- orient providers towards results (in terms of job outcomes) while avoiding problems with incentives to cream or park clients?
- balance the inherent principles of compulsion in active labor-market policies with the public-management ideology of empowering clients as consumers choosing services?
- ensure transparency, equal treatment, and open competition without generating more public regulation and incurring higher transaction costs?

Policymakers' decisions in response to these dilemmas can lead to change in "governance." By this we mean the overall principles animating an area of government activity, such as the rationale of authority, the control mechanisms used, and the focus of provider activities. Drawing on the international literature on employment services (Considine and Lewis 2003; Jantz et al. 2015; Breidahl and Larsen 2015), we distinguish three governance types. "Market governance," which underpins marketization, emphasizes particular results and the price of achieving them, uses contracts and competition to attain them, and focuses provider attention on targets and costs. "Network governance" underpins most non-marketized external provision; its rationale comes from the ethos of the network, uses co-production between provider and funder to develop services, and orients providers to respond in a flexible way to the complex needs of clients. "Procedural governance," the traditional principles of administering in-house public services, emphasizes formal rules and their universal application, uses top-down hierarchical control to implement them, and focuses providers on standardization.

The following sections will discuss four dilemmas: 1) price versus quality, 2) payment by results versus equal access to services, 3) user choice versus public control and client compulsion, and 4) openness and transparency versus transaction costs. Then, we will discuss the step-wise abolition of the market and internalization of services by the public authority as one solution. Based on Danish and German examples we can show that this is a real possibility in employment services, albeit one whose consequences are not well understood. Finally, we will show how these dilemmas matter for governance principles and the problems and opportunities for market, network, and procedural governance under marketization.

Price versus Quality

The idea that high-quality low-cost services can be achieved through market competition is a mainstay of public-sector management rhetoric. Competition is assumed to lead to innovation, and innovation is assumed to lead to higher quality of welfare services. In our sample, however, squeezing prices siphons resources out of services that could be used to employ qualified workers on the front line, and the standardization of services that this requires drains the capacity of providers to innovate.

Public authorities try to mitigate these problems by changing the way that quality is measured or through tighter regulation and monitoring. But changing quality measurements may simply mean allowing lower quality, as in Britain where it is redefined as the quantity of job outcomes, and—as discussed in Appendix B—the funder cannot adequately monitor the services. Tighter regulation through more detailed descriptions of what constitutes high quality can allow for low prices but increases transaction costs, both for purchaser and provider (Larsen and Wright 2014). Time spent by provider staff in documenting interactions with clients is lost for such interactions themselves, as we saw in the German case in Chapter 5.

There does not appear to be a way out of this dilemma.

In Denmark, the flux in the market is partly a function of this dilemma. Over the decade of marketization experiments governments have tried to reduce costs while commissioning services that were both innovative and personalized. The evaluation evidence shows mixed results (AMS 2009; Deloitte 2009; National Audit Office 2013; Skou et al. 2008) reflecting changing ways of balancing these two prerogatives. Under the second wave of marketization (2005–10) price competition between providers was very hard, in response to allegations of profiteering during the first wave. Price became the most important selection criterion and quality assurance took the form of performance-related pay and a requirement that clients "be in activation" 40 percent of the time. The legislation kept the exact description of the work vague, i.e. some form of subsidized work, training, education, and job-search activities, with considerable discretion for providers in designing the services. Because the providers themselves had to pay for all types of activities, most of them chose to only offer low-cost activities often in the form of job-search activities.

The 2005 reform had effects on services that led to a scandal both in the print news media and in the blogs. Dagpengeland.dk ("the land of unemployment benefit") provided a very popular depiction of how a young man just graduated from a five-year university education is taught (in-house at a private provider) basic skills such as how to create an email account; subsequently this was published as a popular book and play.

The Conservative Minister of Employment responded to this in a newspaper interview: "I'm really annoyed every time I hear about these kinds of examples. It is a waste of tax money and not least human resources" (Broberg and Jensen 2010). Both right- and left-wing politicians became increasingly skeptical towards the use of private providers in the employment service, which indirectly paved the way for the dissolution of the national tendering system and a significant reduction in the volume of contracting out in employment services.

After 2011, under the abolition of the national tendering system, central oversight was weakened, and this dynamic changed in many municipalities. Our survey shows that with reduced price competition there was a strong emphasis on service quality, including specialized and individualized services. Simultaneously there was an increased dialogue and partnership collaboration between the purchasers in the municipalities (where most of the municipalities assess that the relation to providers has become more partnership-based) and the reduced use of tendering (see Chapter 2). Despite considerable variation in practice, it leaves open questions of what quality means, how quality strategies change over time, and whether there is a connection between reducing price-based competition and promoting quality.

One of the municipalities we visited has a practice which is very similar to the former national tendering system. Private providers are mainly used as a capacity buffer and they mainly deliver generalist and standardized services targeted at the unemployed at the high end of the labor market (high-skilled unemployed), including interviews and job-search activities. The purchaser believes in this setup that it is possible to ensure low costs and high quality through tight price-based competition. Quality is referred to as objective criteria listed in tendering documents subject to scores which, among others, includes effects (employment outcome) from the past, the composition of policy instruments, and experiences and competences among the staff. Over the course of the two-year contract, the purchaser monitors monthly whether the providers deliver the specified services at the right time, the amount of time used on activation, and employment outcomes; there are meetings between the purchaser and provider at least three times per year over the course of contracts, more frequently if there are problems. As explained by one of the executives in the municipality:

> Other municipalities have had problems running it this way, but we have managed to create a meeting structure and culture with the providers focusing toughly on results, where in other places it becomes very complicated when you discuss methods and content in services, and you need to supervise how the providers work. There our model is very clear-cut...This is a more pure market model. (DK purchaser 1)

In another municipality the response to the abolition of the national tendering system was to change the services it contracted out and its way of doing so. Executives were critical of the old tendering system and argued in interviews that excessive attention on prices made it difficult for providers to improve their services: "If you only focus on prices, there is a huge risk of not getting anything at all. And seen from previous experiences they didn't deliver what we ourselves couldn't do better" (DK purchaser 3). Instead the municipality insourced generalist services and organized close collaborative contracting relationships with providers for developing more specialized services. Because they saw the kinds of contracted-out services needed as more complex than the standard mass-processing services aimed primarily at the job outcome, municipal executives found it difficult to formulate precise standards for services. This meant experimental projects initiated by providers in areas where in-house services were not performing well, which when performance did not improve led to the insourcing of the work. Although increasing the possibilities for the public purchaser to influence quality, this of course entails the risk of creating a less transparent market with less competition (and thereby higher prices).

The providers we interviewed confirmed the general tendency towards less price competition and the stronger focus on individualized and innovative services as a consequence of putting the municipalities in charge of marketization. Their views on municipal control were complex. Although the previous system had allowed what one director called "quick and dirty money" by letting the providers process the easy-to-place through the system (in a pay-for-performance system), they also pointed at the problems with balancing low prices and high quality. They generally prefer to compete around quality rather than price, and they are aware that quality problems during the first and second waves of marketization have given the whole branch of private providers a very bad reputation. Furthermore the expectations from the providers are that the emphasis on more specialized services (targeting the more hard-to-place) will increase prices. The tendency towards a more partnership-based model is seen as positive from many of the providers (see also Chapter 4).

The Danish case illustrates very well how hard price competition can lead to problems with innovating and targeting individual needs, as the providers mostly tried to live up to minimum requirements in the contracts. Some municipalities still prefer hard price competition in combination with contract-based standardized minimum requirements. However, more and more municipalities seem to prefer less price competition in more partnership-based relations attempting to create more innovative and individualized services.

Germany is another case of a squeeze on prices leading to quality problems, in particular the draining of the capacities of providers to innovate. In order to make prices comparable inputs rather than outcomes are used. Tender documents specify the services to be delivered in great detail, in terms of both quantity (e.g. hours of instruction) and quality (e.g. professional degrees and experience of staff, characteristics of the premises). Contracts tend to be small and tightly defined for particular locales, target groups, and legally defined instruments of active labor-market policy. Often they are standardized by the REZen, whose procurement services include the definition of "Standardprodukte." Indeed, to the extent that innovation takes place, it is here in the definition of programs by the REZ.

Interviewees described numerous ways in which their capacities to innovate were paralyzed. One was the squeeze on resources. Providers have to respond to the detailed tender description; if they promise innovative service elements up and above the tender description, they either implement those elements free of charge or price themselves out of competition. While there in principle is scope for providers to organize services according to individual needs beyond those defined in the tendering documents—for example large integrated providers such as the church-affiliated charities that combine a very wide range of social and health services—they face both strict financial constraints as well as legal constraints in terms of transferring unemployed between projects under different contracts. As we saw in Chapter 5, the squeeze on prices also made it difficult to adhere to collective agreements, leading to the creation of a sectoral minimum wage for training providers operating under contract with the BA.

The tendering system also corrodes pre-existing networks. In the past, services were designed jointly by frontline professionals in job centers and project developers of providers. Such collaboration requires more flexibility than is allowed when the work is defined in detail up front. It is also frustrated by the economic problem of competition: after expending resources on a pilot project the provider faces the possibility that it will be outflanked by a competitor in the tendering process for future iterations of the process. This happened in one municipality we visited, for example, where a longstanding network of providers combining intensive social work with job-placement services collapsed when competitive tendering was introduced, including competition to carry out the work of other members of the network.

In interviews with the funder and policymakers it was clear that there were some efforts to mitigate some of these problems in the tendering process. As discussed in Appendix B, the funder has attempted to respond in various ways to the frequently heard accusation that price pressures are reducing the quality of services. For example, while we were carrying out our interviews lawmakers were in the process of revising public procurement rules (the Seventh Procurement Ordinance, passed in July 2013) to allow purchasers to take into account the track record of providers. This creates considerable uncertainty for incumbents: whereas they may be penalized for a project that went wrong, newcomers will start with a clean slate.

With voucher schemes, the tendency has been toward the intensification of regulation. For job-placement vouchers an accreditation requirement has been introduced, which has increased the administrative costs facing mainly small providers. For training vouchers the BA has set new controls on prices, which providers criticized as stifling innovation. Between the introduction of training vouchers and their reform in 2012, it was quite straightforward for a provider to create a new course that combined a range of services but cost extra money. This would be certified independently of its cost. In 2012 this changed with the introduction of nationwide indicative fees. Typically this would be an amount per hour, per participant, which varied by occupational group (e.g. industrial mechanics have their fee set at €7.85 per person per hour, assuming fifteen participants in a course). Schemes that are more expensive require approval by the BA, and applications have according to interviewees a 50 percent acceptance rate. According to managers we interviewed this makes it difficult or impossible to create new combined services—say a training course with a particular kind of counseling—in response to labor-market demand, certain client groups' specific learning problems and discussions with local job-center management. Cost containment thus restricts innovation under the training voucher scheme.

In Great Britain the funder has attempted to sidestep the price-quality dilemma through incentives and discretion. Quality in the bidding process mainly concerned the provider's capacity to roll out, and manage the risks of, delivery models over large areas; once the program was up and running quality meant large numbers of sustained job-placement outcomes. While there was some regulation of minimum standards for clients being "parked," we see in Appendix C that it was weak. The shift away from purchasing clearly defined products from the market was motivated by a desire to maximize outcomes using knowledge not available to the public purchaser. As one senior civil servant told us:

> we were paying a lot of money, we weren't really paying for outcomes; we were paying for a lot of pre-specified activities which in a way is a weird thing to do, is to kind of contract out but then tell the contractor what to do and then pay them for doing the activities rather than the outcome, it's an odd way of using the private sector really.   (GB purchaser 7)

The funder hoped to achieve good outcomes for a low price using price-based competition by asking for "discounts" in the tendering process and assigned price points on this basis. It was also because the quality scoring criteria did not discriminate between delivery models that relied on high versus low levels of staffing (GB manager 2). As we see in Chapter 3 and Appendix C, the funder was extremely effective in reducing its costs through this price-based competition in the bidding process for the Work Programme.

Price pressure, mixed with high levels of discretion, led even more than in Denmark under the second wave of marketization, to standardized mass-processing models of provision. As we will see in the next section, providers responded not only through minimalist support for clients overall but also through "creaming and parking," i.e. the neglect of clients furthest from the labor market. While the funder had established a complex pricing system in which those classified more distant from the labor market attracted a far higher payment than mainstream claimants of jobseeker benefits, there was little evidence that this had created incentives to focus resources on those distant from the labor market. Our interviewees at providers, including for-profit ones, were disappointed by the kinds of provision that emerged:

> I have led the design of [several] delivery models under ERSS programmes both as a potential prime and subcontractor. All have become generic in that they have been changed to include an immediate diagnostic phase when the unemployed person comes in to the programme and as a first action, is assessed in terms of what needs to be done to get them into a job and to keep them there. This is a common feature throughout all delivery of ERSS programmes and is often known as the "diagnostic phase." This is normally followed by "individual action planning" where a timetable of bespoke intervention is prescribed, such as basic skills training, motivational or "attitude" problems are addressed, personal presentation and interview techniques are considered and timetabled job search is delivered.
>
> (GB manager 2)

The innovation that took place under the Work Programme thus took the form of large-scale models of delivery, with sophisticated information technology systems, rolled out over large and very diverse geographies and client groups. These were rolled out on a large scale in "contract package areas" with two or three prime providers, some of them like Scotland with a population approaching that of Denmark. There was insufficient money to pay for labor-intensive services for disadvantaged hard-to-reach clients. They were also kept in place over the course of a five-year contract. While our DWP interviewees were unwilling to criticize this, it was a serious problem for many of the managers we interviewed in providers, especially those with considerable experience in this area. While some saw this as the implementation of best practice, others saw it as a serious constraint on the ability of providers to create services customized for the clientele.

On price versus quality, the overall preference in all three countries is for low prices rather than high quality. Denmark is a partial exception, because it has experienced a general increase in prices alongside a desire of some municipalities to develop specialized services in partnership with providers; but there are other municipalities that continue the low-cost mass-processing models engendered by the national labor-market authorities in the earlier marketization wave. Germany has maintained a clear preference for squeezing prices in procurement alongside very detailed specification of the work and of staff qualifications. The BA's intention to hold up quality against the price squeeze is self-deceptive because of its effects on innovation by providers and because of the difficulty of distinguishing between quality described in the bid and real quality in service delivery. In Britain quality has merely been redefined as quantity of job outcomes and innovation as the rollout of standardized services; while this did reduce spending it created serious quality concerns, especially for clients most distant from the labor market.

Payment by Results versus Equal Access to Services

Payment by results (PbR)—i.e. linking the amount of payment to the number of job placements—is one way of changing the specification of quality, and one that is highly consistent with the ethos of market governance. This payment model, however, bears the risk of creaming and parking. Providers might focus all their resources on easy-to-place clients (creaming), and might neglect those who are furthest from the labor market (parking) (Bredgaard and Larsen 2008). This results in unequal access of customers to services, with the consequence that the labor-market chances of the most disadvantaged jobseekers are not improved by the service. For providers PbR creates a financial risk (of not achieving outcome-related payments) as well as an opportunity (of claiming payments for clients close to the labor market). If those who cream and park achieve higher job outcomes they receive higher remuneration with lower investment costs, placing them at a very strong advantage compared to providers that refuse to cream and park. For the funder it means not only potentially losing certain providers from the market but also paying for outcomes not caused by the services (i.e. dead-weight effects).

There are numerous ways to mitigate this risk. The first is to create differentiated funding models that attempt to pay providers for the extra spending that is needed for clients close to the labor market; the British case shows that this has been ineffective, for reasons discussed in this section. Based on our German and Danish cases we see three conditions under which creaming and parking is unlikely: (1) where the element of PbR in the overall payment model is reduced, (2) where PbR is impossible due to the lack of a measurable outcome (as with most training courses), and (3) where there is a relatively homogeneous client group (and hence a smaller contract).

In *Denmark* the 2005 reform introduced, along with mandatory competitive tendering, a requirement that 80 percent of pay be for performance, nationwide changing the incentives and risks facing providers. The combination of price competition, high risk, delays of up to six months for full payment, and the probability of creating at least some short-term employment outcomes with limited services led to very poor services, such as replicating the tried and tested methods or "in-house" activities as job-searching activities, as discussed above. After municipalities were given flexibility to decide upon the level of performance-related payment themselves in 2011 we observe from here major variations in its use. Some of the municipalities visited were still using the 80 percent performance-related payment model for clients assessed as close to the labor market and therefore not in need of intensive individualized services.

Our survey shows a general decrease in the use of performance-related payment and in interviews; executives cited problems of low-cost and low-quality services as among their motives for increasing the importance of fixed payments. Also the providers we interviewed reported that under the municipalized system the trend has been away from performance-related payment. Managers perceive this change as positive overall and state that high performance-related payment, along with intense price competition, can lead to low-quality services. The for-profit providers also state that the way they organize their services (the kind of services, the staff's educational background, performance-related wages or not, etc.) depends on the setup of the market at the local level in the municipalities. If the municipalities demand individualized and specialized services, this is what they provide (including higher prices), and if the municipalities demand more generalized services this is also something they bid for. The trend is apparently toward more specialized services that do not involve PbR.

Where PbR remains in use in Demark, we do not have any indications of creaming and parking taking place. This could be for a number of reasons. One is that because the lots tend to be for particular groups (e.g. university graduates or particular "heavy" groups), the clientele was too homogeneous for the sorting of clients to have an effect. Another is that, because of the high value placed on equal treatment as a cultural norm our interviewees hid the problem of creaming and parking and denied that it exists. On balance, it seems that performance-related pay created problems with responsiveness rather than equity; under the standardized "people-processing" services that resulted, everybody seems to have been treated equally badly.

Germany, by contrast, has adopted only a very cautious and limited version of payment by results, using two mechanisms: placement vouchers and procured job-placement schemes. Placement vouchers involve no payment except in the case of a job placement. Although unemployed jobseekers with a claim to insurance-based unemployment benefits have the right to request a placement voucher after having been unemployed for at least six weeks, placement vouchers represent less than 1 percent of total spending on active measures in 2013. Procured schemes involving job placement, by contrast, have become a significant part of the German employment-services landscape making up 13 percent of total spending. They usually comprise a combination of activation and placement services, with only the placement component paid by results at the same rate as placement vouchers.

Within the BA there are concerns about the quality of provision by firms operating under the placement vouchers regime. Providers tend to be small, often unemployed people who set up a small business. As we showed in Chapter 5, the provider we visited had an extremely quick and informal way of sorting job-ready clients from those distant from the labor market. This, according to front-line staff we interviewed, was based on a reflex developed over time in which they use basic information and subtle cues to filter out voucher holders who would be unsuitable for the jobs on offer. Creaming, or selection for employability, was thus evident. Parking, however, was less in evidence, since clients turned away because they were deemed unsuitable for the available jobs would still be registered with, and presumably served by, their local job center or employment agency.

Procured job-placement schemes have diverse payment models, with both up-front payments and PbR in arrears, or merely a stipulated minimum placement rate. Although these measures can create strong financial pressures to place clients in jobs, we found no evidence of creaming and parking in the non-profit provider we visited delivering this scheme. There are two possible reasons mentioned by interviewees.

Interviewees on the front line suggested that tensions between the occupational ethos of the social and work-first welfare policies played a role. These workers viewed the human needs that need to be dealt with as rather complex and also wanted to strengthen the agency of clients rather than using sanctions to force them into a particular job. Management interviewees in a non-profit organization, whose staff had a strong social-work ethos, told us that they did not know how to adapt services to be financially sustainable under payment by results. Because the BA commonly requires trained social workers for these kinds of schemes in its tendering documents, we can expect this to be a common pattern at these providers.

Another barrier to creaming and parking in German procured activation schemes may be, like in Denmark, small contracts and relatively homogeneous clientele. These schemes are organized at the local level for particular client groups in the locale such as single mothers, young people, or older people, usually in a particular city. In practice, client groups are never as homogeneous as laid down in the contract; nevertheless, the range of client profiles within a contract is far narrower, demographically and geographically, than Britain's "black box" system, leaving much smaller scope for creaming and parking.

In Great Britain, where PbR represents the vast majority of funding for external employment services, we do find strong evidence of creaming and parking. This is consistent with other studies on performance-related pay in British welfare-to-work schemes, some of them funded by the DWP (e.g. Hudson et al. 2010) and some independent (National Audit Office 2014; Rees et al. 2014), as well as the Work Programme's performance data. The latter reveal worse performance for ESA than JSA claimants, and Chapter 5 discusses the organization-level dynamics behind this. Unlike Denmark and Germany PbR has been rolled out nationwide across an extremely diverse clientele; in addition Work Programme providers have much stronger discretion in the number and kind of staff they deploy to deliver the contract. The situation is put well by one of our interviewees from the for-profit sector:

> So you get less people into work, and because you're getting less people into work you target, and because it's outcome based, you're going to target your resources at those people who are easiest to help. So you're going to aggressively park and cream. You cream by targeting the easy ones, you park by identifying the people you can't help and ignore them. (GB manager 2)

Policymakers were aware from the outset that this could be a problem, and the DWP has two main ways to mitigate it.

The first is minimum standards written out for each of the Work Programme's contractors. This can include a minimum frequency of contact of clients with staff, either monthly or fortnightly, to make and monitor job-search action plans or a general commitment to "regular" contact. Most providers also promise access to electronic resources, such as online courses, information on job openings, or an email account. Also common is a promise to quickly contact clients referred to them and convert 85–95 percent of "referrals" into "attachments." These guidelines, however, vary from contractor to contractor, are mostly vague, and have a strong emphasis on speed, standardization, and use of IT tools (rather than, for example, intensive one-to-one counseling).

The second is differential pricing, in which the DWP divides the clientele into seven different "price groups," classified by age and benefit claimed. Prices are highest for claimants of Employment Support Allowance who in the past received Incapacity Benefit and are required to attend, and they are considerably lower for JSA claimants who have never received Incapacity Benefit. The intention is that providers that focus attention on those disabled clients deemed to be furthest from the labor market will reap rich financial rewards in the long run. The problem is that, while this may compensate providers for the extra effort of aiding clients distant from the labor market, it cannot compensate the risk involved in doing so. As manager 2 argues, "the risk of spending staff time and resource on the graduate is far less than the risk associated with the person who has little chance of getting a job without a major investment of time and money."

Some of the reasons for creaming and parking have to do with program design. The diversity of the clientele creates wide scope for sorting for employability. An opposition member of parliament we interviewed thought this was the core problem, and that the solution to creaming and parking was to create separate contracts for disabled and mainstream jobseekers. Second, performance-related pay also creates a problem with resource scarcity for services. It intensifies the need to divert resources in a very instrumental way, to invest in services where a return is likely, i.e. clients classified as close to the labor market. This restricts funding for so-called "wraparound services" which contractors could provide or purchase for their clients or other forms of assistance traditionally provided to clients, for example, transportation, or clothes for job interviews.

Other reasons have to do with the kinds of providers who have the power and discretion to decide what the services will be and who is served. While government rhetoric emphasizes the mixed landscape of provision—with non-profit, for-profit, and public-sector providers delivering the Work Programme—the prime providers are commercial organizations. They are under pressure to provide a return on investment and—as we saw in Chapter 5—have sophisticated systems to do so.

On payment by results versus equal access to services, there is far more evidence of creaming and parking in Britain than in the other two countries. Some Danish municipalities report ending payment by results due to quality problems; others continue to use payment by results. In Germany there is creaming under the placement vouchers scheme; this market segment is marginal and clients are not being "parked" but rather sent back to the job center. In German schemes using PbR, the size of the bonus is kept relatively small precisely because of fears of creaming and parking, according to interviewees in the BA. In Britain, despite the complex incentives and published minimum service standards, creaming and parking is widespread in the Work Programme.

User Choice versus User Compulsion

While a key justification for marketization in general is user choice, principles of consumerism are difficult to reconcile with the principles of compulsion built into the work-first welfare state. User choice is expected to be an essential precondition of a well-functioning quasi-market, to ensure high-quality services, as the cornerstone of market-based respect, and as the basis of empowerment (Le Grand 2006). In most of the quasi-markets in our sample, however, jobless clients are represented in the market by a public purchaser, which also refers clients to the provider under the threat of sanctioning. This is because clients may not know the landscape of providers (Bredgaard and Larsen 2008), but also because if they did have that knowledge, the most popular service among them might not be the same one that the funder preferred, especially where providers report to the funder on breaches of clients' obligations. Hipp and Warner (2008) summarize the problems identified by the evaluation literature on voucher systems in employment services: "First, preference misalignment due to different preferences of public providers, private deliverers, and jobseekers; second, information asymmetries leading to high transaction costs and preference error; and third, failure of market formation leading to lack of choice" (83). German voucher systems are exceptional and are themselves limited in terms of how they empower clients.

In very limited ways, Danish policymakers have tried to promote user choice. In the first phase of marketization from 2002 to 2005, some of the regional public employment service agencies tried to incorporate a free choice of provider. However, a 2004 evaluation showed that 67 percent of the clients asked reported not having a choice; 8 percent reported a (full) free choice (also including the public employment services); 11 percent a choice between private/non-public providers but not the public service; and 9 percent were offered the possibility of a different provider if they were dissatisfied (AMS 2004, 6). The government's 2005 action plan for employment services urged user choice and instructed the PES staff and management to inform clients about alternative providers. The PES responded by offering clients who had been referred to specific providers the possibility to complain and be sent to a different provider. Where customers were able to exercise this choice, it was limited to the few providers that already had a contract with the purchaser.

When we asked Danish public authorities and providers about user choice, it became clear that it is not seen as an important part of marketization. Providers reported in interviews that they were caught between acting in the interests of employers (who want the best person for the job) and the choices of disadvantaged jobseekers (who want to be referred to a desirable job). Another concern, historically, was that customers might vote with their feet for union-affiliated providers with the hope of looser policing of their job-search activities.

Although policymakers in Britain apply the label of "customer" to clients, choice has always been limited to non-existent. In 1990–2001, long before the present market took shape, there was an experiment with user choice in employment services, as a voucher scheme for unemployed young people known for most of its existence as the Youth Credit. Evaluators found that voucher holders played a passive role and that the credits did not actually encourage competition between providers (see Unwin 1993 and West et al. 2000: 29–39). The scheme failed to open the market to new providers, since customers were referred to the very same incumbent firms already operating under contract with the funder (the Training and Enterprise Councils). There is at present no talk of increasing user choice in British employment services.

One major reason for this lack of trust in user choice is the ongoing escalation of compulsion in the British employment services, which came up again and again in our interviews. At Work Programme providers we visited, non-attendance of meetings could trigger sanctions almost automatically. Front-line staff would log non-attendance on an electronic system by raising a "doubt" with the DWP, which (often with much delay) would lead to a sanction. Subsequent schemes were also introduced, all of which were mandatory and backed up by sanctions. Compulsion is very strongly embedded in British policy discourse: the opposition politician we interviewed made the point that the Coalition Government had increased sanctioning excessively, but when we asked what the alternative was, the reply was more flexibility in the administration of sanctions.

In Germany, the training and placement vouchers go much further in providing user choice than anything seen in Britain or Denmark, and a far wider range of clients are eligible for vouchers in Germany than was ever the case in Britain. In principle front-line workers in the BA are not allowed to influence the choice of clients in choosing providers, because doing so would distort the consumer market. In practice it seems to be standard practice where vouchers are redeemed in large numbers. Outside urban agglomerations, there may be just one provider able to deliver a particular course specified on a training voucher, so in practice there can be limited customer/user choice. The public authority does have some room to decide which courses are funded (at the local level) and to cap their costs (at the national level); and the extent to which they are actually used depends heavily on support from front-line BA staff, whose attitudes toward vouchers and providers varies widely (Doerr and Kruppe 2014).

The connection between vouchers and compulsion is complex. On the one hand, private training providers and placement firms can be included in a jobseekers' agreement and therefore in principle be backed up by sanctions. On the other hand, our interviewees told us that the condition could be satisfied for the client without actually using the service. This would be the case at a training provider that the client approaches for a course but does not have the numbers of trainees needed to actually carry through the course. As one provider told us, "The person did their duty when they bring the voucher to a provider but the provider says: I can't justify this course financially because there are only five participants" (German manager 7). It could also be at a placement firm that sees the client as acting in good faith in looking for work but which cannot match the client with a job. In the latter case front-line staff reported in interviews a problem with jobseekers approaching them for the signature to fulfil the jobseekers' agreement, but without being strong candidates for the jobs on offer.

Compulsion is therefore easier to police when services are directly purchased and clients referred—without a choice—to a specific provider. As with Danish and British employment services, this takes place under the direct threat of sanction. Compared to vouchers this gives the BA far more control over which services are provided. The German case may be the system with the highest degree of user choice, but it also reflects the dilemma of marketization through client (customer) choice conflicting with the political intention of compulsion.

In these countries public authorities overwhelmingly favor compulsion over customer choice, despite the place of consumerism in public management thinking. In Danish and British employment services, choice has always been marginal at best, and in recent years the element of compulsion has increased in Britain. Germany is a partial exception with its voucher arrangements—which represent a similar volume of work to purchased schemes—although the BA and its staff shape how vouchers are used through formal rules and the way they advise potential users of the vouchers.

Openness and Transparency versus Transaction Costs

One claim of NPM is that public bureaucracy can be reduced significantly using market mechanisms. However, as employment services are still part of public policies with political objectives and only one buyer, the onus is still on the public authority to organize the market, which inevitably generates transaction costs. Whereas a private purchaser can choose an optimum between the competing goals of achieving the best buy and keeping down transaction costs, the public purchaser has other legal obligations, e.g. to demonstrate that the most economically advantageous choice is made and that the procedure is transparent, fair, and open to newcomers and facilitates the participation of small and medium-sized enterprises (Williamson 1999). The public authority must continuously generate tendering processes, which include designing tender documents, administering, and assessing incoming bids (including the efforts wasted from both sides in unsuccessful bids), negotiating contracts, monitoring services and outcomes, establishing payment according to performance, and so forth. This ongoing process involves high costs and extensive bureaucracy.

Many attempts have been made to reduce transaction costs and the public bureaucracy related to marketization (Bredgaard and Larsen 2007, 2008), but these attempts often result in limiting the scope of market mechanisms. Germany, where the REZ has become a market-making bureaucracy, represents a strong contrast with Britain which has handed control of the market to a few large firms and Denmark which has moved control of the market into municipalities. Our qualitative findings suggest that the more perfectly a public authority emulates a free and competitive market, the higher transaction costs it will incur.

In Denmark, despite many attempts at cutting transaction costs, public regulation over contractors—and therefore bureaucracy—increased from 2005to 2010 when control over the market was centralized. The centralization reduced transaction costs by reducing the number of tendering processes and increasing the length of the contract period. However, the monitoring and control mechanism increased as the central level was to be held accountable more directly, not only by the national audit office, but also by the providers. When the national tendering from 2010 gradually was replaced with municipal autonomy, the municipalities ended up having varying ways of handling transactions, their costs, and their political risks. In one of the municipalities we visited, executives reported that price competition is accompanied by several kinds of instruments in monitoring and control (sanctioning, user satisfaction, announced and unannounced visits, etc.). Interviewees emphasized how their tendering processes and procurement practices involved a high level of bureaucracy and transaction costs. In another municipality, by contrast, the public bureaucracy related to tendering processes and monitoring is limited. In an interview a municipal executive told us how transaction costs involved in monitoring and controlling the non-public providers led to a reduction of non-public provision after 2011. There seemed to be an increased use of "framework contracting" in which a contract awarded by one municipality is extended to another municipality without a competitive tendering exercise. For those providers remaining, contracting was managed through more informal partner-based relations. It remains to be seen whether the spread of this less marketized approach leads to new scandals over nepotism and murkiness in the awarding of contracts.

In the wake of the Hartz reforms Germany experienced a stepwise intensification of central control over external providers that has not been reversed. The REZen are the principal place in which administration has been built up to manage the market. The BA's aim has been to create a dedicated purchasing function with a professional staff that can design tendering documents and manage the procurement process while avoiding past mistakes. The REZ has taken a number of steps to ensure that the process is legitimate. One is the creation of a formula that determines outcomes of tendering based on quality and price criteria; another is the creation of an appeals procedure, a response to the need in procurement law to justify its decisions in court. These allow the BA to counter the criticism that contracts are given based on anything other than objective criteria.

Bureaucracy has also expanded in Germany to ensure legitimacy in term of quality. This includes tight and detailed contract monitoring, which expands to the degree that the work is specified in a detailed way. Our interviews with front-line staff revealed that filling in online forms was taking up as much time as meeting face to face with clients. A second example has been the rise of accreditation arrangements; these already existed from shortly after the Hartz reforms for training vouchers. In 2012 they were introduced for placement vouchers in response to criticisms of private job-placement companies as not necessarily "serious," and new requirements were placed to scrutinize costs for training vouchers. Our interviewees reported that accreditation for a training scheme could take place once and then be used for three years.

In Britain, the "black box" model can be seen as an attempt to avoid the problem of transaction costs but at the same time reflects a lack of transparency. The regulation of the providers' work by the state is intentionally loose, and the contrast with Germany is stark: rather than creating in-house capacity to directly purchase schemes, most of the procurement work is contracted out to the "primes." While this is intended to reduce the complexity of government contracting by reducing the number of contracts, it does not eliminate bureaucracy. The prime contractors have extremely tight performance management for both their internal staff and their contractors, as shown in Chapter 5. Services contracted out to other providers are subject to a management fee, which though confidential, is estimated by our interviewees as ranging between 12 percent and 25 percent depending on the contract.

There have been some scandals with these more autonomous private providers. In early 2012, payments came to light to A4e's largest shareholder, Emma Harrison, of £11 million between 2009 and 2011. These included her salary, payments to rent her house to the firm, and a dividend payout (Boffey and Helm 2012). While this apparently led to the collapse of A4e's bid to take over services for ex-offenders, it did not apparently affect its employment-services contracts. Nor is it clear that A4e is any different from its competitors in this regard.

British employment-services providers, however, are shielded from the usual pressures for legitimacy that might lead to change in other countries. In their own subcontracting, prime providers are exempt from public procurement rules, since they are private organizations and not public authorities. In this way the government evades legal responsibility for most of the contracts on the Work Programme, and contracting can take place along the lines of private-sector supply-chain management. This may eliminate the transaction costs that are specific to public purchasers, but it also increases the arbitrary power of large private firms and thereby paradoxically by lack of public regulation the extent of free market conditions. Furthermore, private providers are exempt from the rules to promote transparency in the public sector, including the Freedom of Information Act, making them exempt from scrutiny in other areas. While the millions of pounds paid to A4e's top executive may be extreme, the loss of resources from the system through bonuses, dividends, and other forms of profiteering may exceed any savings in transaction costs.

On openness and transparency versus transaction costs, all three countries have moved to reduce transaction costs by allowing the length of contracts to increase. Nevertheless, Germany has a relatively high degree of bureaucratic state control, while Denmark and Great Britain have far looser control and less transparency. While the abolition of the national tendering system in Denmark may reduce overall transaction costs and transparency, municipalities have very different approaches. Some maintain a highly marketized and bureaucratic approach, while others prefer more informal partnership arrangements with providers. Germany is a clear case of creating a national machinery in order to strengthen legitimacy. Local job-center managers, however, are free to use alternative procurement arrangements, some of which are designed to get around the rigid legalism of the national system. Great Britain has made the opposite choice. It has privatized procurement in order to reduce in-house bureaucracy; the result, however, is a murky landscape of provision not subject to the degree of scrutiny seen in the other countries.

Insourcing as a Response to the Dilemmas

We have shown how marketization generates dilemmas that cannot be resolved easily, if at all; one option is to take services out of the market. In line with research on municipal public-service outsourcing, we find examples of public authorities "insourcing" external work (Hefetz and Warner 2004). But critical points were raised by our interviewees concerning in-house capacity building and effects on external providers, and we know little about the real differences between these services and the external ones they replace.

In Denmark this has been done by making the municipalities responsible for managing provision, and letting them decide upon if and how they will use non-public providers in the employment services. Since 2011 it is the municipalities that make choices in relation to the above-described dilemmas. Providers are mainly used as a capacity buffer or as partners with whom they develop and deliver services, but sometimes municipalities insource services that were previously contracted out. Much of the insourced work is standardized work carried out by low-skilled workers, and much of the external work that remains in the market is specialized work carried out by high-skilled workers.

Insourcing, however, is not without problems; the main one highlighted by Danish interviewees was the buildup of organizational capacity within the public sector that is needed to take over services. This was especially a problem in two large municipalities with large numbers of university-educated clients that previously had been required to use external providers. Because of a lack of expertise it was difficult to build up in-house capacity, at least in the short run. In smaller municipalities it was much easier to insource work, because it involved smaller groups, some of which had not been subject to requirements to use external providers.

In Germany a trend for local managers to insource work started after we ended our field research, leading to much public discussion. According to job-center managers in a follow-up discussion, this takes two forms. First, financial resources from the budget for external services can be rededicated to the personnel budget in order to reduce caseloads at the front line. Second, job centers can obtain certification to carry out normally externalized services with their own staff, which enables them to pay themselves from the program budget. This relates mainly to activation and placement measures and not to training or make-work schemes.

Why is this taking place? It is not a central decision but is motivated by the widespread perception in local job centers that they can carry out job-placement work at least as well as external providers if given the same resources. It is also encouraged by human-resource policies within the job centers. Because of long-term and widespread use of fixed-term contracts ever since the Hartz reforms, and legal requirements to convert them into permanent contracts or lose meanwhile experienced staff with the expiration of fixed-term contracts, local job-center managers are looking for funding to create additional permanent positions. This is reinforced by the end of a large ten-year program in which local management was allowed to decide how much insourcing and outsourcing to do for older jobseekers (Knuth 2014a). Finally, insourcing is related to procurement legislation and procedures. As one job-center manager told us, "With a call for tender we do not know who will be our partner to do the job in the end of the process; with insourcing we decide to whom of our staff we assign the task" (German purchaser 6). Incentives for insourcing are transactions costs, uncertainty of outcomes, and more flexible and rapid decisions possible through "hierarchy" as compared to decisions exerted through "market" mechanisms.

This reversal of marketization in Germany does not lead to the old-fashioned symbiosis between the state and the third sector encapsulated in the subsidiarity principle (Chapter 2), but rather to the stepwise exclusion of certain providers from state funding. But providers do not publicly protest, and their written response does not question the main substantive reasons for insourcing; their criticism focuses on the threat to the subsidiarity principle and a demand for transparency in assessing effectiveness (Hoffmann 2014). This may be because insourcing affects "activation and placement" schemes, which are a fairly recent invention and are tainted with "pushing" and "policing" and outside of the historic competency of most providers (which are training and make-work schemes). On the question of insourcing, Germany and Denmark differ sharply from Great Britain. In the former, some localities have shifted employment services work back into the public sector, partly in response to bad quality by external providers and partly in order to retain skilled staff. This has generally taken place as a creeping process and not as a centralized strategic decision, although in Germany it reflects a general negative view of providers expressed by policymakers we interviewed. In Great Britain, by contrast, there has been a clear choice against building up internal state capacity to deliver, or even to purchase, employment services that has accompanied the centralization of the market.

Some important questions about insourcing remain unanswered. First, our Danish respondents raise the difficulty of building in-house capacity. How can this take place given finite funding and the cost of hiring skilled staff? Second, our German respondents point out that it exacerbates the resource squeeze facing external providers. Is there a tradeoff between insourcing and maintaining the capacity of neighborhood-based non-profits whose role was previously justified by the subsidiarity principle? Finally, while it is clear that marketization does not deliver on its promises, and that public authorities have some legitimate reasons for insourcing, it is not clear that insourcing will produce better services. Will these services be susceptible to the old accusation of hierarchical services, i.e. that they are insufficiently focused on outcomes and cost savings, unable to innovate, unresponsive to users, and therefore represent poor value for money? We doubt that the answer is so straightforward; it is a matter for future research.

Marketization as a Governance Problem

The chapter has shown how in all three countries market mechanisms were introduced and led to a range of problems. Denmark responded to the problems of centrally enforced competition through municipalization, allowing a general shrinkage of the market and expansion of insourcing and network governance. Germany has responded to its problems through increasingly tight centralized control by the public authority, which it has extended as much as possible to voucher arrangements. Britain responded to its problems through centralization and then handing control over provision to for-profit firms.

Differences in market organization had consequences for the policy principles governing the services. In Denmark marketization was shaped by municipalization and Danish municipalities varied. In municipalities where local government preferred working in partnership with providers, market governance was augmented by network governance. Tough competition has thus been a tool of top-down management by the BA, and market governance has been mixed with procedural governance. Britain was steadfast in its use of privatized market governance with a surprisingly weak element of market discipline over providers.

How does intensified competition at the level of the transactions shape overall governance principles in employment services?

Marketization does not produce a stable form of market governance, in part because it does not deliver on its promises. In this chapter we have attempted to explain why it is not a panacea: namely, marketization generates dilemmas. Reducing prices has consequences for quality; payment by results has consequences for equality; user choice is limited by the compulsory nature of the services; and openness and transparency increase costs. In Denmark this had the effect of very dramatic changes to the market over the period in study, while Germany and Britain have had more incremental change since the market was established in its present form. While it may be argued that governments are on a learning curve and eventually will learn to resolve these dilemmas, in our countries policymakers have been grappling with them for 10–15 years.

In each case, we documented policymakers' attempts to mitigate the problem. One approach was to reduce marketization, e.g. addressing creaming and parking by reducing PbR, as is common in Germany and Denmark. Another was to choose one of the undesirable options, e.g. accepting a lack of customer choice as in Denmark and Britain. A third was to sidestep the problem and create a new one, e.g. addressing the price-quality dilemma through PbR, which just created a different quality problem, as in Britain.

Network governance sits uneasily with marketization, since competition undermines the foundation of local networks, including trust, flexibility, and reliable funding, as we saw in some German cases. Marketization is also part of the defunding of the agencies and providers that animated past network governance, as in Germany and Britain. Finally, network governance may be a favored alternative to market governance where municipalities are leading, as in Denmark, possibly because local politicians and administrators are more likely to be part of the network of providers than their national counterparts are.

Procedural governance has shortcomings that were supposed to be addressed by marketization, including innovation, responsiveness, and cost.

But marketization can also have serious drawbacks on these dimensions. Procedural governance may be the favored alternative to market governance when central agencies are empowered in managing the market, as in Germany. The German landscape is extremely diverse, so generalizations have to be qualified. But the expanding role of the REZ, the intensified control over prices and provider quality in the voucher schemes, and the insourcing of contracted-out placement services by job centers may mark the rise of a hybrid of market and procedural governance, where competition is used as a tool of top-down management by a public agency.

We do not know how policymakers will respond to the problems above. In Britain there is a strong political consensus behind the fundamental principles of the market, but there are serious problems with the services that are unlikely to be resolved using intensified competition. The power and influence of providers in itself could prevent that. If the German and Danish case studies are any indication, reversals of marketization are led at the local level but take new hybrid forms in which elements of procedural and network governance are added to the market. Marketization apparently leads to combinations of policy principles and tools associated with market, network, and hierarchy.

Conclusion

In this chapter we have discussed dilemmas and tradeoffs resulting from marketization. Our intention is to move beyond the polarized discussion of the potential powers of the market versus the empirical weaknesses of marketization to deliver on promises. The purpose is not to balance criticism with affirmation, but rather to add to what has already been found out in what is a rather large literature.

First, we show here what marketization does. We are not centrally focused on the potential promise of marketization; in our view it is time for an assessment based on the facts, including unintended consequences usually ignored by evaluation studies. Nor do we want merely to repeat what many critics and many evaluation studies have found—that marketization does not live up to its promises. Instead we want to unpack what the consequences are, with a focus on the specifics of what marketization entails for governance (the interaction of funders and providers), and workplaces (where clients and staff interact). We point to a range of unintended consequences and a number of thorny dilemmas, in all three countries.

Second, we show that from the point of view of the management—whether in the funders or the providers—there are problems with marketization. We hear from funders that the services have in the past not performed well

161

enough, and this has led not only to the creation of markets but also to their stepwise modification. In Britain they responded by creating contracting arrangements that gave for-profit providers stronger incentives and greater flexibility to produce large numbers of job outcomes. In Germany they responded by tightening regulation in various ways to keep costs under control and assure the quality of services and in some cases the quantity of job outcomes. In Denmark responses to quality problems changed from tight central regulation of the market in the second wave of marketization to the subsequent delegation of decision making to municipalities, who took varying paths to address past problems. In each case problems remain: most notably creaming and parking in Britain, the squeezing of provider capacities to innovate in Germany, and the difficulty of monitoring the decentralized market in Denmark. Marketization of employment services may lead to injustices, but it is also of limited utility to those whose job it is to make it work.

Many examples can be found of funders reducing the amount of competition and even taking services out of the market. Danish and German municipalities insource certain services where they think they can create in-house capacities stronger than those of external providers. German municipalities continue to favor hand-picked procurement over competitive tendering for certain complex services, despite the rise of the REZ, and even under competitive tendering regulation and prescription by the funder remains tight. Some Danish municipalities responded to the end of the requirement to use competitive tendering by switching to a more partnership-based form of contracting. Even Britain, where there is an ideological attachment to the market as the solution to problems that cannot be addressed effectively by in-house public provision, reduced the degree of marketization by creating longer contracts, reducing prescriptions, and allowing the market to concentrate. This in response to the commercial concerns of the prime contractors, on whom this structure makes the government increasingly dependent.

7

Conclusion

In the past, many training, counseling, and job-placement schemes for the unemployed were delegated by governments to the social institutions or movements present where the needy clientele was. Churches, trade unions, employers, municipalities, and the non-profits that emerged out of the so-called new social movements carried out services funded through grants to carry out a task. Part of this task was carried out in-house by a public employment service in connection with its job placement and often benefits-payment functions. Funding was not marketized and provision not commercialized.

Beginning in the 1990s these services became infused with market principles. Rather than paying providers via grants to carry out some mission or legal obligation, funders increasingly used purchasing and voucher arrangements to pay for particular services or job outcomes. This meant that prices became more important, services more clearly defined and measured, funding decisions less certain, and competition increasingly open to for-profit firms. The assumption was that market competition would produce more responsive, innovative, and high-performing services at a lower price.

The market did not deliver on this promise. This point is hardly original and is borne out by the international evaluation evidence on the performance effects of privatization and contracting out, which shows that these effects are overdetermined by other features of program design and resourcing (Krug and Stephan 2016). The effects of activation schemes overall are, to some of their leading advocates, disappointingly small (e.g. Schmid 2008), and they are contingent on a list of program design, labor market, and client characteristics (Card et al. 2015). A critical literature shows that marketization and privatization diffuses between countries more due to a mixture of political, administrative, and ideological factors than due to any evidence of effectiveness (Peck 2001; Davies 2008). Much of this literature unpicks particular difficulties in employment-services markets such as payment by results (Rees et al. 2014) and the weighting of price and quality in competitive tendering (Ferber 2015).

In this book we argue that these failures are due in large part to the effects of funding practices that constitute the market on both managers and workers in the organizations that are supposed to be activating the unemployed. This concluding chapter summarizes our findings about the specific practices of market making at the level of the transaction and their consequences within organizations and for governance overall in the three countries. Then we discuss some questions raised about employment services that cannot be adequately addressed in this book, either because they are outside the scope of the study or because they concern future developments (at least from the perspective of the interviewees we met in 2011–14). We conclude with lessons for the changing role of markets in Europe more generally.

How Marketization Has Reshaped Employment Services

Through chapters above we develop an argument about how marketization affects services, starting with criteria for distinguishing marketized transactions from non-marketized ones. In employment services marketization presupposes an organizational divide between purchaser and provider. Under marketization grant making—either one-off project grants or ongoing annual grants—gives way to one of two alternative transaction modes. One is public purchasing, in which the public authority retains control over much of the process, but is also constrained by procurement law. The other is vouchers, in which the authority to select providers is handed in principle to the voucher-holding client or "customer." In Chapter 3 we discuss the specific features of transactions in our sample.

We find that vouchers and public purchasing both vary and change in terms of the degree of marketization. Both can be opened to new market players, or restricted by accreditation or pre-qualification. Both can structure transactions as more or less frequent, although this is easier to control under public purchasing using contract length and extension provisions than it is under vouchers. Prices can be made more or less important in the selection of providers and can be squeezed through competition, legislation, or administrative fiat. And the services can be defined in a way that is more or less prescribed and standardized, and therefore commoditized and conducive to market exchange.

In combination, these features of transactions determine the extent to which the market generates resource scarcity and uncertainty for providers. A market that has been opened is inherently more uncertain than one that remains closed; and more frequent transactions create greater uncertainty than infrequent transactions. Prices that float according to supply and demand create uncertainty. In the competitive markets we are looking at they produce a resource squeeze; but fixed prices can have the same effect if they are kept low. The prescription of services also intensifies uncertainty (because it facilitates price-based competition) and the squeeze on resources (because it leads to more monitoring, which is time consuming for staff in providers).

Transactions matter for a second reason as well: as we show in Chapter 4, they redistribute power. The Danish case shows that fluctuation in all of these variables, as well as the overall volume of work, is a recipe for a relatively weak sector with little lobbying power. The German case shows that tight prescription and small contracts can also lead to a weak sector, fragmented by kind of work, region, and political orientation. The British case shows that it is possible to empower providers, even under conditions of a price squeeze, by prescribing the work only very loosely, designing contracts with an eye to the long-term commercial considerations of bidders, and creating a dualized contracting structure in which "prime contractors" can shift risks further onto "subcontractors." This approach empowers prime contractors vis-à-vis both the funder and their subcontractors, i.e. hundreds of mostly specialized and local incumbent providers that existed prior to this market structure.

Commercial providers respond to constraints and opportunities of the market by extending top-down managerial control into the labor process, as we show in Chapter 5. It is in for-profit providers and non-profits that mimic their practices that we observe tight performance management, the devaluing of professions, and changes to staff–client interactions including speeding up, a focus on work activities, and creaming and parking. While such organizations exist in all three of our countries, we observe variation. While commercial providers dominate the British and Danish landscape, they are present to a much more limited extent in Germany; and in all three countries non-commercial employment-services providers were still in existence.

The trend towards management control in the labor process has been accompanied in Germany and Britain by the disorganization of employment-relations institutions. This means a weakening of worker voice mechanisms and the emergence of providers with no collective worker voice at all. It also means the spread of individualized pay, both in the form of downward deviations from collective agreements to reduce costs and upward deviations in order to improve incentives. Third, we see in all three countries job insecurity, which can be purely due to the coming and going of contracts, but in some establishments in Germany and Britain as part of punitive low-road human-resource practices. While these trends are not universal, they do emerge very clearly from interviews as key adaptations made by non-profits to market pressures and/or features of emerging commercial providers.

These changes in markets and organizations create dilemmas, discussed in Chapter 6. The first is that, while policymakers would like both low cost and high quality, squeezing prices invariably leads to fewer or less qualified staff, and using clearly defined descriptions of work to ensure quality tends to sap the capacities of providers to innovate. Second, while funders would like to strengthen incentives for performance by paying for job outcomes (i.e. not for ineffective services), this payment by results can lead to neglect of the neediest clients. This is especially problematic in the Work Programme with its diverse clientele, commercial providers, and loose regulation of providers by the funder. Third, while the doctrines of public management favor client choice, the reality is that for work-first welfare policies compulsion is a substantive element, with clear implications for implementation. Even in Germany where vouchers have been rolled out on a large scale, job-center and BA workers have to advise clients to find services, even if it distorts the consumer market. Fourth, the norms of transparency, openness, and equal treatment found in procurement law tend to clash with the prerogative to reduce transaction costs. Tight competition requires tight regulation, which comes out most clearly in the in-house purchasing function of the BA. Insourcing of external-ized services, which we observe in both Germany and Denmark, is one way out of these dilemmas, even if it may not be a panacea.

What Is New Here?

In order to arrive at the above conclusions, we had to deal with three difficult problems faced by comparative studies of marketization generally. This book contributes a definition of marketization, a specification of its effects, and a mapping of the phenomenon comparatively as a way through these problems.

The Meaning of Marketization

While it is common in the literature to use this term without a formal defin-ition, the meaning is not self-evident. Marketization has been defined as an overall logic of "governance" (e.g. Jantz et al. 2015), a change in public-sector or non-profit organizations to be more like private-sector ones (see Hermann and Flecker 2012, and Eikenberry and Kluver 2004, respectively), the simula-tion of competition by management within a firm or workplace (Brinkmann 2011), a list of changes specific to the particular context being studied (as in most employment-relations studies), or a synonym for privatization, neo-liberalism, deregulation, liberalization, and/or capitalism.

Without a common definition of marketization the literature is confined to either denouncing the neoliberal restructuring of services in general or dis-cussing particular cases of it empirically in isolation. The problem is that it is difficult to draw lessons from one context to apply to others. Our solution focuses on the features of the transaction between funder and provider, because relations with the funder were of central importance in interviews, because this focus on the transaction is a well-trodden theoretical path in institutional economics, and because these same dimensions matter in other industrial sectors and areas of welfare provision.

Defining marketization and its dimensions allows us to identify three different transaction modes: grants, purchasing, and vouchers. Grants place strict limits on the degree of competition, since the work cannot be prescribed, prices have to be calculated based on costs, and a priori quality assessments necessarily include the reputation of the provider and require trust between funder and provider. While grant making can be used to invite newcomers, the importance of trust generally favors incumbents.

Under vouchers and purchasing, by contrast, it is relatively straightforward to organize price- or cost-based competition. Purchasing and voucher markets tend to be more open than grant markets, since any provider can participate, subject to administrative requirements such as accreditation. Purchasing and voucher markets also create additional opportunities for squeezing prices, standardizing services, and exiting the funder–provider relationship after a particular exchange. In purchasing this happens through the public authority's own decision making in the selection of providers and the necessarily time-bounded nature of contracts. In vouchers it happens through its specification of the services in the voucher, the regulation of how the client exercises his or her decision-making power as a consumer of services, and the ongoing nature of competition.

Our specification of marketization allows us to show how purchasing and vouchers can be modified to create more or less competition. These markets can be opened or closed using changes to pre-qualification, licensing, and accreditation or by advertising the services or calls for tender more widely using online platforms. Prices can be made more or less important by squeezing them (through competition, legislation, or administrative fiat) or by increasing their weight in selection of the provider (in our sample this is only possible with purchasing). The services they entail can be standardized or customized through the description of work on the voucher or in the tendering documents and by creating spaces for partnership between purchaser and provider. The time horizon and level of uncertainty can be altered by changing the frequency of the transaction, i.e. by lengthening or shortening contracts or the length of the service.

The Effects of Marketization on Services

For policymakers an important question is: what are the effects of marketization on clients? The evaluation literature uses quantitative techniques to assess program effects in terms of the intended outcomes. Sometimes the change of interest is whether the provider is in-house or external. What is the probability of the client being in work, having more income, and receiving fewer benefits under marketized as opposed to non-marketized provision? The critical literature questions the basic assumptions of policymakers, focuses on problems identified in marketized or privatized services, and uses qualitative techniques to assess them in terms of what kind of services the client is receiving and how this changes their entitlements as citizens. These literatures provide little reason to think that marketization will produce major improvements in services.

Nevertheless, it was apparent from the beginning of our field research that marketization was having an effect in the day-to-day work of our interviewees. We asked managers and front-line workers about their work and how it was shaped by the funding arrangements (i.e. the organization of the transaction by the funder). We looked at the complex processes that our interviewees described within the provider organizations. Of particular interest to us were (1) differences between marketized and (formerly) non-marketized kinds of work and (2) policy dilemmas created that affected the evolution of the way services were governed.

Services that had grown up under marketized transactions differed in numerous ways from those under less market pressure, or where marketization was a recent introduction. In Britain, Germany, and Denmark we saw examples of for-profit companies with tight management control over staff, and in Britain and Germany they lacked trade unions and collective bargaining. These kinds of providers grew up under market changes aimed at re-engineering services—the predecessors of Britain's Work Programme, Germany's placement vouchers, and the national tendering system in Denmark—and in Britain and Denmark they gained a dominant position in the market. These providers had severe quality problems: creaming and parking in Britain, cherry picking in Germany, and an overall problem of standardization and lack of innovation.

However in some ways older forms of provision remained resilient in the face of marketization. In Britain some of the municipal and non-profit providers retained their basic ethos, in some cases because they had core funding and were not dependent exclusively on the Work Programme market. In Germany many of the non-profit providers contracting with the BA retained their past social-work-oriented approach in the face of a price squeeze, partly because of requirements by the funder to employ certain numbers of qualified staff with a clear professional profile. In Denmark, trade union providers had lost market share; but for-profit and non-profit providers alike were increasing the degree of professionalization in response to an increase in less-marketized partnership contracting arrangements.

These changes in markets and organizations posed dilemmas for policymakers. The funder had the power to alter the transaction to extract low prices, but this could lead to quality problems because of its consequences for staffing and planning of services. There were also payment-by-results schemes, but this could lead to creaming and parking because of the risks this entailed and the way that organizations—especially commercial ones—calculated and avoided it. Funders could reduce transaction costs, but not without sacrificing principles of transparency and equal treatment, as in Britain's "Black Box." Key decisions could be shifted to the clientele using vouchers, but not without watering down the compulsion built into the work-first welfare state or the free-market logic of voucher schemes.

After the market structure had been created, funders typically responded to these problems through a step-wise reduction in the degree of marketization. One example of this, common to all three countries, was lengthening contracts: by reducing the number of tendering exercises, the funder can reduce transaction costs and make it more straightforward to private-sector investors to plan and make a return. In Denmark municipalization led to the replacement of competitive tendering in many municipalities with less prescriptive and less competitive partnership contracting. In Germany and Denmark, furthermore, some municipalities took services out of the market altogether through insourcing.

Similarities and Differences between the Three Countries

Denmark, Great Britain, and Germany represent, according to the dominant theories of comparative social science, three very different "worlds" of capitalism and welfare provision. Fundamental to welfare regimes and varieties of capitalism theories is the assumption that markets work differently in these three kinds of societies. Great Britain is more market-driven, and Denmark and Germany for different reasons and in different ways restrain market competition. How, then, can market logic be introduced in this area in all three of the countries? Does the label "marketization" deceptively suggest similarities between what are, fundamentally, different worlds?

This is a real challenge, since the tradition of comparative research points to differences that are present in our data. Social-democratic Denmark, for example, has much more government spending per client than the other two countries and a much more active state—at both local and national levels—in altering the parameters of the market. Conservative Germany still has a strong insurance principle for the short-term unemployed and extensive provision by the churches, municipalities, and non-profits in services for jobless people deemed to be further from the labor market. Liberal Britain has empowered private providers far more and allowed both spending and the level of service to drop under a payment-by-results system. The continued power of Danish government, German social insurance, and British private sectors would suggest that there is no convergence on a single deregulated liberal model.

To leave it at this, however, would ignore some puzzling but important features of the cases. Why did providers affiliated with Danish unions exit the market, and why is the Danish trajectory so volatile? Why has Germany replaced the subsidiarity logic of funding with a commercial logic of purchasing and vouchers, and why are German employment-services markets so varied? Why did the British market structure emerge last and create a relatively centralized, concentrated, and non-competitive market? In addition to failing to explain some between-country differences, the standard toolbox of comparative social science leaves open the question of within-country differences. Why are there different commercial and non-commercial models co-existing within each country, how do they differ, and is one replacing the other?

It is not possible to answer these questions in employment services without understanding government funding practices. As we showed in Chapter 2, the structure of the state—in particular the centralization of power and authority—matters a great deal. Both the task and the organization of the transaction are shaped by a division of labor between central and other levels of government. The division of task into market segments with different kinds of transactions leads to different constraints for management and workers, which vary by market segment.

Denmark stands out for the volatility of the rules of the market, its players, and its size; this reflects the pro-market ideology built into NPM ideas in the first two waves of marketization followed by a loss of faith in the market at the national level and a broader trend towards municipal control of services in the third wave. One consequence is that, at the time of our study, some municipalities were insourcing services or switching to partnership contracting due to concerns over poor quality, while others continued past practices of competitive tendering. Another consequence was reportedly widespread job insecurity; worker pay was stabilized by high union membership, a lack of a reported price squeeze from the funder, and pressure providers—especially commercial ones—to attract the best employees for particular contracts.

Germany stands out for the fragmentation of the market and the diversity of transactions. While the Hartz reforms centralized the relevant part of the market in some ways by creating a common apparatus for purchasing services and a common set of voucher arrangements, authority concerning how to use these instruments remained in the hands of local managers. This reflected the decentralized landscape of the German state—strong state and local government and self-administration in social insurance—but in the wake of the reforms, diversity in transactions increased, since the BA produced three very different modes of transaction. Voucher markets were highly volatile, leading to precarious employment; grants had been a source of stability for non-profits until the volume of work they funded was sharply reduced; and purchasing overall had the effect of squeezing the resources of providers to such a great extent that there was a major discussion of the devaluing of professions in employment services and a statutory minimum wage was established for training providers.

Britain stands out for the centralization of the market, the dualized structure of the sector, and control by the private sector. The Work Programme was the result of a decade of experimentation with privatized welfare-to-work schemes as well as a radical approach to using for-profit providers. It could only be rolled out across all of Great Britain because the state was highly centralized, and its effects on incumbent providers were extreme because numerous regional and local funders were abolished or had their funding reduced. The core of the sector, the "prime contractors," turned out not to be very volatile and these providers did develop new models of commercial provision with tight methods of management control. The periphery of the sector was much more volatile, with providers—many of them unionized local government agencies and voluntary-sector bodies—coming and going in accordance with the supply-chain management practices of the prime contractors.

Future Directions in Employment Services

There are a few questions about employment services that we could not adequately address in this book. Some concern the marketization phenomenon in employment services as it has played out historically, others to ongoing processes that were too recent for us to assess.

The first is how the outcomes of services were changed due to marketization. The evaluation literature has not pinpointed marketization as a cause of relative success or failure. Instead, studies typically compare private with public providers. Such studies may reveal the effects of differing ownership but do not tell us about the effects of the actions of public authorities in organizing transactions. We have shown that external providers behave differently depending on the funding arrangements, and changing the transaction mode or other parameters is probably much easier for public authorities than privatization or insourcing.

In response to the question of whether marketization was positive or negative for the performance of services we posed dilemmas. But are they thornier under conditions of marketization than under traditional networks or public-sector service provision? In Denmark and Germany this question could be answered through further research that takes advantage of the wide within-country diversity in funding practices and resulting availability of comparators.

A second question concerns the effects of choices relating to the specific dilemmas. Is there, for example, some optimal balance of price and quality?

Would some compulsory services (using purchasing) perform better with greater customer choice (using vouchers)? What is the payoff of creating a strong in-house procurement function like the REZ, as opposed to outsourcing it to primes? Creaming and parking may violate principles of equal treatment and targeted interventions on disadvantaged clients, but how damaging is this really to different groups of clients' employment chances?

The third question is why marketization is observed less in some countries and more in others. We have left unexplained the puzzling fact that marketization began in the Netherlands and Australia and was rolled out later, and to a more limited extent in terms of the share of employment-services work, in Germany, Denmark, and Britain. We have also deliberately excluded countries where marketization has experienced severe setbacks or simply not taken place.

One starting point suggested by work on France is that marketization initiated at a central level can be frustrated by strong networks of providers, funders, and policymakers at the local level (Schulte et al. 2016). But religious traditions may also matter (none of the countries subject to marketized employment services are Catholic-dominant), as may the level of development and coverage of the welfare state (fiscal and political pressures that build up over time may be conducive to marketization).

A fourth question is how citizens effectively resist marketization and prevent it from taking place. Resistance could come from trade unionists or claimant organizers representing potential "losers" of the process, but it could also come from policymakers, managers, and front-line workers who see it as wasteful and ineffective.

The issue of resistance has not been at the center of our analysis, but we do find examples of it. In Denmark, for example, trade union campaigners were deeply involved in efforts to expose the flaws of the market and effective in accelerating the loss of faith in the market at the national level. In Britain, disability campaigners and claimants groups have been highly effective in disrupting particular contracts, including the Work Capability Assessment carried out by Atos Healthcare (leading to the contract collapsing) and Mandatory Work Activity (which may be responsible for the scheme remaining relatively small).

Comparative qualitative research on examples of resistance could answer a number of questions. Under what conditions do trade unionists and service users campaign against marketization or privatization, to what extent do they succeed in working together, and when do they succeed in their aims or disrupting the market? How does this differ between countries? And how do different parts of the welfare state in the same country—e.g. those only serving jobseekers as opposed to those like healthcare that serve the entire population—differ from one another?

A fifth question concerns the relationship between austerity and marketization. The overall trend in spending on active labor-market services has been downward in these countries, and the effect has been that providers are competing for increasingly scarce resources. From the perspective of purchasers this has the advantage that the markets are relatively competitive, even if they have difficulty attracting outside players and are working mainly with incumbents (as is the case in Germany and Denmark). But austerity may not always be conducive to marketization. It could be, as with the National Health Service in England, that the squeezing of prices and the increase in uncertainty stunts the development of the market by discouraging private investors (Krachler and Greer 2015). Future research could look at the conditions under which austerity contributes to, or frustrates, market competition in employment services.

A sixth question concerns the reversal of marketization due to the internal dynamics of the market. There are several reasons to believe in general that markets in contracted-out public services are uncompetitive (Van Slyke 2003). One is the tendency of markets to concentrate and for governments to become dependent on a small number of providers. While this has happened in Britain, market concentration is not possible at a national level in the more fragmented German and Danish markets. It is unclear whether German and Danish funders would allow concentration even if they could, since the supposed improvements in price and quality produced by markets arise from competition.

What are the conditions under which governments allow these markets to become more or less competitive? Are German funders more consequent in their promotion of competition than their British counterparts, and if so, why? Will British practice gravitate towards less competition with Brexit and the declining influence of EU market-making public procurement rules?

A seventh question concerns why insourcing takes place. It is tempting to see it as part of a learning process in which public managers learn from their failures in realizing value in contracting (Warner 2008) or the result of a Polanyian counter-movement in which societies push back against market forces (Warner and Clifton 2014). There are several alternative explanations, as well. One is that privatization can lead to the destruction of in-house capacities thus making insourcing unlikely due to lock-in effects, and that insourcing is more likely where privatization was more recent or where the work being privatized is similar to other work being done in-house. Another is that there are administrative reasons for insourcing, such as the need to hoard labor in-house, especially if—as in Germany—layoffs are made expensive by civil-service rules, employment-protection legislation, or collective agreements. A third is the degree of centralization: the search for public value may be more pronounced in municipalized services than those under strong central control. As we show in this book, the degree of local control varies between countries and can change over time.

A final question concerns what happens after insourcing takes place. Mainstream policy discourse would see it as a return to the bad old days of unresponsive services in the hands of public-sector bureaucrats. A different starting point would be that "there is a rebalancing of government reform that capitalizes on the efficiency of markets, the technical expertise of planning, and the social choice of democracy without the problems of accountability and decision cycling that occur under any of these strands alone" (Warner 2008: 164). This would suggest that the new services created in-house are fundamentally different because they simultaneously draw on the advantages of local networks, central administrative control by the state, and market competition. But alternatively, the new governance mix may be afflicted by the disadvantages of various approaches, for example combining the murkiness of network governance with the perverse incentives of market governance.

Newly municipalized and renationalized employment services have yet to be studied in any depth. Are these best conceptualized as hybrids or as new models with their own logic distinct from previous models? Is this a benign balancing act reflecting the virtues of deliberation and democracy, or a political and administrative trajectory that leads to the worst of many worlds?

Broader Lessons on the Changing Role of Markets in Europe

In this book we have attempted to provide a vocabulary for discussing marketization that can be used in the comparative social sciences, especially in applied fields where the central focus is on learning from the mistakes and good practices of other countries. But to what extent can lessons be drawn from employment services in our three countries? In this section we discuss how employment services compare with other economic sectors in terms of marketization and how our concepts can serve as a starting point for research more broadly.

Employment services are in some ways not unusual sectors of economic activity. Our three transaction modes account for a high percentage of externalized public services and a substantial share of economic activity overall. Public purchasing accounts for 14 percent of the GDP of the European Union, according to the European Commission.[1] Additional services are purchased by grants, vouchers, or voucher-like funding arrangements such as social-insurance reimbursements for health services. Many services are funded by some mixture of transaction modes. A hospital, for example, may receive a grant to pay for investment, while working under contract with a public

[1] https://ec.europa.eu/growth/single-market/public-procurement/strategy_en, accessed September 28, 2016.

funder, and claiming back reimbursements for treatments (using a similar logic to vouchers). We can therefore expect marketized employment services to have lessons for other kinds of government-funded services.

But these three modes do not exhaust the possible variation in interorganizational transactions in services. One obvious difference is that we are examining the "quasi-markets" of public purchasers and not markets created by private actors. While Williamson (1999) draws on economic theory to argue that the former are less efficient than the latter, the difference between the two is not well understood empirically. Our material suggests that, far more than their private-sector counterparts, public purchasers are expected to make decisions that they can legitimize in terms of equal treatment and transparency. In such a case, the legitimacy of a decision may have a higher priority than the rationality of its outcome. Public purchasers can, however, evade these principles somewhat through private-sector-managed supply chains (as with the Work Programme), opting out from EU procurement law (as with Denmark), or delegating the decision to clients (as with German vouchers).

Furthermore, we are dealing with external services and therefore the simulation of markets between organizations. Our transaction modes therefore exclude the simulation of markets within organizations such as competitive arrangements to distribute investment to locations within private multinational firms, "purchaser-provider splits" within Britain's National Health Service, or seemingly market-like NPM methods within public employment services. Again, while there are theoretical reasons why transactions in an internal market may differ from those in an external one, there is little empirical evidence on what they are.

Nevertheless, much of our analytical framework, beyond the transaction modes, can apply to other sectors. The four dimensions we use to define marketization also matter in other sectors (Greer and Doellgast forthcoming). Openness is an obvious example, given the globalization of product markets and the creation of a single European market for goods, services, capital, and labor.

The other three dimensions, though less researched, seem equally relevant to understanding the transformative power of markets. In British social care, for example, the increasing frequency of transactions between municipalities and providers has led to the rise of zero-hours contracts and unpaid overtime (Bessa et al. 2013; Rubery et al. 2015). In Canadian social services the spread of quantitative indicators of service quality has led to work intensification and deskilling (Baines 2004). In German health care the increasing transparency of prices brought about by standardized rates for diagnoses has led to a wave of cost cutting and privatizations of entire hospital systems (Greer et al. 2013).

The four governance dilemmas may be more acute in employment services than in other kinds of marketized work, but this deserves future research. The tradeoff between cost and quality in employment services is due in part to the labor and skill intensity of the service. The problem of transaction costs is closely related not only to the complexity of the task but also to the degree to which the state regulates its own activities including its simulation of fair and transparent markets. The creaming and parking issue presupposes a quantitatively measurable outcome that can be rewarded. The choice between consumerism and compulsion may be decided differently in a service that is not primarily for low-income working-class individuals.

What is the future of marketization in Europe? Are we studying a phenomenon that has reached its limit?

We find that marketization at the level of the transaction is reversible. This can happen for many reasons: marketization fails to deliver on its promises, it creates political opposition or unruly social movements, or it generates undesirable side effects such as creaming and parking. It can happen in diverse ways. The funder might reverse it in an incremental way by merely changing the workings of the transaction or imposing some other form of regulation like a statutory minimum wage. Or it can take the services out of the market through insourcing.

But our findings give little ground for the faith that the marketization trend is over. The bulk of employment services in these three countries are still delivered in-house. There is thus further scope for increasing the element of marketization in the governance mix of these services, including expanding the share of services that can be marketized and increasing competition for those services that are external.

Marketization, in addition, has its own normative logic that is yet to be defeated. Billions of pounds, kronor, euros, and dollars are spent annually on public services to deal with difficult or intractable social problems. Because services do not usually eliminate the problem they are supposed to address, funders are pressed to justify the spending. It is difficult to argue against the propositions that competition should be fair and transparent and that services should be held to account in terms of their performance. Indeed, providers' criticisms of the market tend to reflect, rather than reject, these ideas. Market principles will probably endure for some time into the future as an ingredient in the organization of publicly funded services.

European societies and their elites may experience a sudden loss in their faith in the market; this could happen due to the next economic crisis, the continued rise of populist political parties, or the decline of US and British influence in the wake of Brexit. If this happens there will be many ways in which they will be able to reduce the role of price-based competition, of which financing employment services will be only one. But it remains to be seen when this will happen, who will bring it about, and what comes next.

Bibliography

Arbejdsmarkedsstyrelsen (AMS). (2004). *Erfaringsopsamling vedrørende inddragelsen af andre aktører i beskæftigelsesindsatsen.* Copenhagen: Rambøll Management.

Arbejdsmarkedsstyrelsen (AMS). (2009). *Evaluering af brugen af anden aktør under Service- og LVU-udbuddene.* Copenhagen: Deloitte.

Baadsgaard, K., Henning, J., Iben, N., and Søren, P. O. (2014). *Jobcentre og klemte kvalifikationer.* Aalborg: Aalborg Universitetsforslag.

Baccaro, L. and Howell, C. (2011). A common neoliberal trajectory: The transformation of industrial relations in advanced capitalism. *Politics and Society,* 39, 521–63.

Bach, S. and Bordogna, L. (2011). Varieties of new public management or alternative models? The reform of public service employment relations in industrialized democracies. *International Journal of Human Resource Management,* 22(11), 2281–94.

Baines, D. (2004). Pro-market, non-market: The dual nature of organizational change in social services delivery. *Critical Social Policy,* 24(1), 5–29.

Barbier, J.-C. and Knuth, M. (2011). Activating social protection against unemployment: France and Germany compared. *Sozialer Fortschritt* 60(1–2), 15–24.

Barton-Ziemann, M. (2012). *Umsetzung der Instrumentenreform. Kostenzustimmung der BA bei FbW und andere Änderungen.* Presentation at the BBB-Fachgespräch, February 14, Nuremburg, <http://www.bildungsverband.info/de/system/files/dateien/fachg-barton-ziemann.ppt>.

Batt, R., Doellgast, V., Kwon, H., and Agrawal, V. (2005). Service management and employment systems in US and Indian call centers (with comment and discussion). In *Brookings Trade Forum* (pp. 335–72). Washington, DC: Brookings Institution Press.

Bechter, B., Brandl, B., and Meardi, G. (2012). Sectors or countries? Typologies and levels of analysis in comparative industrial relations. *European Journal of Industrial Relations,* 18(3), 185–202.

Benassi, C. and Dorigatti, L. (2014). Straight to the core—explaining union responses to the casualization of work: The IG Metall campaign for agency workers. *British Journal of Industrial Relations,* 53(3), 533–55.

Berger, S. and Piore, M. J. (1980). *Dualism and Discontinuity in Industrial Societies.* Cambridge: Cambridge University Press.

Bernhard, S. and Kruppe, T. (2010). *Vermittlungsgutscheine für Arbeitslose: Oft ausgegeben und selten eingelöst.* Nuremburg: IAB.

Bessa, I., Forde, C., Moore, S., and Stuart, M. (2013). *The National Minimum Wage, Earnings and Hours in the Domiciliary Care Sector.* London: University of Leeds and Low Pay Commission.

Bishop, V., Korczynski, M., and Cohen, L. (2005). The invisibility of violence constructing violence out of the job centre workplace in the UK. *Work, Employment and Society*, 19(3), 583–602.

Blank, F. and Schulz, S. (2015). *Soziale Sicherung unter dem Brennglas: Altersarmut und Alterssicherung bei Beschäftigten im deutschen Sozialsektor*. Bonn: FES.

Bode, I. (2003). Flexible response in changing environments: The German third sector model in transition. *Nonprofit and Voluntary Sector Quarterly*, 32(2), 190–210.

Boffey, D. and Helm, T. (2012). Welfare boss Emma Harrison made a pile renting out her stately home to A4E. *Guardian*, February 25.

Bredgaard, T. and Larsen, F. (2006). *Udlicitering af beskæftigelsespolitikken: Australien, Holland og Danmark—Markedets usynlige eller statens synlige hånd?* Copenhagen: Jurist og Økonomforbundets Forlag.

Bredgaard, T. and Larsen, F. (2007). Implementing public employment policy: What happens when non-public agencies take over? *International Journal of Sociology and Social Policy*, 27(7/8), 287–301.

Bredgaard, T. and Larsen, F. (2008). Quasi-markets in employment policy in Australia, the Netherlands and Denmark: Do they deliver on promises? *Social Policy and Society*, 7(3), 341–52.

Breidahl, K. N. and Larsen, F. (2015). The developing trajectory of the marketization of public employment services in Denmark. *European Policy Analysis*, February.

Breidahl, K. and Seemann, J. (2009). *Jobcenteret som organisatorisk fænomen*. Oslo: Frydenlund Academika.

Brinkmann, U. (2011). *Die unsichtbare Faust des Marktes: Betriebliche Kontrolle und Koordination im Finanzmarktkapitalismus*. Berlin: edition sigma.

Brinkmann, U. and Nachtwey, O. (2013). Postdemokratie, mitbestimmung und industrielle bürgerrechte. *Politische Vierteljahresschrift*, 54(3), 506–33.

Broberg, M. B. and Jensen, K. Ø. (2010). Legoklodser og fugle skal få ledige i job. *Jyllands-Posten*, October 25.

Brodkin, E. Z. and Marston, G. (eds). (2013). *Work and the Welfare State: Street-Level Organizations and Workfare Politics*. Washington, DC: Georgetown University Press.

Brown, W., Bryson, A., and Forth, J. (2008). *Competition and the Retreat from Collective Bargaining*. Cambridge: University of Cambridge.

Bundesagentur für Arbeit. (2012). *Kostenzustimmung der BA bei FbW*. Nuremburg: BA.

Bundesagentur für Arbeit. (2016). Pressemitteilung: Keine Vorgaben der BA zu den Mindestlohnbedingungen für Auftragsleistungen der BA. March 22.

Bundesagentur für Arbeit—Statistik. (2014a). *Eingliederungsbilanz nach § 11 SGB III*. Deutschland, Berichtsjahr 2013, Datenstand: März.

Bundesagentur für Arbeit—Statistik. (2014b). *Eingliederungsbilanz nach § 54 SGB II*. Deutschland—ohne Daten der zugelassenen kommunalen Träger. Berichtsjahr: 2013, Datenstand: März.

Bundesverband der Traeger Beruflicher Bildung. (2014). *Info-Brief*. February. <http://www.bildungsverband.info/de/system/files/dateien/bbb-info_02_2014.pdf>.

Card, D., Kluve, J., and Weber, A. (2015). *What Works? A Meta Analysis of Recent Active Labor Market Program Evaluations*. Washington, DC: National Bureau of Economic Research.

Carney, T. and Ramia, G. (2002). *From Rights to Management: Vol. 18: Contract, New Public Management and Employment Services*. Alphen aan den Rijn: Kluwer Law International.

Carter, B., Danford, A., Howcroft, D., Richardson, H., Smith, A., and Taylor, P. (2011). "All they lack is a chain": Lean and the new performance management in the British civil service. *New Technology, Work and Employment*, 26(2), 83–97.

Clarke, J. and Newman, J. (1997). *The Managerial State*. London: Sage.

Commons, J. (1909). American shoemakers, 1648–1895: A sketch of industrial evolution. *Quarterly Journal of Economics*, 39–84.

Considine, M. (2001). *Enterprising States: The Public Management of Welfare-to-Work*. Cambridge: Cambridge University Press.

Considine, M. and Lewis, J. M. (2003). Bureaucracy, network, or enterprise? Comparing models of governance in Australia, Britain, the Netherlands, and New Zealand. *Public Administration Review*, 63(2), 131–40.

Cooke, F. L., Earnshaw, J., Marchington, M., and Rubery, J. (2004). For better and for worse: Transfer of undertakings and the reshaping of employment relations. *International Journal of Human Resource Management*, 15(2), 276–94.

Crawford, E. and Perry, F. (2010). *Professionalising the Welfare to Work Industry: Developing a Framework for Action*. London: CESI.

Cunningham, I. and James, P. (eds). (2011). *Voluntary Organizations and Public Service Delivery*. London: Routledge.

Cunningham, I., Hearne, G., and James, P. (2013). Voluntary organisations and marketisation: A dynamic of employment degradation. *Industrial Relations Journal*, 44(2), 171–88.

Davies, S. (2008). Contracting out employment services to the third and private sectors: A critique. *Critical Social Policy*, 28(2), 136–64.

Deloitt (2009). Evaluering af brugen af anden aktør under Service- og LVU-udbuddene. Delrapport 2, supplerende dataanalyse-. Copenhagen: Deloitte.

Department for Work and Pensions (DWP). (2008). *Commissioning Strategy*. London: DWP.

Department for Work and Pensions (DWP). (2010a). Framework for the Provision of Employment Related Support Services: Specification of the Commercial Requirement. August.

Department for Work and Pensions (DWP). (2010b). The Work Programme Prospectus. November.

Dobischat, R., Fischell, M., and Rosendahl, A. (2009). *Beschäftigung in der Weiterbildung. Prekäre Beschäftigung als Ergebnis einer Polarisierung in der Weiterbildungsbranche?* Duisberg: Universität Duisburg-Essen.

Dobischat, R., Fischell, M., and Rosendahl, A. (2010). Professionalität bei prekärer Beschäftigung? Weiterbildung als Beruf im Spannungsfeld von professionellem Anspruch und Destabilisierungen im Erwerbsverlauf. In *Neue Lebenslaufregimes–neue Konzepte der Bildung Erwachsener?*, 163–81. Berlin: VS Verlag für Sozialwissenschaften.

Doellgast, V. (2012). *Disintegrating Democracy at Work*. Ithaca, NY: ILR Press.

Doellgast, V. and Greer, I. (2007). Vertical disintegration and the disorganization of German industrial relations. *British Journal of Industrial Relations*, 45, 55–76.

Doellgast, V., Batt, R., and Sørensen, O. H. (2009). Introduction: Institutional change and labour market segmentation in European call centres. *European Journal of Industrial Relations*, 15(4), 349–71.

Doerr, A. and Kruppe, T. (2014). Training vouchers, local employment agencies, and policy styles. *Journal for Labour Market Research*, 1–16.

Dörre, K., Scherschel, K., Booth, M., Marquardsen, K., Haubner, T., and Schierhorn, K. (2013). *Bewaehungsproben fuer die Unterschicht?* Frankfurt: Campus.

Dunlop, J. T. (1993). *Industrial Relations Systems*. Boston, MA: Harvard Business School.

Eikenberry, A. M. and Kluver, J. D. (2004). The marketization of the nonprofit sector: Civil society at risk? *Public Administration Review*, 64(2), 132–40.

Ellguth, P. and Kohaut, S. (2016). Tarifbindung und betriebliche Interessenvertretung: Ergebnisse aus dem IAB-Betriebspanel 2015. *WSI-Mitteilungen*, 4, 283–91.

Emmenegger, P., Häusermann, S., Palier, B., and Seeleib-Kaiser, M. (2012). How we grow unequal. In P. Emmenegger, S. Häusermann, B. Palier, and M. Seeleib-Kaiser (eds), *The Age of Dualization*, 3–26. Oxford: Oxford University Press.

Enggruber, R. and Mergner, U. (eds). (2007). *Lohndumping und neue Beschäftigungsbedingungen in der Sozialen Arbeit*. Berlin: Frank and Timme.

Entwistle, T., Bristow, G., Hines, F., Donaldson, S., and Martin, S. (2007). The dysfunctions of markets, hierarchies and networks in the meta-governance of partnership. *Urban Studies*, 44(1), 63–79.

Esbenshade, J., Vidal, M., Fascilla, G., and Ono, M. (2016). Customer-driven management models for choiceless clientele? Business process reengineering in a California welfare agency. *Work, Employment and Society*, 30(1), 77–96.

Esping-Andersen, G. (1990). *The Three Worlds of Welfare Capitalism*. Cambridge: Polity Press.

Estevez-Abe, M., Iversen, T., and Soskice, D. (2001). Social protection and the formation of skills: A reinterpretation of the welfare state. In P. Hall and D. Soskice (eds), *Varieties of Capitalism: The Institutional Foundations of Comparative Advantage*, 145. Oxford: Oxford University Press.

Felstead, A. (1995). The gender implications of creating a training market. In J. Rubery and J. Humphries (eds), *The Economics of Equal Opportunities*, 177–201. Manchester: Equal Opportunities Commission.

Ferber, T. (2015). *Bewertungskriterien und -matrizen im Vergabeverfahren. Wie erziele ich ein optimales Zuschlagsergebnis?* Köln: Bundesanzeiger Verlag.

Finn, D. (2015). *Welfare to Work Devolution in England*. York: Joseph Rowntree Foundation.

Foster, S., Riley, T., Foster, R., and Colechin, J. (2013). *Evaluation of the Institute of Employability Professionals Growth and Innovation Fund Project*. London: CESI.

Foster, S., Metcalf, H., Purvis, A., Lanceley, L., Foster, R., Lane, P., and Garlick, M. (2014). *Work Programme Evaluation: Operation of the Commissioning Model, Finance and Programme Delivery*. London: Department for Work and Pensions.

Freud, D. (2007). *Reducing Dependency, Increasing Opportunity: Options for the Future of Welfare to Work*. London: DWP.

Gautié, J. and Schmitt, J. (eds). (2010). *Low-Wage Work in the Wealthy World*. New York: Russell Sage Foundation.

Gershon, P. (2004). *Releasing Resources to the Front Line: Independent Review of Public Sector Efficiency*. London: HM Stationery Office.

Gingrich, J. (2011). *Making Markets in the Welfare State: The Politics of Varying Market Reforms*. Cambridge: Cambridge University Press.

Gold, M. and Veersma, U. (2011). Public sector reform and employment relations in Europe. In S. Corby and G. Symon (eds), *Working for the State*, 23–42. London: Palgrave Macmillan.

Grambow, T. (2013). Die betriebsverfassungsrechtliche Behandlung von Vereinen, Stiftungen und gGmbHs. *Zeitschrift für Stiftungs- und Vereinswesen*, 11(11), 161–200.

Greer, I. (2016). Welfare reform, precarity and the re-commodification of labour. *Work, Employment, and Society*, 30(1), 162–73.

Greer, I. and Doellgast, V. (forthcoming). Marketization, inequality, and institutional change. Toward a new framework for comparative employment relations. *Journal of Industrial Relations*.

Greer, I. and Hauptmeier, M. (2016). Management whipsawing: The staging of labor competition under globalization. *Industrial and Labor Relations Review*, August.

Greer, I., Greenwood, I., and Stuart, M. (2011). Beyond national "varieties": Public-service contracting in comparative perspective. In I. Cunningham and P. James (eds), *Voluntary Organizations and Public Sector Delivery*, 153–67. New York: Routledge.

Greer, I., Schulten, T., and Böhlke, N. (2013). How does market making affect industrial relations? Evidence from eight German hospitals. *British Journal of Industrial Relations*, 51(2), 215–39.

Gregg, P. (2008). *Realising Potential: A Vision for Personalised Conditionality and Support*. London: Department for Work and Pensions.

Grimshaw, D., Rubery, J., and Marino, S. (2012). Public sector pay and procurement in Europe during the crisis: The challenges facing local government. Unpublished Manuscript, University of Manchester.

Grugulis, I. (2003). The contribution of National Vocational Qualifications to the growth of skills in the UK. *British Journal of Industrial Relations*, 41(3), 457–75.

Hall, P. and Soskice, D. (2001). *Varieties of Capitalism*. Oxford: Oxford University Press.

Hartlapp, M., Metz, J., and Rauh, C. (2014). *Which Policy for Europe? Power and Conflict inside the European Commission*. Oxford: Oxford University Press.

Hartz Commission. (2002). *Modern services on the labour market*. Report of the Commission. Federal Ministry for Employment and Economic Affairs, Berlin.

Hassel, A. and Schiller, C. (2010). Sozialpolitik im Finanzföderalismus–Hartz IV als Antwort auf die Krise der Kommunalfinanzen. *Politische Vierteljahresschrift*, 51(1), 95–117.

Hauptmeier, M. (2010). Reassessing markets and employment relations. *Reassessing the Employment Relationship*, 171.

Hefetz, A. and Warner, M. (2004). Privatization and its reverse: Explaining the dynamics of the government contracting process. *Journal of Public Administration Research and Theory*, 14(2), 171–90.

Hegele, D. (2009). *Der Vermittlungsgutschein: Entwicklung von 2002 bis 2008 und Fortführung des erfolgreichen Instruments der Arbeitsvermittlung*. Berlin: BWV Verlag.

Heidenrich, M. and Rice, D. (2016). Integrating Social and Employment Policies in Europe: Active Inclusion and Challenges for Local Welfare Governance. Cheltenham: Edward Elgar.

Hengsbach, F. (2011). Letzte Ausfahrt Dritter Weg? Zur aktuellen Lage kirchlicher Arbeitsverhältnisse. Transcript of lecture given on the 20th anniversary of the creation of worker representation (MAV) in the archdiocese of Cologne and the 15th anniversary of MAV in the archdiocese of München und Freising. Frankfurt: Oswald von Nell-Breuning Institut für Wirtschafts- und Gesellschaftsethik.

Hermann, C. and Flecker, J. (2012). *The Privatization of Public Services*. London: Routledge.

Hipp, L. and Warner, M. (2008). Market forces for the unemployed? Training vouchers in Germany and the USA. *Social Policy and Administration*, 42(1), 77–101.

Hodkinson, P. and Sparkes, A. (1995). Markets and vouchers: The inadequacy of individualist policies for vocational education and training in England and Wales. *Journal of Education Policy*, 10(2), 189–207.

Hoffmann, T. (2014). *Fachinformation des Paritätischen Gesamtverbandes zu den sog. "Inhouse-Maßnahmen der Jobcenter."* Berlin: Paritaetischer Gesamtverband.

Holst, H. (2014). "Commodifying institutions": Vertical disintegration and institutional change in German labour relations. *Work Employment and Society*, May.

Höpner, M. (2011). Der Europäische Gerichtshof als Motor der Integration: Eine akteursbezogene Erklärung. *Berliner Journal für Soziologie*, 21(2), 203–29.

Höpner, M., Petring, A., Seikel, D., and Werner, B. (2009). *Liberalisierungspolitik: eine Bestandsaufnahme von zweieinhalb Dekaden marktschaffender Politik in entwickelten Industrieländern.* Cologne: Max Planck Institute for the Study of Societies.

Hudson, M., Phillips, J., Ray, K., Vegeris, S., and Davidson, R. (2010). The influence of outcome-based contracting on provider-led pathways to work. Research Report 638. London: Department for Work and Pensions.

Ingold, J. and Stuart, M. (2015). The demand-side of active labour market policies: A regional study of employer engagement in the Work Programme. *Journal of Social Policy*, 44(3), 443–62.

Jaehrling, K. (2015). The state as a "socially responsible customer"? Public procurement between market-making and market-embedding. *European Journal of Industrial Relations*, 21(2), 149–64.

Jaehrling, K. and Méhaut, P. (2013). "Varieties of institutional avoidance": Employers' strategies in low-waged service sector occupations in France and Germany. *Socio-economic Review*, 11(4), 687–710.

Jantz, B., Larsen, F., Klenk, T., and Wiggan, J. (2014). Marketisation and varieties of accountability relationships in employment services: Comparing Denmark, Germany and Great Britain. *Administration and Society*, 125.

Jessop, B. (1999). The changing governance of welfare: Recent trends in its primary functions, scale, and modes of coordination. *Social Policy and Administration*, 33(4), 348–59.

Katz, H. C. and Darbishire, O. R. (2000). *Converging Divergences: Worldwide Changes in Employment Systems*. Ithaca, NY: Cornell University Press.

Kerr, C., Dunlop, J. T., and Harbison, F. H. (1960). *Industrialism and Industrial Man: The Problems of Labor and Management in Economic Growth*. Cambridge, MA: Harvard University Press.

Klenk, T. (2015). Zur Ambivalenz der neuen Subsidiarität. *Sozialer Fortschritt*, 64(6), 144–9.

Klenk, T. and Pavolini, E. (eds). (2015). *Restructuring Welfare Governance*. London: Edward Elgar.

Knuth, M. (2009). Path shifting and path dependence: Labour market policy reforms under German federalism. *International Journal of Public Administration*, 32(12), 1048–69.

Knuth, M. (2011). Widersprüchliche Dynamiken im deutschen Arbeitsmarkt. *WSI-Mitteilungen*, 64(11), 580–7.

Knuth, M. (2014a). Broken hierarchies, quasi-markets and supported networks: A governance experiment in the second tier of Germany's public employment service. *Social Policy and Administration*, 48(2), 240–61.

Knuth, M. (2014b). *"The Impossible Gets Done at Once; the Miraculous Takes a Little Longer." Labour Market Reforms and the "Jobs Miracle" in Germany*. Strasbourg: European Parliament.

Knuth, M. and Larsen, F. (2010). Increasing roles for municipalities in delivering public employment services: The cases of Germany and Denmark. *European Journal of Social Security*, 12, 174.

Kochan, T. A., Katz, H. C., and McKersie, R. B. (1986). *The Transformation of American Industrial Relations*. Ithaca, NY: Cornell University Press.

Köngeter, N. (2013). *Ausschreibungspraxis und Perspektiven—Auswirkung auf die Qualität der Bildungsangebote*. Presentation Fachtagung ver.di. November 13.

Krachler, N. and Greer, I. (2016). When does marketisation lead to privatisation? Profit-making in English health services after the 2012 Health and Social Care Act. *Social Science and Medicine*, 124, 215–23.

Kreß, H. (2014). *Die Sonderstellung der Kirchen im Arbeitsrecht—sozialethisch vertretbar? Ein deutscher Sonderweg im Konflikt mit Grundrechten*. Baden-Baden: Nomos Verlagsgesellschaft.

Krug, G. and Stephan, G. (2016). Private and public placement services for hard-to-place unemployed results from a randomized field experiment. *ILR Review*, 69(2), 471–500.

Kruppe, T. (2009). Bildungsgutscheine in der aktiven Arbeitsmarktpolitik. *Sozialer Fortschritt*, 58(1), 9–19.

Lane, P., Foster, R., Gardiner, L., Lanceley, L., and Purvis, A. (2013). *Work Programme Evaluation: Procurement, Supply Chains and Implementation of the Commissioning Model*. London: Department for Work and Pensions.

Larsen, F. and Wright, S. (2014). Interpreting the marketisation of employment services in Great Britain and Denmark. *Journal of European Social Policy*, 24(5), 455–69.

Le Grand, J. (2006). *Motivation, Agency, and Public Policy: Of Knights and Knaves, Pawns and Queens*. Oxford: Oxford University Press.

Lethbridge, J., Greer, I., Kretsos, L., Umney, C., and White, G. (2014). *Industrial Relations in Central Public Administration: Recent Trends and Features*. Dublin: Eurofound.

Lillie, N. (2010). Bringing the offshore onshore. *International Studies Quarterly*, 54, 685–706.

Lipsky, M. (1980). *Street-Level Bureaucracy: Dilemmas of the Individual in Public Services*. New York: Russell Sage Foundation.

Local Government Association. (2013). *Future Funding Outlook for Councils from 2010/11 to 2019/20*. London: LGA.

Lødemel, I. and Moreira, A. (eds). (2014). *Activation or Workfare? Governance and Neoliberal Convergence*. Oxford: Oxford University Press.

Lødemel, I. and Trickey, H. (eds). (2001). *An Offer You Can't Refuse: Workfare in International Perspective*. Cambridge: Policy Press.

Lonsdale, C., Kirkpatrick, I., Hoque, K., and De Ruyter, A. (2010). Supplier behaviour and public contracting in the English agency nursing market. *Public Administration*, 88(3), 800–18.

McGuinness, F. and Dar, A. (2014). *Remploy*. London: House of Commons Library.

McGurk, P. (2014). *Employer engagement: A human resource management perspective*. Unpublished paper, University of Greenwich.

Marchington, M., Grimshaw, D., Rubery, J., and Willmott, H. (eds). (2005). *Fragmenting Work*. Oxford: Oxford University Press.

Marshall, T. H. (1950). *Citizenship and Social Class*. Cambridge: Cambridge University Press.

Meyer, D. (1999). *Wettbewerbliche Neuorientierung der freien Wohlfahrtspflege*. Berlin: Duncker and Humblot.

Morton, A. (2012). *European Union Public Procurement Law, the Public Sector and Public Service Provision*. Tralee: European Services Strategy Unit.

National Audit Office. (2012). *The Introduction of the Work Programme*. London: NAO.

National Audit Office. (2013). *Beretning til Statsrevisorerne om effekten og kvaliteten af andre aktøres beskæftigelsesindsats*. Copenhagen: Rigsrevisionen.

National Audit Office. (2014). *The Work Programme*. London: NAO.

Pattar, A. K. (2012). Sozialhilferechtliches Dreiecksverhältnis. Rechtsbeziehungen zwischen Hilfebedürftigen, Sozialhilfeträgern und Einrichtungsträgern. Einführung in die rechtlichen Grundlagen. *Sozialrecht Aktuell*, 16(3), 85–99.

Paugam, S. (2003). *La société française et ses pauvres*. Paris: Presses Universitaires de France.

Peck, J. (2001). *Workfare States*. New York: Guilford Publications.

Peck, J. and Theodore, N. (2007). Variegated capitalism. *Progress in Human Geography*, 31(6), 731–72.

Plimmer, G. (2014). Providence buys unemployment adviser Ingeus for $225m. *Financial Times*, April 1.

Polanyi, K. (1944). *Origins of Our Time: The Great Transformation*. London: Gollancz.

Pollert, A. and Charlwood, A. (2009). The vulnerable worker in Britain and problems at work. *Work, Employment and Society*, 23(2), 343–62.

Prasad, M. (2006). *The Politics of Free Markets: The Rise of Neoliberal Economic Policies in Britain, France, Germany, and the United States*. Chicago, IL: University of Chicago Press.

Przeworski, A. and Teune, H. (1970). *The Logic of Comparative Social Inquiry*. New York: Wiley.

Ranald, P. (1999). Impacts on employees of the competitive tendering of employment services. J. Teicher Public Sector Industrial Relations: Australian and International Perspectives. Melbourne, NKCIR, Monash University, 232–56.

Rees, J., Taylor, R., and Damm, C. (2013). Does sector matter? Understanding the experiences of providers in the work programme. Working paper. Birmingham: TSRC.

Rees, J., Whitworth, A., and Carter, E. (2014). Support for all in the UK Work Programme? Differential payments, same old problem. *Social Policy and Administration*, 48(2), 221–39.

Robinson, K. and Egert, W. (2014). Vermartklichung der Leistungserbringung in beruflicher Teilhabe? Ein Bericht aus der Praxis. *Sozialrecht Aktuell*, annual special issue, 58–63.

Rogowski, S. (2011). Managers, managerialism and social work with children and families: The deformation of a profession? *Practice: Social Work in Action*, 23, 157–67.

Rosendahl, A. (2013). *Finanzierungs- und Vergabemodalitäten ausgewählter Qualifizierungsangebote zur Erleichterung des Übergangs Schule-Beruf. Expertise zu den Ländern Dänemark, England und Österreich*. Frankfurt: Internationaler Bund und BAG ÖRT.

Rothstein, B. (1998). *Just Institutions Matter: The Moral and Political Logic of the Universal Welfare State*. Cambridge: Cambridge University Press.

Rubery, J., Grimshaw, D., Hebson, G., and Ugarte, S. M. (2015). "It's all about time": Time as contested terrain in the management and experience of domiciliary care work in England. *Human Resource Management*, 54(5), 753–72.

Sachße, C. (1998). Entwicklung und Perspektiven des Subsidiaritätsprinzips. In R. Strachwitz (ed.), *Dritter Sektor–Dritte Kraft: Versuch einer Standortbestimmung*, 369–82. Düsseldorf: Versuch einer Standortbestimmung.

Scherschel, K., Streckeisen, P., and Krenn, M. (eds). (2012). *Neue Prekarität. Die Folgen aktivierender Arbeitsmarktpolitik—europäische Länder im Vergleich*. Frankfurt: Campus.

Schmid, G. (2008). *Full Employment in Europe: Managing Labour Market Transitions and Risks*. Cheltenham: Edward Elgar Publishing.

Schulte, L., Greer, I., Umney, C., Iankova, K., and Symon, G. (2016). Insertion as an alternative to workfare: Active labour market schemes in the Parisian suburbs. Unpublished manuscript. London: University of Greenwich.

Seibel, W. (1991). Erfolgreich scheiternde Organisationen Zur politischen Ökonomie des Organisationsversagens. *Politische Vierteljahresschrift*, 479–96.

Siddique, H. (2014). Atos quits £500m work capability assessment contract early. *Guardian*, March 27.

Simmonds, D. (2015). *Review of the Merlin Standard*. London: DWP.

Skou, M., Beer, F., and Winter, S. C. (2008). Udlicitering af sagsbehandling—Andre aktører i beskæftigelsesindsatsen, SFI rapport 08:20.

Sol, E. and Westerveld, M. (eds). (2005). *Contractualism in Employment Services: A New Form of Welfare State Governance*. Amsterdam: Kluwer.

Stefaniak, A. (2011). *Kirchliche Arbeitgeber—angekommen in der Normalität von Markt und Wettbewerb*. Dortmund: ver.di.

Stephan, G. and Pahnke, A. (2008). A pairwise comparison of the effectiveness of selected active labour market programmes in Germany. Discussion Paper 29. Nurnberg: IAB.

Stolz-Willig, B. and Christoforidis, J. (eds). (2011). *Hauptsache billig? Prekarisierung der Arbeit in den sozialen Berufen.* Münster: Westfälisches Dampfboot.

Streeck, W. (2008). *Re-Forming Capitalism: Institutional Change in the German Political Economy: Institutional Change in the German Political Economy.* Oxford: Oxford University Press.

Thelen, K. (2014). *Varieties of Liberalization and the New Politics of Social Solidarity.* Cambridge: Cambridge University Press.

Unwin, L. (1993). Training Credits: The pilot doomed to succeed. In W. Richardson, J. Woolhouse and D. Finegold (eds), *The Reform of Educational and Training in England and Wales,* 205–23. London: Longman.

Van Berkel, R. and van der Aa, P. (2005). The marketization of activation services: A modern panacea? Some lessons from the Dutch experience. *Journal of European Social Policy,* 15(4), 329–43.

Van Slyke, D. M. (2003). The mythology of privatization in contracting for social services. *Public Administration Review,* 63(3), 296–315.

Vincent, S. and Grugulis, I. (2009). Employment relations, cost minimisation and inter-organisational contracting. *Industrial Relations Journal,* 40(1), 40–59.

Warner, M. E. (2008). Reversing privatization, rebalancing government reform: Markets, deliberation and planning. *Policy and Society,* 27(2), 163–74.

Warner, M. E. and Clifton, J. (2014). Marketisation, public services and the city: The potential for Polanyian counter movements. *Cambridge Journal of Regions, Economy and Society,* 7(1).

Webb, S. and Webb, B. (1897). *Industrial Democracy.* London: Longmans.

Webb, S. and Webb, B. (1909). *The Break-Up of the Poor Law.* London: Longmans.

Weil, D. (2014). *The Fissured Workplace.* Boston, MA: Harvard University Press.

West, A., Sparkes, J., and Balabanaov, T. (2000). *Demand-Side Financing—a Focus on Vouchers in Post-Compulsory Education and Training: Discussion Paper and Case Studies.* Thessalonica: CEDEFOP.

Wiehler, A. (2013). Neue Vergabeverordnung: bieterbezogene Qualitätsmerkmale sollen als Zuschlagskriterien zugelassen warden. Vergabeblog.de vom 15/07/2013, Nr. 16314.

Wiggan, J. (2009). Mapping the governance reform of welfare to work in Britain under New Labour. *International Journal of Public Administration,* 32(12), 1026–47.

Wiggan, J. (2014). Active labour market policy under the UK Conservative-Liberal Coalition Government: An autonomist Marxist analysis. Working paper, University of Edinburgh.

Wiggan, J. (2015). Varieties of marketisation in the UK: Examining divergence in activation markets between Great Britain and Northern Ireland 2008–2014. *Policy Studies,* 36(2), 115–32.

Williamson, O. E. (1985). *The Economic Institutions of Capitalism.* London: Simon and Schuster.

Williamson, O. E. (1999). Public and private bureaucracies: A transaction cost economics perspectives. *Journal of Law, Economics, and Organization*, 15(1), 306–42.

Yoon, Y. and Chung, H. (2015). New forms of dualization? Labour market segmentation patterns in the UK from the late 90s until the post-crisis in the late 2000s. *Social Indicators Research*, 1–23.

Zimmermann, K., Aurich, P., Graziano, P., and Fuertes, V. (2014). Local worlds of marketization–employment policies in Germany, Italy and the UK compared. *Social Policy and Administration*, 48(2), 127–48.

Index